Nietzsche

VOLUME I

The Will to Power as Art

Harper & Row Editions of
MARTIN HEIDEGGER

Basic Writings
Being and Time
Discourse on Thinking
Early Greek Thinking
The End of Philosophy
Hegel's Concept of Experience
Identity and Difference
Nietzsche: Volume I, The Will to Power as Art
On the Way to Language
On Time and Being
Poetry, Language, Thought
The Question Concerning Technology and Other Essays
What Is Called Thinking?

MARTIN HEIDEGGER

Nietzsche

Volume I: The Will to Power as Art

Translated from the German, with Notes and an Analysis, by

DAVID FARRELL KRELL

With a Facsimile Page from the Original Manuscript

1817

Published in San Francisco by

HARPER & ROW, PUBLISHERS

NEW YORK, HAGERSTOWN, SAN FRANCISCO, LONDON

Martin Heidegger's text was originally published in *Nietzsche,* Erster Band, © Verlag
Günther Neske, Pfullingen, 1961.

NIETZSCHE. *Volume I: The Will to Power as Art.* Copyright © 1979 by Harper & Row,
Publishers, Inc. Appendix and Analysis Copyright © 1979 by David Farrell Krell. All
rights reserved. Printed in the United States of America. No part of this book may be
used or reproduced in any manner whatsoever without written permission except in the
case of brief quotations embodied in critical articles and reviews. For information address
Harper & Row, Publishers, Inc., 10 East 53rd Street, New York, N.Y. 10022. Published
simultaneously in Canada by Fitzhenry & Whiteside Limited, Toronto.

FIRST EDITION

Designed by Jim Mennick

Library of Congress Cataloging in Publication Data

Heidegger, Martin, 1889–1976.
NIETZSCHE.

   CONTENTS: v. 1.   The will to power as art.
   1.   Nietzsche, Friedrich Wilhelm, 1844–1900.
B3317.H3713 1979   193   78-19509
ISBN 0-06-063847-8 (v. 1)

79 80 81 82 83 10 9 8 7 6 5 4 3 2 1

Contents

Editor's Preface

From 1936 to 1940 Martin Heidegger offered four lecture courses at the University of Freiburg-im-Breisgau on selected topics in Nietzsche's philosophy. During the decade 1936–1946 he composed a number of individual lectures and essays on that thinker. After lecturing again on Nietzsche during the early 1950s Heidegger determined to publish these and the earlier materials; in 1961 the Neske Verlag released two large volumes of Heidegger's early lectures and essays on Nietzsche.* The present book, the first of four English volumes, provides a translation of the first lecture course, *Nietzsche: Der Wille zur Macht als Kunst,* taught during the winter semester of 1936–37.

The Neske edition (referred to throughout as NI, NII, with page number) derives from Heidegger's handwritten lecture notes. Heidegger collated these notes with the help of a number of assistants and approved the final typescript in spring of 1961. Since access to the original notes is restricted, and because the notes themselves are fascinating documents, I have prepared a description of one complete page of the notes and a comparison of it to the relevant pages of the Neske edition as an Appendix to the present volume. (See also a photographic facsimile of that page following p. 223.) There is one serious error on this page as transcribed in the Neske edition, volume one, page 51, line 22. An examination of the holograph page (listed in the Marbach Archive as no. A 33/14) shows that line 22 ends one of Heidegger's long emendations designed for insertion into the body of the text.

---

*Martin Heidegger, *Nietzsche,* 2 vols. (Pfullingen: Verlag Günther Neske, 1961).

The line is difficult to read with certainty; it is easy to see how the error in the published text occurred. But the sense of the holograph page is clear, and with the aid of the only extant *Abschrift* or typescript (Archive no. II 19/27) an accurate reconstruction is possible. With the support of F.-W. von Herrmann, I propose the following reading:

> *strike line 22 of NI, 51, and insert:* Streben auf. Wille dagegen, [als] Entschlossenheit zu sich, ist immer über sich *etc.*

I have adopted this reading for the translation, p. 41, lines 13–14. A more detailed discussion appears in the Appendix.

The only other serious error in the Neske edition of which I am aware is the duplication of the word *nicht* at NI, 189, line 5 from the bottom, which ought to read:

> Sinnlichen, als ein Nichtseiendes und Nicht-sein-sol- *etc.*

Occasional typographical errors in the Neske edition and minor inaccuracies in the quotations I have corrected without drawing attention to them.

I have translated all passages from Nietzsche's works in Heidegger's text, as well as the quotations from Hegel, Wagner, Dilthey, and others. But I am grateful to have had the translation of *The Will to Power* by Walter Kaufmann and R. J. Hollingdale (New York: Random House, 1967) for reference and comparison.

Heidegger's many references to *Der Wille zur Macht* are cited in these English volumes as WM, followed by aphorism—not page— number, e.g.: (WM, 794). His references to all other Nietzschean texts are to the *Grossoktavausgabe* (Leipzig, 1905 ff.); in the body of the text they are cited simply by volume and page, e.g.: (XIV, 413–67); in my own explanatory footnotes I cite the *Grossoktavausgabe* as GOA. In those notes the letters CM refer to the new *Kritische Gesamtausgabe* of Nietzsche's works and letters, edited by Giorgio Colli and Mazzino Montinari (Berlin: Walter de Gruyter, 1967 ff.). I have checked as many of Heidegger's references to the GOA in CM as time, the incompleteness of CM, and its one-way concordances allowed. Where no major discrepancies emerged I let the GOA text stand. However, readers who wish to focus on a specific reference by Heidegger to the GOA should themselves check CM carefully before proceeding. Heidegger's text contains no footnotes; all notes in the present volume are my own. I have tried to keep them to a minimum, since it is hard to know when such notes are helpful and when they are a nuisance. I hope that readers who have difficulties with the editorial matter or any aspect of the translation will write me about them in care of the publisher. As for the translation itself, its apologist is Jerome, whose *Preface to Eusebius' Chronicle* William Arrowsmith has rendered (in *Arion,* New Series, 2/3, 1975, p. 359):

Jerome to Vincentius and Gallienus: Greetings

. . . It is difficult, when you are following in another man's footsteps, to keep from going astray somewhere. And it is extremely difficult to preserve in translation the particular verbal felicities of a foreign language. The original meaning, for instance, may be conveyed in a single word—a word which has no single Latin equivalent. If the translator tries to catch the full meaning, he must resort to lengthy paraphrase. To these difficulties must be added the problems of word-order, differences in case and rhetorical figures, and finally, the *native* genius of the language itself. If I translate word for word, the result is ludicrous; if I am forced to change the words or rearrange them, it will look as though I had failed in my duty as a translator.

So, my dear Vincentius and Gallienus, I beg of you, if you find signs of haste and confusion, to read this work rather as friends than critics.

I owe thanks to Friedrich-Wilhelm von Herrmann for expert counsel in all textual and editorial matters; to Joachim W. Storck of the Heidegger Archive for answers to my queries on the manuscript of the lecture course and for providing the photograph of A 33/14; to Sherry Gray, Frank A. Capuzzi, and John B. Shopp, who made many improvements in the manuscript; to John Sallis for his thought and his thoughtfulness; to Jochen Barkhausen, Helmbrecht Breinig, and Ulrich Halfmann, my colleagues in the Universität-Mannheim and on the Max-Joseph-Strasse, for their support and friendship; to Friederike Born for her careful work on the typescript; and to Elfride Heidegger for her constant helpfulness.

While the translation was in preparation, on October 29, 1977, Glenn Gray died at his home in Colorado Springs, Colorado. I owe more to his steadfast friendship and Hieronymic wisdom than I can say. This translation of Heidegger's *Nietzsche* is dedicated to his memory.

D.F.K.

die Säge
St. Ulrich

Plan of the English Edition

Volume I: The Will to Power as Art
  1. Author's Foreword to All Volumes [NI, 9–10].
  2. "Will to Power as Art," a lecture course delivered at the University of Freiburg during the winter semester of 1936–37 [NI, 11–254].

Volume II: The Eternal Recurrence of the Same
  1. "The Eternal Recurrence of the Same," a lecture course delivered at the University of Freiburg during the summer semester of 1937 [NI, 255–472].
  2. "Who Is Nietzsche's Zarathustra?," a lecture to the Bremen Club on May 8, 1953, printed in *Vorträge und Aufsätze* (Pfullingen: G. Neske, 1954), pp. 101–26, added here as a supplement to the *Nietzsche* material.

Volume III: Will to Power as Knowledge and as Metaphysics
  1. "Will to Power as Knowledge," a lecture course delivered at the University of Freiburg during the summer semester of 1939 [NI, 473–658].
  2. "The Eternal Recurrence of the Same and Will to Power," the concluding lecture to all three lecture courses cited above, written in 1939 but not delivered [NII, 7–29].
  3. "Nietzsche's Metaphysics," a typescript dated August–December 1940, apparently deriving from an unscheduled and heretofore unlisted course on Nietzsche's philosophy [NII, 257–333].*

---

*"Nietzsche's Metaphysics" appears as the title of a lecture course for the the winter semester of 1941–42 in all published lists of Heidegger's courses. The prospectuses of

Volume IV: Nihilism
1. "European Nihilism," a lecture course delivered at the University of Freiburg during the first trimester of 1940 [NII, 31–256].
2. "The Determination of Nihilism in the History of Being," an essay composed during the years 1944–46 but not published until 1961 [NII, 335–398].

The three remaining essays in volume two of the Neske edition, "Metaphysics as History of Being" [NII, 399–457], "Sketches for a History of Being as Metaphysics" [NII, 458–80], and "Recollection of Metaphysics" [NII, 481–90], all from the year 1941, appear in English translation in Martin Heidegger, *The End of Philosophy*, tr. Joan Stambaugh (New York: Harper & Row, 1973). *The End of Philosophy* also contains the essay "Overcoming Metaphysics" (1936–46), related thematically and chronologically to the *Nietzsche* material, an essay originally published in *Vorträge und Aufsätze*, pp. 71–99. The lecture in which Heidegger summarizes much of the material in volume two of *Nietzsche*, "The Word of Nietzsche: 'God is Dead'" (1943), appears in English translation in Martin Heidegger, *The Question Con-*

---

the Klostermann publishing firm cite such a lecture course as volume 52 of the Heidegger "Complete Edition" (*Gesamtausgabe*). But the Heidegger Archive of the Schiller-Nationalmuseum in Marbach contains no manuscript for such a course. It does contain the sixty-four-page typescript in question, with many handwritten alterations, composed in August 1940 and revised during the months of September, October, and December of that year. One of the typescript's several title pages refers to the winter semester of 1938–39, in all probability not to any lecture or seminar in the published lists but to an unlisted *Übung* [exercise] entitled "Toward an Interpretation of Nietzsche's Second 'Untimely Meditation,' *On the Use and Disadvantage of History for Life*." On September 29, 1975, I asked Heidegger about the discrepancy of the dates for "Nietzsche's Metaphysics" in the Neske edition (1940) and in the published lists and catalogues of his courses (winter semester 1941–42). (At the time of our conversation on this matter the above information, supplied by the Archive, was unknown to me.) Heidegger reaffirmed the date 1940 as the time of composition. He explained that the material had been prepared during a seminar, title and date not specified, and conceded that he might have employed the same material for the WS 1941–42 lecture course.

The problem awaits the more patient scrutiny of the Archive's curators. But this may suffice to explain why Heidegger cites 1940 (and not 1942, as the catalogues would lead us to expect) as the closing date for his early lectures on Nietzsche.

cerning *Technology and Other Essays,* tr. William Lovitt (New York: Harper & Row, 1977). Other references to Nietzsche in Heidegger's works are listed in the second, revised edition of Hildegard Feick, *Index zu Heideggers "Sein und Zeit"* (Tübingen: M. Niemeyer, 1968), p. 120.

Author's Foreword to All Volumes

Nietzsche himself identifies the experience that determines his thinking:
"Life ... more mysterious since the day the great liberator came over me—the thought that life should be an experiment of knowers."
The Gay Science 1882
(Book IV, no. 324)

"Nietzsche"—the name of the thinker stands as the title for *the matter* of his thinking.

The matter, the point in question, is in itself a confrontation. To let our thinking enter into the matter, to prepare our thinking for it—these goals determine the contents of the present publication.

It consists of *lecture courses* held at the University of Freiburg-im-Breisgau during the years 1936 to 1940. Adjoined to them are *treatises* which originated in the years 1940 to 1946. The treatises further extend the way by which the lecture courses—still at that time under way—paved the way for the confrontation.

The text of the lectures is divided according to content, not hours of presentation. Nevertheless, the lecture character has been retained, this necessitating an unavoidable breadth of presentation and a certain amount of repetition.

It is intentional that often the same text from Nietzsche's writings is discussed more than once, though each time in a different context. Much material has been presented that may be familiar and even well known to many readers, since in everything well known something worthy of thought still lurks. The repetitions are intended to provide occasions for thinking through, in ever renewed fashion, those several thoughts that determine the whole. Whether, and in what sense, with what sort of range, the thoughts remain worthy of thought becomes clear and is decided through the confrontation. In the text of the lectures unnecessary words and phrases have been deleted, involuted sentences simplified, obscure passages clarified, and oversights corrected.

For all that, the written and printed text lacks the advantages of oral presentation.

Considered as a whole, the publication aims to provide a view of the path of thought I followed from 1930 to the "Letter on Humanism" (1947). The two small lectures published just prior to the "Letter," "Plato's Doctrine of Truth" (1942) and "On the Essence of Truth" (1943), originated back in the years 1930–31. The book *Commentaries on Hölderlin's Poetry* (1951), which contains one essay and several lectures from the years between 1936 and 1943, sheds only indirect light on that path.

Whence the confrontation with the "Nietzsche matter" comes and whither it goes may become manifest to the reader when he himself sets off along the way the following texts have taken.

M. H.

Freiburg-im-Breisgau
May, 1961

Nietzsche

VOLUME I

The Will to Power as Art

"Well-nigh two thousand years and not a single new god!"
The Antichrist 1888
(VIII, 235–36)

1. Nietzsche as Metaphysical Thinker

In *The Will to Power,* the "work" to be treated in this lecture course, Nietzsche says the following about philosophy (WM, 420):

> I do not wish to persuade anyone to philosophy: it is inevitable and perhaps also desirable that the philosopher should be a *rare* plant. I find nothing more repugnant than didactic praise of philosophy as one finds it in Seneca, or worse, Cicero. Philosophy has little to do with virtue. Permit me to say also that the man of knowledge is fundamentally different from the philosopher. —What I desire is that the genuine concept of the philosopher not perish utterly in Germany. . . .

At the age of twenty-eight, as a professor in Basel, Nietzsche writes (X, 112):

> There are times of great danger in which philosophers appear—times when the wheel rolls ever faster—when philosophers and artists assume the place of the dwindling *mythos.* They are far ahead of their time, however, for the attention of contemporaries is only quite slowly drawn to them. A people which becomes aware of its dangers produces the genius.

The Will to Power—the expression plays a dual role in Nietzsche's thinking. First, it serves as the title of Nietzsche's chief philosophical work, planned and prepared over many years but never written. Second, it names what constitutes the basic character of all beings. "Will to power is the ultimate *factum* to which we come" (XVI, 415).

It is easy to see how both applications of the expression "will to power" belong together: only because the expression plays the second role can and must it also adopt the first. As the name for the basic character of all beings, the expression "will to power" provides an answer to the question "What is being?" Since antiquity that question has been *the* question of philosophy. The name "will to power" must therefore come to stand in the title of the chief philosophical work of a thinker who says that all being ultimately is will to power. If for Nietzsche the work of that title is to be the philosophical "main structure," for which *Zarathustra* is but the "vestibule," the implication is that Nietzsche's thinking proceeds within the vast orbit of the ancient guiding question of philosophy, "What is being?"

Is Nietzsche then not at all so modern as the hubbub that has surrounded him makes it seem? Is Nietzsche not nearly so subversive as he himself was wont to pose? Dispelling such fears is not really necessary; we need not bother to do that. On the contrary, the reference to the fact that Nietzsche moves in the orbit of the question of Western philosophy only serves to make clear that Nietzsche knew what philosophy is. Such knowledge is rare. Only great thinkers possess it. The greatest possess it most purely in the form of a persistent question. The genuinely grounding question, as the question of the essence of Being, does not unfold in the history of philosophy as such; Nietzsche too persists in the guiding question.

The task of our lecture course is to elucidate the fundamental position within which Nietzsche unfolds the guiding question of Western thought and responds to it. Such elucidation is needed in order to prepare a confrontation with Nietzsche. If in Nietzsche's thinking the prior tradition of Western thought is gathered and completed in a decisive respect, then the confrontation with Nietzsche becomes one with all Western thought hitherto.

The confrontation with Nietzsche has not yet begun, nor have the prerequisites for it been established. For a long time Nietzsche has been either celebrated and imitated or reviled and exploited. Nietzsche's thought and speech are still too contemporary for us. He and we have not yet been sufficiently separated in history; we lack the distance necessary for a sound appreciation of the thinker's strength.

Confrontation is genuine criticism. It is the supreme way, the only way, to a true estimation of a thinker. In confrontation we undertake to reflect on his thinking and to trace it in its effective force, not in its weaknesses. To what purpose? In order that through the confrontation we ourselves may become free for the supreme exertion of thinking.

But for a long time it has been declaimed from chairs of philosophy in Germany that Nietzsche is not a rigorous thinker but a "poet-philosopher." Nietzsche does not belong among the philosophers, who think only about abstract, shadowy affairs, far removed from life. If he is to be called a philosopher at all then he must be regarded as a "philosopher of life." That rubric, a perennial favorite, serves at the same time to nourish the suspicion that any other kind of philosophy is something for the dead, and is therefore at bottom dispensable. Such a view wholly coincides with the opinion of those who welcome in Nietzsche the "philosopher of life" who has at long last quashed abstract thought. These common judgments about Nietzsche are in error. The error will be recognized only when a confrontation with him is at the same time conjoined to a confrontation in the realm of the grounding question of philosophy. At the outset, however, we ought to introduce some words of Nietzsche's that stem from the time of his work on "will to power": "For many, abstract thinking is toil; for me, on good days, it is feast and frenzy" (XIV, 24).

Abstract thinking a feast? The highest form of human existence? Indeed. But at the same time we must observe how Nietzsche views the essence of the feast, in such a way that he can think of it only on the basis of his fundamental conception of all being, will to power. "The feast implies: pride, exuberance, frivolity; mockery of all earnestness and respectability; a divine affirmation of oneself, out of animal plenitude and perfection—all obvious states to which the Christian may not honestly say Yes. *The feast is paganism par excellence*" (WM, 916). For that reason, we might add, the feast of thinking never takes place in Christianity. That is to say, there is no Christian philosophy. There is no true philosophy that could be determined anywhere else than from within itself. For the same reason there is no pagan philosophy, inasmuch as anything "pagan" is always still something Christian —the counter-Christian. The Greek poets and thinkers can hardly be designated as "pagan."

Feasts require long and painstaking preparation. This semester we want to prepare ourselves for the feast, even if we do not make it as far as the celebration, even if we only catch a glimpse of the preliminary festivities at the feast of thinking—experiencing what meditative thought is and what it means to be at home in genuine questioning.

2. The Book, *The Will to Power*

The question as to what being is seeks the Being of beings. All Being is for Nietzsche a Becoming. Such Becoming, however, has the character of action and the activity of willing. But in its essence will is will to power. That expression names what Nietzsche thinks when he asks the guiding question of philosophy. And for that reason the name obtrudes as the title for his planned *magnum opus,* which, as we know, was not brought to fruition. What lies before us today as a book with the title *The Will to Power* contains preliminary drafts and fragmentary elaborations for that work. The outlined plan according to which these fragments are ordered, the division into four books, and the titles of those books also stem from Nietzsche himself.

At the outset we should mention briefly the most important aspects of Nietzsche's life, the origins of the plans and preliminary drafts, and the later publication of these materials after Nietzsche's death.

In a Protestant pastor's house in the year 1844 Nietzsche was born. As a student of classical philology in Leipzig in 1865 he came to know Schopenhauer's major work, *The World as Will and Representation.* During his last semester in Leipzig (1868–69), in November, he came into personal contact with Richard Wagner. Apart from the world of the Greeks, which remained decisive for the whole of Nietzsche's life, although in the last years of his wakeful thinking it had to yield some ground to the world of Rome, Schopenhauer and Wagner were the earliest intellectually determinative forces. In the spring of 1869, Nietzsche, not yet twenty-five years of age and not yet finished with his doctoral studies, received an appointment at Basel as associate professor of classical philology. There he came into amicable contact with Jacob

Burckhardt and with the Church historian Franz Overbeck. The question as to whether or not a real friendship evolved between Nietzsche and Burckhardt has a significance that exceeds the merely biographical sphere, but discussion of it does not belong here. He also met Bachofen,* but their dealings with one another never went beyond reserved collegiality. Ten years later, in 1879, Nietzsche resigned his professorship. Another ten years later, in January, 1889, he suffered a total mental collapse, and on August 25, 1900, he died.

During the Basel years Nietzsche's inner disengagement from Schopenhauer and Wagner came to completion. But only in the years 1880 to 1883 did Nietzsche find himself, that is to say, find himself as a thinker: he found his fundamental position within the whole of beings, and thereby the determinative source of his thought. Between 1882 and 1885 the figure of "Zarathustra" swept over him like a storm. In those same years the plan for his main philosophical work originated. During the preparation of the planned work the preliminary sketches, plans, divisions, and the architectonic vision changed several times. No decision was made in favor of any single alternative; nor did an image of the whole emerge that might project a definitive profile. In the last year before his collapse (1888) the initial plans were finally abandoned. A peculiar restlessness now possessed Nietzsche. He could no longer wait for the long gestation of a broadly conceived work which would be able to speak for itself, on its own, as a work. Nietzsche himself had to speak, he himself had to come forth and announce his basic position vis-à-vis the world, drawing the boundaries which were to prevent anyone's confusing that basic position with any other. Thus the smaller works originated: *The Wagner Case, Nietzsche contra Wagner, Twilight of the Idols, Ecce Homo,* and *The Antichrist*—which first appeared in 1890.

But Nietzsche's philosophy proper, the fundamental position on the basis of which he speaks in these and in all the writings he himself

---

*J. J. Bachofen (1815–1887), Swiss historian of law and religion, interested in myths and symbols in primitive folklore, today best known as the author of the classic work on matriarchy, *Das Mutterrecht,* published in 1861.

published, did not assume a final form and was not itself published in any book, neither in the decade between 1879 and 1889 nor during the years preceding. What Nietzsche himself published during his creative life was always foreground. That is also true of his first treatise, *The Birth of Tragedy from the Spirit of Music* (1872). His philosophy proper was left behind as posthumous, unpublished work.

In 1901, a year after Nietzsche's death, the first collection of his preliminary drafts for a *magnum opus* appeared. It was based on Nietzsche's plan dated March 17, 1887; in addition, the collection referred to notes in which Nietzsche himself arranged particular fragments into groups.

In the first and in later editions the particular fragments selected from the handwritten *Nachlass* were numbered sequentially. The first edition of *The Will to Power* included 483 selections.

It soon became clear that this edition was quite incomplete when compared to the available handwritten material. In 1906 a new and significantly expanded edition appeared, retaining the same plan. It included 1,067 selections, more than double the number in the first edition. The second edition appeared in 1911 as volumes XV and XVI of the *Grossoktav* edition of Nietzsche's works. But even these volumes did not contain the amassed material; whatever was not subsumed under the plan appeared as two *Nachlass* volumes, numbered XIII and XIV in the *Collected Works.*

Not long ago the Nietzsche Archive in Weimar undertook to publish a historical-critical complete edition of Nietzsche's works and letters in chronological order. It should become the ultimate, definitive edition.* It no longer separates the writings Nietzsche himself published and the *Nachlass,* as the earlier complete editions do, but collates for each period both published and unpublished materials. The extensive

---

*The *Historisch-kritische Gesamtausgabe der Werke und Briefe* (Munich: C. H. Beck, 1933–42), edited by a group of scholars including H. J. Mette, W. Hoppe, and K. Schlechta, under the direction of Carl August Emge, published fewer than a dozen of the many volumes of works and letters planned. For an account of the "principles" of the edition—with which Heidegger takes issue below—see the Foreword to the Nietzsche *Gesamtausgabe,* I, x–xv.

collection of letters, which thanks to new and rich finds is growing steadily, is also to be published in chronological sequence. The historical-critical complete edition, which has now begun, remains in its foundations ambiguous. First of all, as a historical-critical "complete edition" which brings out every single thing it can find, guided by the fundamental principle of completeness, it belongs among the undertakings of nineteenth-century publication. Second, by the manner of its biographical, psychological commentary and its similarly thorough research of all "data" on Nietzsche's "life," and of the views of his contemporaries as well, it is a product of the psychological-biological addiction of our times.

Only in the actual presentation of the authentic "Works" (1881–89) will this edition have an impact on the future, granted the editors succeed in their task. That task and its fulfillment are not a part of what we have just criticized; moreover, the task can be carried out without all that. But we can never succeed in arriving at Nietzsche's philosophy proper if we have not in our questioning conceived of Nietzsche as the end of Western metaphysics and proceeded to the entirely different question of the truth of Being.

The text recommended for this course is the edition of *The Will to Power* prepared by A. Baeumler for the Kröner pocket edition series. It is a faithful reprint of volumes XV and XVI of the *Grossoktavausgabe*, with a sensible Afterword and a good, brief outline of Nietzsche's life history. In addition, Baeumler has edited for the same series a volume entitled *Nietzsche in His Letters and in Reports by Contemporaries*. For a first introduction the book is useful. For a knowledge of Nietzsche's biography the presentation by his sister, Elisabeth Förster-Nietzsche, *The Life of Friedrich Nietzsche* (published between 1895 and 1904), remains important. As with all biographical works, however, use of this publication requires great caution.

We will refrain from further suggestions and from discussion of the enormous and varied secondary literature surrounding Nietzsche, since none of it can aid the endeavor of this lecture course. Whoever does not have the courage and perseverance of thought required to become involved in Nietzsche's own writings need not read anything *about* him either.

Citation of passages from Nietzsche's works will be by volume and page number of the *Grossoktav* edition. Passages from *The Will to Power* employed in the lecture course will not be cited by the page number of any particular edition but by the fragment number which is standard in all editions. These passages are for the most part not simple, incomplete fragments and fleeting observations; rather, they are carefully worked out "aphorisms," as Nietzsche's individual notations are customarily called. But not every brief notation is automatically an aphorism, that is, an expression or saying which absolutely closes its borders to everything inessential and admits only what is essential. Nietzsche observes somewhere that it is his ambition to say in a brief aphorism what others in an entire book ... do *not* say.

3. Plans and Preliminary Drafts of the "Main Structure"

Before we characterize more minutely the plan on which the presently available edition of *The Will to Power* is based, and before we indicate those passages with which our inquiry shall begin, let us introduce testimony from several of Nietzsche's letters. Such testimony sheds light on the origin of the preliminary drafts for the planned chief work and suggests the fundamental mood from which the work derives.

On April 7, 1884, Nietzsche writes to his friend Overbeck in Basel:

> For the past few months I've been preoccupied with "world history," enchanted by it, in spite of many hair-raising results. Did I ever show you Jacob Burckhardt's letter, the one which led me by the nose to "world history"? If I get to Sils Maria this summer I want to undertake a revision of my *metaphysica* and my epistemological views. Now I must work through a whole series of disciplines step by step, for I am resolved to devote the next five years to the construction of my "philosophy," for which I have in my *Zarathustra* constructed a vestibule.

We should take this opportunity to observe that the common assumption that Nietzsche's *Thus Spoke Zarathustra* was to present his philosophy in poetic form, and that, since *Zarathustra* did not achieve this goal, Nietzsche wanted to transcribe his philosophy into prose for purposes of greater intelligibility, is an error. The planned major work, *The Will to Power,* is in truth as much a poetic work as *Zarathustra* is a work of thought. The relationship between the two works remains one of vestibule and main structure. Nevertheless, between 1882 and 1888 several essential steps were taken which remain wholly concealed in prior collections of the *Nachlass* fragments, such concealment preventing a glimpse into the essential structure of Nietzsche's metaphysics.

In mid-June, 1884, Nietzsche writes to his sister:

> So, the scaffolding for the main structure ought to be erected this summer; or, to put it differently, during the next few months I want to draw up the schema for my philosophy and my plan for the next six years. May my health hold out for this purpose!*

From Sils Maria on September 2, 1884, to his friend and assistant Peter Gast:

> In addition, I have completely *finished* the major task I set myself for this summer—the next six years belong to the elaboration of a schema in which I have outlined my "philosophy." The prospects for this look good and promising. Meanwhile, *Zarathustra* retains only its entirely personal meaning, being my "book of edification and consolation"—otherwise, for Everyman, it is obscure and riddlesome and ridiculous.

To Overbeck, July 2, 1885:

> I have dictated for two or three hours practically every day, but my "philosophy"—if I have the right to call it by the name of something that has maltreated me down to the very roots of my being—is *no longer* communicable, at least not in print.

Here doubts about the possibility of a presentation of his philosophy

---

*According to Karl Schlechta's "Philologischer Nachbericht," in *Friedrich Nietzsche Werke in drei Bänden* (Munich: C. Hanser, 6th ed., 1969), III, 1411, 1417, and 1420–22, this letter, number 379 in the edition by Frau Förster-Nietzsche, is a forgery. More specifically, it appears that Nietzsche's sister altered the addressee (the letter was sent not to her but to Malwida von Meysenbug) and enlarged upon the original contents of the letter. Because she managed to destroy all but a fragment of the original, it is virtually impossible to determine whether or not the words Heidegger cites are Nietzsche's. Nevertheless, the fragment does contain the following lines, relevant to the present issue: ". . . nachdem ich mir diese Vorhalle meiner Philosophie gebaut habe, muss ich die Hand wieder anlegen und nicht müde werden, bis auch der Haupt-Bau fertig vor mir steht." In translation: ". . . now that I have built this vestibule for my philosophy, I must get busy once again and not grow weary until the main structure too stands finished before me."

in book form are already stirring. But a year later Nietzsche is again confident.

To his mother and sister, September 2, 1886:

> For the next four years the creation of a four-volume *magnum opus* is proposed. The very title is fearsome: *"The Will to Power:* Attempt at a Revaluation of All Values." For it I have *everything* that is necessary, health, solitude, good mood, and maybe a wife.*

With this mention of his major work Nietzsche refers to the fact that on the cover of the book that had appeared during that year, *Beyond Good and Evil,* a work with the above-mentioned title was cited as the volume to appear next. In addition, Nietzsche writes in his *Toward a Genealogy of Morals,* which appeared in 1887 (See Division Three, no. 27):

> ... with respect to which [i.e., the question of the meaning of the ascetic ideal] I refer to a work I am now preparing: **The Will to Power,** *Attempt at a Revaluation of All Values.*

Nietzsche himself emphasized the title of his planned work by means of special, heavy print.

To Peter Gast, September 15, 1887:

> I vacillated, to be honest, between Venice and—Leipzig: the latter for learned purposes, since in reference to the major *pensum* of my life, which is presently to be resolved, I still have much to learn, to question, and to read. But for that I would need, not an "autumn," but an *entire winter* in Germany: and, all things considered, my health forcefully discourages such a dangerous experiment for *this* year. Therefore it has turned out to be a matter of Venice and Nice: —and also, as you yourself may judge to be true, I now need the profound isolation which in my case is even more compelling than further study and exploration into five thousand particular problems.

To Carl von Gersdorff, December 20, 1887:

> In a significant sense my life stands right now at *high noon:* one door is closing, another opening. All I have done in the last few years has been a

---

*Schlechta (ibid.) does *not* cite this letter as a forgery.

settling of accounts, a conclusion of negotiations, an adding up of things past; by now I have finished with men and things and have drawn a line under it all. *Who* and what remain for me, whither I must now go, toward the really most important matter of my existence (a transition to which I have *been condemned*), are now capital questions. For, between you and me, the tension in which I live, the pressure of a great task and passion, is now too great for me to allow still more people to approach me. The desert that surrounds me is vast indeed. I really can bear only complete strangers or passers-by, or, on the other hand, people who have been a part of me for a long time, even from childhood. Everyone else has drifted away or has been *repulsed* (there was much violence and much pain in that—).

Here it is no longer simply the matter of a *magnum opus*. Here already are early signs of the last year of his thinking, the year in which everything about him radiates an excessive brilliance and in which therefore at the same time a terrible boundlessness advances out of the distance. In that year, 1888, the plan of the work changes altogether. When madness overwhelms Nietzsche in the first days of January, 1889, he writes to the composer Peter Gast, as a final word to his friend and helper, a postcard dated January 4 with the following contents:

To my maëstro Pietro. Sing me a new song: the world is transfigured and all the heavens rejoice. The Crucified.

Although Nietzsche expresses in them what is most interior, these few pieces of evidence can for us at first be only an extrinsic indication of the fundamental mood in which the planning of the work and its preliminary casting moved. But at the same time we need to refer to the plans themselves and to their transformation; and even that can occur at first only from the outside. The plans and proposals are published in volume XVI, pages 413–67.

Three fundamental positions can be distinguished in the sequence of proposals: the first extends chronologically from 1882 to 1883 (*Thus Spoke Zarathustra*); the second from 1885 to 1887 (*Beyond Good and Evil, Toward a Genealogy of Morals*); the third embraces the years 1887 and 1888 (*Twilight of the Idols, Ecce Homo, The Antichrist*). But these are not stages of development. Neither can the three fundamental positions be distinguished according to their scope: each is concerned with the whole of philosophy and in each one the other two are implied, although in each case the inner configuration and the location of the center which determines the form vary. And it was nothing else than the question of the center that genuinely "maltreated" Nietzsche. Of course, it was not the extrinsic question of finding a suitable connection or link among the handwritten materials available; it was, without Nietzsche's coming to know of it or stumbling across it, the question of philosophy's self-grounding. It concerns the fact that, whatever philosophy is, and however it may exist at any given time, it defines itself solely on its own terms; but also that such self-determination is possible only inasmuch as philosophy always has already grounded itself. Its proper essence turns ever toward itself, and the more original a philosophy is, the more purely it soars in turning about itself, and therefore the farther the circumference of its circle presses outward to the brink of nothingness.

Now, when closely examined, each of the three fundamental positions may be identified by a predominant title. It is no accident that the two titles displaced in each case by the main title recur under that title.

The first fundamental position derives its character from the main title, "Philosophy of Eternal Return," with the subtitle "An Attempt at the Revaluation of All Values" (XVI, 415). A plan pertaining to this title (p. 414) contains as its crowning, concluding chapter (the fifth) "The doctrine of eternal return as *hammer* in the hand of the most powerful man." Thus we see that the thought of power, which always means will to power, extends through the whole simultaneously from top to bottom.

The second fundamental position is marked by the title "The Will to Power," with the subtitle "Attempt at a Revaluation of All Values." A plan pertaining to this title (p. 424, number 7) contains as the fourth part of the work "The Eternal Return."

The third fundamental position transposes what was only the subtitle of the two previous positions to the main title (p. 435), "Revaluation of All Values." The plans pertaining to this title contain as their fourth part the "Philosophy of Eternal Return," and they propose another part, concerning the "yes-sayers," whose place within the whole was not fixed. Eternal Recurrence, Will to Power, Revaluation: these are the three guiding phrases under which the totality of the planned major work stands, the configuration in each case differing.*

Now, if we do not thoughtfully formulate our inquiry in such a way that it is capable of grasping in a unified way the doctrines of the eternal return of the same and will to power, and these two doctrines in their most intrinsic coherence as revaluation, and if we do not go on to comprehend this fundamental formulation as one which is also necessary in the course of Western metaphysics, then we will never grasp Nietzsche's philosophy. And we will comprehend nothing of the twentieth century and of the centuries to come, nothing of our own metaphysical task.

---

*An examination of CM VIII, 1, 2, and 3 reveals that the selection of plans provided as an appendix to the GOA, the edition Heidegger employed, oversimplified the matter of the organization of the *Nachlass*. Yet Heidegger's analysis of the changing stratification of eternal recurrence, will to power, and revaluation in Nietzsche's plans still seems tenable.

4. The Unity of Will to Power, Eternal Recurrence, and Revaluation

The doctrine of the eternal return of the same coheres in the most intimate way with that of will to power. The unity of these teachings may be seen historically as the revaluation of all values hitherto.

But to what extent do the doctrines of the eternal return of the same and will to power belong essentially together? This question must animate us more thoroughly, indeed as the decisive one. For the present, therefore, we offer a merely provisional answer.

The expression "will to power" designates the basic character of beings; any being which is, insofar as it is, is will to power. The expression stipulates the character that beings have as beings. But that is not at all an answer to the first question of philosophy, its proper question; rather, it answers only the final preliminary question. For anyone who at the end of Western philosophy can and must still question philosophically, the decisive question is no longer merely "What basic character do beings manifest?" or "How may the Being of beings be characterized?" but "What is this 'Being' itself?" The decisive question is that of "the meaning of Being," not merely that of the Being of beings. "Meaning" is thereby clearly delineated conceptually as that from which and on the grounds of which Being in general can become manifest as such and can come into truth. What is proffered today as ontology has nothing to do with the question of Being proper; it is a very learned and very astute analysis of transmitted concepts which plays them off, one against the other.

What is will to power itself, and how is it? Answer: the eternal recurrence of the same.

Is it an accident that the latter teaching recurs continually in decisive passages throughout all plans for the philosophical main work? What can it mean when in one plan, which bears the unadorned title "Eternal Return" (XVI, 414), Nietzsche lists the first part under the title "The most difficult thought"? To be sure, the question of Being is the most difficult thought of philosophy, because it is simultaneously its innermost and uttermost thought, the one with which it stands and falls.

We heard that the fundamental character of beings is will to power, willing, and thus Becoming. Nevertheless, Nietzsche does not cling to such a position—although that is usually what we are thinking when we associate him with Heraclitus. Much to the contrary, in a passage purposely and expressly formulated to provide an encompassing overview (WM, 617), Nietzsche says the following: *"Recapitulation:* To *stamp* Becoming with the character of Being—that is the *supreme will to power."* This suggests that Becoming only *is* if it is grounded in Being as Being: "That *everything recurs* is the closest *approximation* of a world of Becoming to one of Being: —peak of the meditation."*

With his doctrine of eternal return Nietzsche in his way thinks nothing else than the thought that pervades the whole of Western philosophy, a thought that remains concealed but is its genuine driving force. Nietzsche thinks the thought in such a way that in his metaphysics he reverts to the beginnings of Western philosophy. More precisely, he reverts to that beginning which Western philosophy became accustomed to seeing in the course of its history. Nietzsche shared in

---

*Heidegger often cites the "Recapitulation" aphorism during the *Nietzsche* lectures and essays. See, for example, NI, 466 and 656; NII, 288. He employs it elsewhere as well, for instance in "The Anaximander Fragment," the first chapter of Martin Heidegger, *Early Greek Thinking,* tr. D. F. Krell and F. A. Capuzzi (New York: Harper & Row, 1975), p. 22. Yet it was not Nietzsche but Peter Gast (Heinrich Köselitz) who supplied the title of the aphorism: see Walter Kaufmann's note in his edition of *The Will to Power,* p. 330, and cf. CM VIII, 1, p. 320, which does not print the title. Furthermore, WM, 617 is a note the *entire* context and contents of which must be carefully examined. The problem will be discussed in the Analysis of volume III in the present series.

such habituation in spite of his otherwise original grasp of pre-Socratic philosophy.

In the popular view, and according to the common notion, Nietzsche is the revolutionary figure who negated, destroyed, and prophesied. To be sure, all that belongs to the image we have of him. Nor is it merely a role that he played, but an innermost necessity of his time. But what is essential in the revolutionary is not that he overturns as such; it is rather that in overturning he brings to light what is decisive and essential. In philosophy that happens always when those few momentous questions are raised. When he thinks "the most difficult thought" at the "peak of the meditation," Nietzsche thinks and meditates on Being, that is, on will to power as eternal recurrence. What does that mean, taken quite broadly and essentially? Eternity, not as a static "now," nor as a sequence of "nows" rolling off into the infinite, but as the "now" that bends back into itself: what is that if not the concealed essence of Time? Thinking Being, will to power, as eternal return, thinking the most difficult thought of philosophy, means thinking Being as Time. Nietzsche thinks that thought but does not think it as the *question* of Being and Time. Plato and Aristotle also think that thought when they conceive Being as *ousia* (presence), but just as little as Nietzsche do they think it as a question.

If we do ask the question, we do not mean to suggest that we are cleverer than both Nietzsche and Western philosophy, which Nietzsche "only" thinks to its end. We know that the most difficult thought of philosophy has only become more difficult, that the peak of the meditation has not yet been conquered and perhaps not yet even discovered at all.

If we bring Nietzsche's "will to power," that is, his question concerning the Being of beings, into the perspective of the question concerning "Being and Time," that does not at all mean that Nietzsche's work is to be related to a book entitled *Being and Time* and that it is to be measured and interpreted according to the contents of that book. *Being and Time* can be evaluated only by the extent to which it is equal or unequal to the question it raises. There is no standard other than the question itself; only the question, not the book, is essential. Furthermore, the book merely leads us to the threshold of the question, not yet into the question itself.

Whoever neglects to think the thought of eternal recurrence together with will to power, as what is to be thought genuinely and philosophically, cannot adequately grasp the metaphysical content of the doctrine of will to power in its full scope. Nevertheless, the connection between eternal recurrence as the supreme determination of Being and will to power as the basic character of all beings does not lie in the palm of our hand. For that reason Nietzsche speaks of the "most difficult thought" and the "peak of the meditation." It is nonetheless true that the current interpretation of Nietzsche does away with the properly philosophical significance of the doctrine of eternal recurrence and thus irremediably precludes a fertile conception of Nietzsche's metaphysics. We will introduce two examples, each quite independent of the other, of such a treatment of the doctrine of eternal return in Nietzsche's philosophy: Alfred Baeumler, *Nietzsche: Philosopher and Politician* (1931), and Karl Jaspers, *Nietzsche: Introduction to an Understanding of His Philosophizing* (1936).* The negative position taken by each author with respect to the doctrine of eternal recurrence—and for us that means the misinterpretation by each—varies in kind and has different grounds.

Baeumler portrays what Nietzsche calls the most difficult thought and the peak of the meditation as an entirely personal, "religious" conviction of Nietzsche's. He says, "Only one can be valid: either the doctrine of eternal return or the doctrine of will to power" (p. 80). He tries to ground this either-or by the following argument: will to power is Becoming; Being is grasped as Becoming; that is the ancient doctrine of Heraclitus on the flux of things and it is also Nietzsche's genuine teaching. His thought of eternal recurrence has to deny the unlimited flux of Becoming. The thought introduces a contradiction into

---

*Alfred Baeumler, *Nietzsche der Philosoph und Politiker* (Leipzig: P. Reclam, 1931), and Karl Jaspers, *Nietzsche. Einführung in das Verständnis seines Philosophierens* (Berlin and Leipzig: Walter de Gruyter, 1936). Both books are discussed in the Analysis (section II) at the end of this volume. The analyses to the later volumes of the present series will treat Baeumler more thoroughly.

Nietzsche's metaphysics. Therefore, either the doctrine of will to power or that of eternal recurrence, only one of them, can define Nietzsche's philosophy. Baeumler writes, "In truth, seen from the point of view of Nietzsche's *system,* this thought is without importance." And on page 82 he opines, "Now, Nietzsche, who is a founder of religion, also accomplishes an Egyptification of the Heraclitean world." According to Baeumler's account, the doctrine of eternal recurrence implies bringing Becoming to a standstill. With his either-or, Baeumler presupposes that Heraclitus teaches the eternal flux of things, in the sense of the ever-ongoing. For some time now we have known that this conception of Heraclitus' doctrine is utterly foreign to the Greek. Just as questionable as the interpretation of Heraclitus, however, is whether Nietzsche's will to power should automatically be taken as Becoming in the sense of the onward-flowing. In the end, such a concept of Becoming is so superficial that we had better not be too quick to ascribe it to Nietzsche. The immediate result of our considerations so far is that there is not necessarily a contradiction between the two statements "Being is Becoming" and "Becoming is Being." Precisely that is Heraclitus' teaching. But assuming that there is a contradiction between the doctrines of will to power and eternal recurrence, we have known since Hegel's day that a contradiction is not necessarily proof against the truth of a metaphysical statement, but may be proof for it. If therefore eternal recurrence and will to power contradict one another, perhaps the contradiction is precisely the demand to *think* this most difficult thought, instead of fleeing into the "religious." But even if we concede that here we have a contradiction which cannot be transcended and which compels us to decide in favor of either will to power or eternal recurrence, why does Baeumler then decide *against* Nietzsche's most difficult thought, the peak of his meditation, and *for* will to power? The answer is simple: Baeumler's reflections on the relationship between the two doctrines do not press toward the realm of actual inquiry from either side. Rather, the doctrine of eternal recurrence, where he fears "Egypticism," militates against his conception of will to power, which, in spite of the talk about metaphysics, Baeumler does not grasp metaphysically but interprets politically.

Nietzsche's doctrine of eternal recurrence conflicts with Baeumler's conception of politics. It is therefore "without importance" for Nietzsche's system. This interpretation of Nietzsche is all the more remarkable since Baeumler belongs among those few commentators who reject Klages' psychological-biologistic interpretation of Nietzsche.*

The second conception of Nietzsche's doctrine of eternal return is that of Karl Jaspers. True, Jaspers discusses Nietzsche's teaching in greater detail and discerns that here we are in the presence of one of Nietzsche's decisive thoughts. In spite of the talk about Being, however, Jaspers does not bring the thought into the realm of the grounding question of Western philosophy and thereby also into actual connection with the doctrine of will to power. For Baeumler the doctrine of eternal recurrence cannot be united with the political interpretation of Nietzsche; for Jaspers it is not possible to take it as a question of great import, because, according to Jaspers, there is no conceptual truth or conceptual knowledge in philosophy.

But if in contrast to all this the doctrine of eternal recurrence is seen to coincide with the very center of Nietzsche's metaphysical thinking, is it not misleading, or at least one-sided, to collate all the preliminary sketches for a philosophical *magnum opus* under the plan that takes as its definitive title "Will to Power"?

That the editors selected the middle one of the three basic positions in the plans testifies to their considerable understanding. For Nietzsche himself first of all had to make a decisive effort to visualize the basic character of will to power throughout beings as a whole. Yet this was never for him the ultimate step. Rather, if Nietzsche was the thinker we are convinced he was, then the demonstration of will to power would always have to revolve about the thought of the Being of beings, which for Nietzsche meant the eternal recurrence of the same.

---

*Ludwig Klages (1872–1956) developed as his life's work a "biocentric metaphysics" which was to clarify once and for all the problem of the body-soul-mind relationship. His major work is the three-volume *Der Geist als Widersacher der Seele* (1929–32); the work Heidegger refers to here is *Die psychologischen Errungenschaften Nietzsches* (1926). Cf. section 17, below, and section II of the Analysis. For a critical edition of Klages' writings see Ludwig Klages, *Sämtliche Werke* (Bonn: Bouvier, 1964 ff.).

But even if we grant the fact that this edition of the preliminary sketches for the major work, dominated by the theme of will to power, is the best edition possible, the book that lies before us is still something supplementary. Nobody knows what would have become of these preliminary sketches had Nietzsche himself been able to transform them into the main work he was planning. Nevertheless, what is available to us today is so essential and rich, and even from Nietzsche's point of view so definitive, that the prerequisites are granted for what alone is important: actually to think Nietzsche's genuine philosophical thought. We are all the more liable to succeed in this endeavor the less we restrict ourselves to the sequence of particular fragments as they lie before us, collected and subsumed into book form. For such ordering of particular fragments and aphorisms within the schema of divisions, a schema which does stem from Nietzsche himself, is arbitrary and inessential. What we must do is think through particular fragments, guided by the movement of thought which occurs when we ask the genuine questions. Therefore, measured against the order established by the text before us, we will jump about within various particular divisions. Here too an arbitrariness, within certain limits, is unavoidable. Still, in all this what remains decisive is to hear Nietzsche himself; to inquire with him and through him *and therefore at the same time against him,* but *for* the one single innermost matter that is common to Western philosophy. We can undertake such a task only if we limit its scope. But the important thing is to know where these limits are to be set. Such limitation does not preclude but expects and demands that in time, with the help of the book *The Will to Power,* you will work through whatever is not explicitly treated in the lectures, in the spirit and manner of our procedure here.

5. The Structure of the "Major Work." Nietzsche's Manner of Thinking as Reversal

Nietzsche's basic metaphysical position may be defined by two statements. First, the basic character of beings as such is "will to power." Second, Being is "eternal recurrence of the same." When we think through Nietzsche's philosophy in a questioning way, along the guidelines of those two statements, we advance beyond the basic positions of Nietzsche and of philosophy prior to him. But such advance only allows us to come back to Nietzsche. The return is to occur by means of an interpretation of *"The Will to Power."*

The plan upon which the published edition is based, a plan Nietzsche himself sketched and even dated (March 17, 1887), takes the following form (XVI, 421):

THE WILL TO POWER
Attempt at a Revaluation of All Values

Book I: *European Nihilism.*
Book II: *Critique of the Highest Values.*
Book III: *Principle of a New Valuation.*
Book IV: *Discipline and Breeding.*

Our inquiry proceeds immediately to the third book and restricts itself to that one. The very title, "Principle of a New Valuation," suggests that here a laying of grounds and an erection of structures are to be brought to language.

Accordingly, in Nietzsche's view, philosophy is a matter of valuation, that is, establishment of the uppermost value in terms of which and according to which all beings are to be. The uppermost value is the one that must be fundamental for all beings insofar as they are beings. A "new" valuation would therefore posit another value, in opposition to the old, decrepit one, which should be determinative for the future. For that reason a critique of the highest values hitherto is advanced beforehand, in Book II. The values in question are religion, specifically, the Christian religion, morality, and philosophy. Nietzsche's manner of speaking and writing here is often imprecise and misleading: religion, morality, and philosophy are not themselves the supreme values, but basic ways of establishing and imposing such values. Only for that reason can they themselves, mediately, be posited and taken as "highest values."

The critique of the highest values hitherto does not simply refute them or declare them invalid. It is rather a matter of displaying their origins as impositions which must affirm precisely what ought to be negated by the values established. Critique of the highest values hitherto therefore properly means illumination of the dubious origins of the valuations that yield them, and thereby demonstration of the questionableness of these values themselves. Prior to this critique, which is offered in Book II, the first book advances an account of European nihilism. Thus the work is to begin with a comprehensive presentation of the basic development of Western history, which Nietzsche recognizes in its range and intensity here for the first time: the development of nihilism. In Nietzsche's view nihilism is not a *Weltanschauung* that occurs at some time and place or another; it is rather the basic character of what happens in Occidental history. Nihilism is at work even—and especially—there where it is not advocated as doctrine or demand, there where ostensibly its opposite prevails. Nihilism means that the uppermost values devalue themselves. This means that whatever realities and laws set the standard in Christendom, in morality since Hellenistic times, and in philosophy since Plato, lose their binding force, and for Nietzsche that always means creative force. In his view nihilism is never merely a development of his own times; nor does it pertain only to the nineteenth century. Nihilism begins in the pre-

Christian era and it does not cease with the twentieth century. As a historical process it will occupy the centuries immediately ahead of us, even and especially when countermeasures are introduced. But neither is nihilism for Nietzsche mere collapse, valuelessness, and destruction. Rather, it is a basic mode of historical movement that does not exclude, but even requires and furthers, for long stretches of time, a certain creative upswing. "Corruption," "physiological degeneration," and such are not causes of nihilism but effects. Nihilism therefore cannot be overcome by the extirpation of those conditions. On the contrary, an overcoming of nihilism would merely be delayed by countermeasures directed toward alleviation of its harmful side effects. In order to grasp what Nietzsche designates in the word "nihilism" we need profound insight and even more profound seriousness.

Because of its necessary involvement in the movement of Western history, and on account of the unavoidable critique of prior valuations, the *new* valuation is necessarily a *re*valuation of all values. Hence the subtitle, which in the final phase of Nietzsche's philosophy becomes the main title, designates the general character of the countermovement to nihilism *within* nihilism. No historical movement can leap outside of history and start from scratch. It becomes all the more historical, which is to say, it grounds history all the more originally, as it overcomes radically what has gone before by creating a new order in that realm where we have our roots. Now, the overwhelming experience derived from the history of nihilism is that all valuations remain without force if the corresponding basic attitude of valuing and the corresponding manner of thinking do not accompany them.

Every valuation in the essential sense must not only bring its possibilities to bear in order to be "understood" at all, it must at the same time develop a breed of men who can bring a new attitude to the new valuation, in order that they may bear it into the future. New requirements and prerequisites must be bred. And this process consumes, as it were, most of the time that is allotted to nations as their history. Great ages, because they are great, are in terms of frequency quite rare and of endurance very brief, just as the most momentous times for individual men often consist of a single moment. A new valuation itself implies the creation and inculcation of requirements and demands that conform to the new values. For that reason the work is to find its conclusion in the fourth book, "Discipline and Breeding."

At the same time, however, it is a basic experience gained from the history of valuations that even the positing of the uppermost values does not take place at a single stroke, that eternal truth never blazes in the heavens overnight, and that no people in history has had its truth fall into its lap. Those who posit the uppermost values, the creators, the new philosophers at the forefront, must according to Nietzsche be experimenters; they must tread paths and break trails in the knowledge that they do not have *the* truth. But from such knowledge it does not at all follow that they have to view their concepts as mere betting chips that can be exchanged at any time for any currency. What does follow is just the opposite: the solidity and binding quality of thought must undergo a grounding in the things themselves in a way that prior philosophy does not know. Only in this way is it possible for a basic position to assert itself over against others, so that the resultant strife will be actual strife and thus the actual origin of truth.* The new thinkers must attempt and tempt. That means they must put beings themselves to the test, tempt them with questions concerning their Being and truth. So, when Nietzsche writes in the subtitle to his work, "attempt" at a revaluation of all values, the turn of phrase is not meant to express modesty and to suggest that what follows is still incomplete; it does not mean an "essay" in the literary sense; rather, in an utterly clearminded way, it means the basic attitude of the new inquiry that grows out of the countermovement against nihilism. "—We are conducting an experiment with truth! Perhaps mankind will perish because of it! Fine!" (XII, 410).

---

*The reference to strife and to the origin of truth is to "Der Ursprung des Kunstwerkes" ["The Origin of the Work of Art"]. See Martin Heidegger, *Holzwege* (Frankfurt/Main: V. Klostermann, 1950), pp. 37–38 ff.; cf. the revised edition (Stuttgart: P. Reclam, 1960), pp. 51–52 ff. Heidegger first reworked this essay during the autumn of 1936, which is to say, while the first Nietzsche course was in session. We will hardly be surprised therefore to hear echoes of each in the other. For an English translation of the essay, see Martin Heidegger, *Poetry, Language, Thought,* tr. Albert Hofstadter (New York: Harper & Row, 1971), pp. 17–87.

We new philosophers, however, not only do we begin by presenting the actual gradations in rank and variations in value among men, but we also desire the very opposite of an assimilation, an equalizing: we teach estrangement in every sense, we tear open gaps such as never were, we want man to become more wicked than he ever was. Meanwhile, we ourselves live as strangers to one another, concealed from one another. It is necessary for many reasons that we be recluses and that we don masks—consequently, we shall do poorly in searching out our comrades. We shall live alone and probably come to know the torments of all seven solitudes. If perchance our paths should cross, you may wager that we will mistake one another or betray one another (WM, 988).

Nietzsche's procedure, his manner of thinking in the execution of the new valuation, is perpetual reversal. We will find opportunity enough to think through these reversals in a more detailed way. In order to clarify matters now we will bring forward only two examples. Schopenhauer interprets the essence of art as a "sedative for life," something that ameliorates the miseries and sufferings of life, that puts the will—whose compulsiveness makes existence miserable—out of commission. Nietzsche reverses this and says that art is the *stimulans* of life, something that excites and enhances life, "what eternally *compels* us to life, to eternal life" (XIV, 370). *Stimulans* is obviously the reverse of sedative.

A second example. To the question "What is truth?" Nietzsche answers, *"Truth is the kind of error* without which a certain kind of living being could not live. The value for *life* ultimately decides" (WM, 493). " 'Truth': this, according to my way of thinking, does not necessarily denote the antithesis of error, but in the most fundamental cases only the position of various errors in relation to one another" (WM, 535). It would of course be utterly superficial to explain such statements in the following way: Nietzsche takes everything that is an error to be true. Nietzsche's statement—truth is error, error truth—can be grasped only in terms of his fundamental position in opposition to all Western philosophy since Plato. If we have grasped this fact, then the statement already sounds less alien. Nietzsche's procedure of reversal at times becomes a conscious mania, if not indeed a breach of good taste. With reference to the expression "Whoever laughs last, laughs best," he says, by way of reversal, "And today whoever laughs best also laughs last" (VIII, 67). In contrast to "Blessed are they who do not see and still believe," he speaks of "seeing and still not believing." This he calls "the primary virtue of knowers," whose "greatest tempter" is whatever is "clear to the eyes" (XII, 241).

One need not penetrate too far into Nietzsche's thought in order to determine without difficulty that his procedure everywhere is one of reversal. On the basis of that determination a basic objection to Nietzsche's procedure and to his entire philosophy has been raised: reversal is merely denial—in setting aside the previous order of values no new values yet arise. With objections of this kind it is always advisable to suppose at least provisionally that the philosopher under consideration was after all alert enough to experience such doubts himself. Nietzsche not only avers that by means of reversal a new order of values should originate; he says explicitly that in this way an order should originate *"of itself."* Nietzsche says, "If the tyranny of previous values has thus been shattered, if we have abolished the 'true world,' then a *new order of values* must follow of itself."* Merely by doing away with the old, something new should eventuate of itself! Are we to ascribe such an opinion to Nietzsche, or do such "abolition" and "reversal" signify something other than what we usually represent to ourselves with the help of everyday concepts?

What is the principle of the new valuation? At the outset it is important to clarify in general the meaning of the title of the third book, to which we are limiting ourselves. "Principle," comes from *principium,* beginning. The concept corresponds to what the Greeks call *archē,* that on the basis of which something is determined to be what it is and how it is. Principle: the ground on which something stands, pervading it, guiding it in its whole structure and essence. We also conceive of principles as fundamental propositions. But these are

---

*Heidegger cites no source, but the passage probably derives from WM, 461. If so, Heidegger misreads the phrase ". . . *Ordnung der Werte"* as "Ordnung der Welt." I have restored Nietzsche's text in the translation.

"principles" only in a derived sense and only because and insofar as they posit something as the fundament of something else within a statement. A statement as such can never be a principle. The principle of a new valuation is that in which valuing as such has its supporting and guiding ground. The principle of a new valuation is that kind of ground which inaugurates a valuing that is new in contrast to previous kinds. The valuing is to be new: not only what is posited as a value but above all else the manner in which values are posited in general. If one objects that Nietzsche was basically uncreative and did not really establish any new values, such an objection first needs to be tested carefully. But however it turns out, the objection itself does not touch what Nietzsche actually wanted to do above all else, namely, to ground anew the manner in which values are posited, to lay a new ground for this purpose. Therefore, if we want to grasp what is thought here, we must read the title of Book III, "Principle of the New Valuation,"* as having the following sense: the new ground from which in the future the manner and kind of valuing will spring and upon which it will rest. How are we to conceive that ground?

If the work as a whole involves will to power, and if the third book is to exhibit the ground-laying and structuring principle of the new valuation, then the principle can only be will to power. How are we to understand this? We said by way of anticipation that will to power is a name for the basic character of all beings. It means precisely *what* properly constitutes the being in beings. Nietzsche's decisive consideration runs as follows: if we are to establish what properly should be, and what must come to be in consequence of that, it can be determined only if truth and clarity already surround whatever *is* and whatever constitutes *Being.* How else could we determine what is to be?

In the sense of this most universal consideration, whose ultimate tenability we must still leave open, Nietzsche says, "Task: to *see* things *as they are!"* (XII, 13). "My philosophy—to draw men away from *semblance,* no matter *what* the danger! And no fear that life will perish!" (XII, 18). Finally: "Because you lie concerning what is, the

---

*Heidegger changes here the indefinite article, *einer,* to the definite, *der,* Cf. p. 25.

thirst for what should come to be does not grow in you" (XII, 279).

Demonstration of will to power as the basic character of beings is supposed to expunge the lies in our experience of beings and in our interpretation of them. But not only that. It is also supposed to ground the principle, and establish the ground, from which the valuation is to spring and in which it must remain rooted. For "will to power" is already in itself an estimating and valuing. If beings are grasped as will to power, the "should" which is supposed to hang suspended over them, against which they might be measured, becomes superfluous. If life itself is will to power, it is itself the ground, *principium,* of valuation. Then a "should" does not determine Being; Being determines a "should." "When we talk of values we are speaking under the inspiration or optics of life: life itself compels us to set up values; life itself values through us *whenever* we posit values. . . ." (VIII, 89).*

To exhibit the principle of the new valuation therefore first of all means to display will to power as the basic character of beings throughout all groups and regions of beings. With a view to that task the editors of *The Will to Power* divided the third book into four divisions:

I. Will to Power as Knowledge.
II. Will to Power in Nature.
III. Will to Power as Society and Individual.
IV. Will to Power as Art.

Several of Nietzsche's sets of instructions could have been used for such a division, for example, Plan I, 7, dated 1885 (XVI, 415): "Will to Power. Attempt at an interpretation of all occurrence. Foreword on the 'meaninglessness' that threatens. Problem of pessimism." Then comes a list of topics arranged vertically: "Logic. Physics. Morals, Art. Politics." These are the customary disciplines of philosophy; the only one that is missing, and not by accident, is speculative theology. For

---

*To this analysis of the "should" compare that in Heidegger's lecture course during the summer semester of 1935, published as *Einführung in die Metaphysik* (Tübingen: M. Niemeyer, 1953), pp. 149–52; in the English translation, Martin Heidegger, *An Introduction to Metaphysics,* tr. Ralph Manheim (Garden City, N.Y.: Doubleday-Anchor, 1961), pp. 164–67.

the decisive stance vis-à-vis Nietzsche's interpretation of beings as will to power it is important to know that from the very start he saw beings as a whole in the perspectives of traditional disciplines of academic philosophy.

As a further aid in apportioning the aphorisms which appear in the handwritten notebooks into the chapters mentioned, the editors employed an index in which Nietzsche himself numbered 372 aphorisms and divided them into particular books cited in a plan which, it is true, originates at a later date (Plan III, 6; XVI, 424). The index is printed in volume XVI, 454–67; it stems from the year 1888.*

The disposition of the third book of *The Will to Power,* as it lies before us today, is accordingly as well grounded as it could be on the basis of the extant handwritten materials.

However, we shall begin the interpretation of Book III not with the first chapter, "Will to Power as Knowledge," but with the fourth and final one, "Will to Power as Art."

This chapter consists of aphorisms 794 to 853. Why we are beginning with the fourth chapter will soon become clear on the basis of that chapter's contents. Our immediate task must be to ask in what way Nietzsche perceives and defines the essence of art. As the very title of the chapter suggests, art is a configuration of will to power. If art is a configuration of will to power, and if within the whole of Being art is accessible in a distinctive way for us, then we should most likely be able to grasp what will to power means from the Nietzschean conception of art. But lest the expression "will to power" remain an empty term any longer, let us delineate our interpretation of the fourth chapter by means of a preliminary observation. This we will do by asking, first, what does Nietzsche mean by the expression "will to power"; and second, why should it not surprise us that the basic character of beings is here defined as *will?*

---

*Karl Schlechta indicates that the list of 372 aphorisms could apply to a number of plans other than that dated March 17, 1887. See Schlechta, *Der Fall Nietzsche* (Munich: C. Hanser, 2nd ed., 1959), pp. 74 ff. and 88 ff.

6. The Being of beings as Will in Traditional Metaphysics

We shall begin with the second question. The conception of the Being of all beings as will is very much in line with the best and greatest tradition of German philosophy. When we look back from Nietzsche our glance falls immediately upon Schopenhauer. His main work, which at first impels Nietzsche toward philosophy but then later repels him, bears the title *The World as Will and Representation*. But what Nietzsche himself understands by "will" is something altogether different. Nor is it adequate to grasp Nietzsche's notion of will as the reversal of the Schopenhauerian.

Schopenhauer's major work appeared in the year 1818. It was profoundly indebted to the main works of Schelling and Hegel, which had already appeared by that time. The best proof of this debt consists in the excessive and tasteless rebukes Schopenhauer hurled at Hegel and Schelling his life long. Schopenhauer called Schelling a "windbag," Hegel a "bumbling charlatan." Such abuse, directed repeatedly against philosophy in the years following Schopenhauer, does not even have the dubious distinction of being particularly "novel."

In one of Schelling's most profound works, the treatise *On the Essence of Human Freedom,* published in 1809, that philosopher writes: "In the final and ultimate instance there is no other Being at all than Willing. Willing is Primal Being" (I, VII, 350).* And in his

---

*During the previous semester (summer 1936) Heidegger had lectured on Schelling. See Martin Heidegger, *Schellings Abhandlung über das Wesen der menschlichen Freiheit (1809),* ed. Hildegard Feick (Tübingen: M. Niemeyer, 1971). Especially useful in

Phenomenology of Spirit (1807) Hegel grasps the essence of Being as knowing, but grasps knowing as essentially identical to willing.

Schelling and Hegel were certain that with the interpretation of Being as will they were merely thinking the essential thought of another great German thinker—the concept of Being in Leibniz. Leibniz defined the essence of Being as the original unity of *perceptio* and *appetitus,* representation and will. Not accidentally, Nietzsche himself referred to Leibniz in two decisive passages of *The Will to Power:* "German philosophy as a whole—Leibniz, Kant, Hegel, Schopenhauer, to name the great ones—is the most thoroughgoing kind of *romanticism* and homesickness that has ever existed: the longing for the best there ever was" (WM, 419). And: "Händel, Leibniz, Goethe, Bismarck —characteristic of the *strong German type*" (WM, 884).

Now, to be sure, one should not assert that Nietzsche's doctrine of will to power is dependent upon Leibniz or Hegel or Schelling, in order by such a pronouncement to cancel all further consideration. "Dependence" is not a concept by which we can understand relationships among the greats. But the small are always dependent on the great; they are "small" precisely because they think they are independent. The great thinker is one who can hear what is greatest in the work of other "greats" and who can transform it in an original manner.

Reference to Nietzsche's predecessors with regard to the doctrine of Being as will is not meant to calculate some sort of dependence; it is rather to suggest that such a doctrine within Western metaphysics is not arbitrary but perhaps even necessary. Every true thinking lets itself be determined by what is to be thought. In philosophy the Being of beings is to be thought. For philosophy's thinking and questioning there is no loftier and stricter commitment. In contrast, all the sciences think always only of *one* being among others, *one* particular region of beings. They are committed by this region of beings only in an indirect manner, never straightforwardly so. Because in philosophical thought

---

the context of Heidegger's reading of Nietzsche are the notes sketched five years later for a seminar on that same treatise. The notes appear in an appendix to Heidegger's *Schelling.* See esp. pp. 224–25.

the highest possible commitment prevails, all great thinkers think the same. Yet this "same" is so essential and so rich that no single thinker exhausts it; each commits all the others to it all the more strictly. To conceive of beings according to their basic character as will is not a view held by particular thinkers; it is a necessity in the history of the Dasein which those thinkers ground.

7. Will as Will to Power

But now, to anticipate the decisive issue, what does Nietzsche himself understand by the phrase "will to power"? What does "will" mean? What does "will to power" mean? For Nietzsche these two questions are but one. For in his view will is nothing else than will to power, and power nothing else than the essence of will. Hence, will to power is will to will, which is to say, willing is self-willing. But that requires elucidation.

With our attempt, as with all conceptual definitions elaborated in a similar fashion which claim to grasp the Being of beings, we must keep two things in mind. First, a precise conceptual definition that ticks off the various characteristics of what is to be defined remains vacuous and false, so long as we do not really come to know in an intimate way what is being talked about and bring it before our mind's eye. Second, in order to grasp the Nietzschean concept of will, the following is especially important: if according to Nietzsche will as will to power is the basic character of all beings, then in defining the essence of will we cannot appeal to a particular being or special mode of Being which would serve to explain the essence of will.

Hence, will as the pervasive character of all beings does not yield any immediate sort of directive from which its concept, as a concept of Being, might be derived. Of course, Nietzsche never explicated this state of affairs systematically and with attention to principles; but he knew quite clearly that here he was pursuing an unusual question.

Two examples may illustrate what is involved. According to the usual view, will is taken to be a faculty of the soul. What will is may be determined from the essence of the psyche. The latter is dealt with in psychology. The psyche is a particular being, distinct from body and mind. Now, if in Nietzsche's view will determines the Being of every sort of being, then it does not pertain to the psyche; rather, the psyche somehow pertains to the will. But body and mind too are will, inasmuch as such things "are." Furthermore, if will is taken to be a faculty, then it is viewed as something that can do something, is in a position to do it, possessing the requisite power and might. Whatever is intrinsically power, and for Nietzsche that is what will is, thus cannot be further characterized by defining it as a faculty or power. For the essence of a faculty is grounded in the essence of will as power.

A second example. Will is taken to be a kind of cause. We say that a man does something not so much by means of his intellect as by sheer willpower. Will brings something about, effects some consequence. But to be a cause is a particular mode of Being; Being as such cannot be grasped by means of causation. Will is not an effecting. What we usually take to be a thing that effects something else, the power of causation, is itself grounded in will (cf. VIII, 80).

If will to power characterizes Being itself, there is nothing *else* that will can be defined *as*. Will is will—but that formally correct definition does not say anything. It is in fact quite deceptive if we take it to mean that things are as simple as the simple phrase suggests.

For that reason Nietzsche can declare, "Today we know that it [i.e., the will] is merely a word" (*Twilight of the Idols,* 1888; VIII, 80). Corresponding to this is an earlier assertion from the period of *Zarathustra:* "I laugh at your free will and your unfree one too: what you call will is to me an illusion; there is no will" (XII, 267). It is remarkable that the thinker for whom the basic character of all beings is will should say such a thing: "There is no will." But Nietzsche means that there is no *such* will as the one previously known and designated as "a faculty of the soul" and as "striving in general."

Whatever the case, Nietzsche must constantly repeat what will is. He says, for example, that will is an "affect," a "passion," a "feeling," and a "command." But do not such characterizations of will as "affect," "passion," and so on speak within the domain of the psyche and of states of the soul? Are not affect, passion, feeling, and command each something different? Must not whatever is introduced in order to illuminate the essence of will itself be adequately clear at the outset? But what is more obscure than the essence of affect and passion, and the distinction between the two? How can will be all those things simultaneously? We can hardly surmount these questions and doubts concerning Nietzsche's interpretation of the essence of will. And yet, perhaps, they do not touch on the decisive issue. Nietzsche himself emphasizes, "Above all else, willing seems to me something *complicated,* something that is a unity only as a word; and precisely in this one word a popular prejudice lurks which has prevailed over the always meager caution of philosophers" (*Beyond Good and Evil;* VII, 28). Nietzsche here speaks primarily against Schopenhauer, in whose opinion will is the simplest and best-known thing in the world.

But because for Nietzsche will as will to power designates the essence of Being, it remains forever the actual object of his search, the thing to be determined. What matters—once such an essence is discovered—is to locate it thoroughly, so that it can never be lost again. Whether Nietzsche's procedure is the sole possible one, whether the singularity of the *inquiry concerning Being* became sufficiently clear to him at all, and whether he thought through in a fundamental manner the ways that are necessary and possible in this regard, we leave open for now. This much is certain: for Nietzsche there was at the time no other alternative—given the ambiguity of the concepts of will and the multiplicity of prevailing conceptual definitions—than to clarify what he meant with the help of what was familiar and to reject what he did not mean. (Cf. the general observation concerning philosophical concepts in *Beyond Good and Evil;* VII, 31 ff.)

If we try to grasp willing by that peculiarity which, as it were, first forces itself upon us, we might say that willing is a heading toward . . . , a going after . . . ; willing is a kind of behavior directed toward something. But when we look at something immediately at hand, or observantly follow the course of some process, we behave in a way that can be described in the same terms: we are directed toward the thing by way of representation—where willing plays no role. In the mere observation of things we do not want to do anything "with" them and do not expect anything "from" them; we let things be just as they are. To be directed toward something is not yet a willing, and yet such directedness is implied in willing. . . .

But we can also "want" [i.e., will-to-have] some thing, e.g., a book or a motorbike. A boy "wills" to have a thing, that is, he would like to have it. This "would like to have" is no mere representation, but a kind of striving after something, and has the special characteristic of wishing. But to wish is not yet to will. Whoever only wishes, in the strict sense of the word, does not will; rather, he hopes that his wish will come true without his having to do anything about it. Is willing then a wishing to which we add our own initiative? No, willing is not wishing at all. It is the submission of ourselves to our own command, and the resoluteness of such self-command, which already implies our carrying out the command. But with this account of willing we have suddenly introduced a whole series of definitions that were not given in what we first discussed, namely, directing oneself toward something.

Yet it seems as though the essence of will would be grasped most purely if this "directing oneself toward," as pure willing, were canceled abruptly in favor of a directing oneself toward something in the sense of sheer desire, wishing, striving, or mere representing. Will would thus be posited as the pure relation of a simple heading toward or going after something. But this approach is misconceived. Nietzsche is convinced that Schopenhauer's fundamental error is his belief that there is such a thing as pure willing, a willing that becomes purer as what is willed is left more and more indeterminate and the one who wills left more and more decisively out of the picture. Much to the contrary, it is proper to the essence of willing that what is willed and the one who wills be brought into the willing, although not in the extrinsic sense in which we can say that to every striving belongs something that strives and something that is striven for.

The *decisive question* is this: how, and on what grounds, do the willed and the one who wills belong to the willing to will? Answer: on the grounds of willing and by means of willing. Willing wills the one who wills, as such a one; and willing posits the willed as such. Willing is resoluteness toward oneself, but as the one who wills what is posited in the willing as willed. In each case will itself furnishes thoroughgoing determinateness to its willing. Someone who does not know what he wants does not want anything and cannot will at all. There is no willing-in-general. "For the will, as an affect of command, is the decisive distinguishing mark of self-mastery and force" (*The Gay Science,* Bk. V, 1886; V, 282). In contrast, striving can be indeterminate, both with respect to what is actually striven for and in relation to the very one who strives. In striving and in compulsion we are caught up in movement toward something without knowing what is at stake. In mere striving after something we are not properly brought before ourselves. For that reason it is not possible for us to strive beyond ourselves; rather, we merely strive, and get wholly absorbed in such striving. By way of contrast, will, as resolute openness to oneself, is always a willing out beyond oneself. If Nietzsche more than once emphasizes the character of will as command, he does not mean to provide a prescription or set of directions for the execution of an act; nor does he mean to characterize an act of will in the sense of resolve. Rather, he means resoluteness—that by which willing can come to grips with what is willed and the one who wills; he means coming to grips as a founded and abiding decisiveness. Only he can truly command—and commanding has nothing to do with mere ordering about —who is always ready and able to place himself under command. By means of such readiness he has placed himself within the scope of the command as first to obey, the paragon of obedience. In such decisiveness of willing, which reaches out beyond itself, lies mastery over . . . , having power over what is revealed in the willing and in what is held fast in the grips of resoluteness.

Willing itself is mastery over . . . , which reaches out beyond itself; will is intrinsically power. And power is willing that is constant in itself. Will is power; power is will. Does the expression "will to power" then have no meaning? Indeed it has none, when we think of will in the sense of Nietzsche's conception. But Nietzsche employs this expression anyhow, in express rejection of the usual understanding of will, and especially in order to emphasize his resistance to the Schopenhauerian notion.

Nietzsche's expression "will to power" means to suggest that will as we usually understand it is actually and only will to power. But a possible misunderstanding lurks even in this explanation. The expression "will to power" does not mean that, in accord with the usual view, will is a kind of desiring that has power as its goal rather than happiness and pleasure. True, in many passages Nietzsche speaks in that fashion, in order to make himself provisionally understood; but when he makes will's goal power instead of happiness, pleasure, or the unhinging of the will, he changes not only the goal of will but the essential definition of will itself. In the strict sense of the Nietzschean conception of will, power can never be pre-established as will's goal, as though power were something that could first be posited outside the will. Because will is resolute openness toward itself, as mastery out beyond itself, because will is a willing beyond itself, it is the strength that is able to bring itself to power.

The expression "to power" therefore never means some sort of appendage to will. Rather, it comprises an elucidation of the essence of will itself. Only when we have clarified Nietzsche's concept of will in these respects can we understand those designations Nietzsche often chooses in order to exhibit the complicated nature of what that simple word "will" says to him. He calls will—therefore will to power—an "affect." He even says, "My theory would be that *will to power* is the primitive form of affect, that all other affects are but its configurations" (WM, 688).* Nietzsche calls will a "passion" as well, or a "feeling." If we understand such descriptions from the point of view of our common psychology—something that always seems to happen—then we might easily be tempted to say that Nietzsche abandons the essence of will to the "emotional," or that he rescues it from the rationalistic misinterpretations perpetrated by Idealism.

Here we must ask two things. First, what does Nietzsche mean when

---

*Walter Kaufmann notes that the phrase "My theory would be" stems from the editors, not from Nietzsche himself. See his edition of *The Will to Power*, p. 366, n. 73.

he emphasizes the character of will as affect, passion, and feeling? Second, when we believe we have found that the idealistic conception of will has nothing to do with Nietzsche's, how are we understanding "Idealism"?

8. Will as Affect, Passion, and Feeling

In the passage last cited Nietzsche says that all affects are "configurations" of will to power. If we ask what will to power is, Nietzsche answers that it is the original affect. Affects are forms of will; will is affect. That is called a circular definition. Common sense feels itself superior when it discovers such "errors of logic" even in a philosopher. Affect is will and will is affect. Now, we already know—at least roughly —that the question of will to power involves the question concerning the *Being of beings;* Being itself can no longer be determined by any given beings, since it is what determines them. Therefore, if any designation of Being is brought forward at all, and if it is supposed to say the same as Being, yet not in a merely empty way, then the determination brought to bear must of necessity be drawn from beings—and the circle is complete. Nevertheless, the matter is not all that simple. In the case at hand Nietzsche says with good grounds that will to power is the original form of affect; he does not say that it is simply one affect, although we often find such turns of phrase in his hastily composed argumentative presentations.

To what extent is will to power the original form of affect, i.e., that which constitutes the Being of an affect in general? What is an affect? To this, Nietzsche provides no clear and precise answer. Just as little does he answer the questions as to what a passion or a feeling may be. The answer ("configurations" of will power) does not immediately conduct us any farther. Rather, it assigns us the task of divining what it is in what we know as affect, passion, and feeling that signifies the essence of will to power. In that way we could derive particular characteristics which are suitable for making clearer and richer the previous attempts to define the essential concept of will. This work we must do ourselves. Yet the questions (what are affect, passion, and feeling?) remain unanswered. Nietzsche himself often equates the three; he follows the usual ways of representing them, ways still accepted today. With these three words, each an arbitrary substitute for the others, we depict the so-called irrational side of psychic life. For customary representational thought that may suffice, but not for true knowledge, and certainly not if our task is to determine by such knowledge the Being of beings. Nor is it enough to revamp the current "psychological" explanations of affects, passions, and feelings. We must above all see that here it is not a matter for psychology, nor even for a psychology undergirded by physiology and biology. It is a matter of the basic modes that constitute Dasein, a matter of the ways man confronts the *Da*, the openness and concealment of beings, in which he stands.

We cannot deny that the things physiology grapples with—particular states of the body, changes in internal secretions, muscle flexions, occurrences in the nervous system—are also proper to affects, passions, and feelings. But we have to ask whether all these bodily states and the body itself are grasped in a metaphysically adequate way, so that one may without further ado borrow material from physiology and biology, as Nietzsche, to his own detriment, so often did. The one fundamental point to realize here is that no result of any science can ever be applied *immediately* to philosophy.

How are we to conceive of the essence of affect, passion, and feeling, indeed in such a way that in each case it will be fruitful for an interpretation of the essence of will in Nietzsche's sense? Here we can conduct our examination only as far as illumination of Nietzsche's characterization of will to power requires.

Anger, for instance, is an affect. In contrast, by "hate" we mean something quite different. Hate is not simply another affect, it is not an affect at all. It is a passion. But we call both of them "feelings." We speak of the feeling of hatred and of an angry feeling. We cannot plan or decide to be angry. Anger comes over us, seizes us, "affects" us. Such a seizure is sudden and turbulent. Our being is moved by a kind of excitement, something stirs us up, lifts us beyond ourselves, but in such a way that, seized by our excitement, we are no longer masters of ourselves. We say, "He acted on impulse," that is to say, under the influence of an affect. Popular speech proves to be keensighted when it says of someone who is stirred up and acts in an excited manner, "He isn't altogether himself." When we are seized by excitement, our being "altogether there" vanishes; it is transformed into a kind of "falling apart." We say, "He's beside himself with joy."

Nietzsche is obviously thinking of that essential moment in the affect when he tries to characterize will in its terms. Such being lifted beyond ourselves in anger, the seizure of our whole being, so that we are not our own master, such a "not" does not at all mean to deny that in anger we are carried beyond ourselves; such "not being master" in the affect, in anger, distinguishes the affect from mastery in the sense of will, for in the affect our being master of ourselves is transformed into a manner of being beyond ourselves where something is lost. Whatever is contrary we call "counter." We call anger a counter-will that subsists beyond us, in such a way that in anger we do not remain together with ourselves as we do when willing, but, as it were, lose ourselves. Here will is a counter-will. Nietzsche turns the state of affairs around: the formal essence of the affect is will, but now will is visualized merely as a state of excitement, of being beyond oneself.

Because Nietzsche says that to will is to will out beyond oneself, he can say that, in view of such being beyond oneself in the affect, will to power is the original form of affect. Yet he clearly wants to add the other moment of the affect for the sake of the essential characterization of will, that moment of seizure in the affect by which something comes over us. That too, and precisely that, in a manifold and Protean sense of course, is proper to the will. That we can be beyond or outside ourselves in this or that way, and that we are in fact constantly so, is possible only because will itself—seen in relation to the essence of man—is seizure pure and simple.

Will itself cannot be willed. We can never resolve to have a will, in the sense that we would arrogate to ourselves a will; for such resoluteness is itself a willing. When we say, "He wants to have his will carried out in this or that matter," it means as much as, he really wants to stand firm in his willing, to get hold of himself in his entire being, to be master over his being. But that very possibility indicates that we are always within the scope of will, even when we are unwilling. That genuine willing which surges forward in resoluteness, that "yes," is what instigates the seizure of our entire being, of the very essence within us.

Nietzsche designates will as passion just as often as affect. We should not automatically conclude that he identifies affect and passion, even if he does not arrive at an explicit and comprehensive clarification of the essential distinction and connection between these two. We may surmise that Nietzsche knows the difference between affect and passion. Around the year 1882 he says regarding his times, "Our age is an agitated one, and precisely for that reason, not an age of passion; it heats itself up continuously, because it feels that it is not warm—basically it is freezing. I do not believe in the greatness of all these 'great events' of which you speak" (XII, 343). "The age of the greatest events will, in spite of all that, be the age of the most meager effects if men are made of rubber and are all too elastic." "In our time it is merely by means of an echo that events acquire their 'greatness'—the echo of the newspapers" (XII, 344).

Usually Nietzsche employs the word "passion" interchangeably with "affect." But if anger and hate, for example, or joy and love, not only are different as one affect is from another, but are distinct as affects and passions respectively, then here too we need a more exact definition. Hate too cannot be produced by a decision; it too seems to overtake us—in a way similar to that when we are seized by anger. Nevertheless, the manner in which it comes over us is essentially different. Hate can explode suddenly in an action or exclamation, but only because it has already overtaken us, only because it has been growing within us for a long time, and, as we say, has been nurtured in us. But something can be nurtured only if it is already there and is alive. In contrast, we do not say and never believe that anger is nurtured. Because hate lurks much more deeply in the origins of our being it has a cohesive power; like love, hate brings an original cohesion and perdurance to our essential being. But anger, which seizes us, can also release

us again—it "blows over," as we say. Hate does not "blow over." Once
it germinates it grows and solidifies, eating its way inward and consum-
ing our very being. But the permanent cohesion that comes to human
existence through hate does not close it off and blind it. Rather, it
grants vision and premeditation. The angry man loses the power of
reflection. He who hates intensifies reflection and rumination to the
point of "hardboiled" malice. Hate is never blind; it is perspicuous.
Only anger is blind. Love is never blind: it is perspicuous. Only infatua-
tion is blind, fickle, and susceptible—an affect, not a passion. To
passion belongs a reaching out and opening up of oneself. Such reaching out occurs even in hate, since the hated one is pursued everywhere
relentlessly. But such reaching out in passion does not simply lift us up
and away beyond ourselves. It gathers our essential being to its proper
ground, it exposes our ground for the first time in so gathering, so that
the passion is that through which and in which we take hold of ourselves and achieve lucid mastery over the beings around us and within
us.

Passion understood in this way casts light on what Nietzsche calls
will to power. Will as mastery of oneself is never encapsulation of the
ego from its surroundings. Will is, in our terms, resolute openness, in
which he who wills stations himself abroad among beings in order to
keep them firmly within his field of action.* Now the characteristic
traits are not seizure and agitation, but the lucid grip which
simultaneously gathers that passionate being.

Affect: the seizure that blindly agitates us. Passion: the lucidly gathering grip on beings. We talk and understand only extrinsically when
we say that anger flares and then dissipates, lasting but a short time,

---

*Perhaps a word is needed concerning the traditional translation of *Entschlossenheit,*
"resoluteness." Heidegger now hyphenates the German word to emphasize that *Entschlossenheit,* far from being a sealing-off or closing-up of the will in decision, means
unclosedness, hence a "resolute openness." The word thus retains its essential ties to
Erschlossenheit, the disclosure of Being in Dasein. On *Entschlossenheit* see Martin
Heidegger, *Sein und Zeit,* 12th ed. (Tübingen: M. Niemeyer, 1972), esp. p. 297; "Vom
Wesen der Wahrheit," in *Wegmarken* (Frankfurt/Main: V. Klostermann, 1967), p. 90;
and *Gelassenheit* (Pfullingen: G. Neske, 1959), p. 59. Cf. *Martin Heidegger: Basic
Writings,* ed. D. F. Krell (New York: Harper & Row, 1977), p. 133 n.

while hate lasts longer. No, hate and love not only last longer, they bring perdurance and permanence for the first time to our existence. An affect, in contrast, cannot do that. Because passion restores our essential being, because it loosens and liberates in its very grounds, and because passion at the same time reaches out into the expanse of beings, for these reasons passion—and we mean great passion—possesses extravagance and resourcefulness, not only the ability but the necessity to submit, without bothering about what its extravagance entails. It displays that self-composed superiority characteristic of great will.

Passion has nothing to do with sheer desire. It is not a matter of the nerves, of ebullition and dissipation. All of that, no matter how excited its gestures, Nietzsche reckons as attrition of the will. Will is what it is only as willing out beyond itself, willing more. Great will shares with great passion that serenity of unhurried animation that is slow to answer and react, not out of insecurity and ponderousness, but out of the broadly expansive security and inner buoyancy of what is superior.

Instead of "affect" and "passion" we also say "feeling," if not "sensation." Or, where affects and passions are distinguished, the two are conjoined in the genus "feeling." Today if we apply the term "feeling" to a passion, it is understood as a kind of reduction. For we believe that a passion is not a mere feeling. Nevertheless, the simple fact that we refrain from calling passions feelings does not prove that we possess a more highly developed concept of the essence of passion; it may only be a sign that we have employed too paltry a concept of the essence of feeling. So it is in fact. But it may seem that here we are merely inquiring into word meanings and their appropriate applications. Yet the *matter* that is here in question is, first, whether what we have now indicated as being the essence of affect and of passion exhibits an original, essential connection between these two, and second, whether this original connection can truly be understood if only we grasp the essence of what we call "feeling."

Nietzsche himself does not shy from conceiving willing simply as feeling: "Willing: a compelling feeling, quite pleasant! It is the epiphenomenon of all *discharge of energy*" (XIII, 159). To will—a feeling of pleasure? "Pleasure is only a symptom of the feeling of power attained, a consciousness of difference (—it [a living creature] does not strive for pleasure: rather, pleasure enters on the scene when it achieves what it is striving for: pleasure accompanies, it does not motivate—)" (WM, 688). Is will accordingly but an "epiphenomenon" of energy discharge, an accompanying feeling of pleasure? How does that jibe with what was said about the essence of will in general, and in particular with respect to the comparison with affect and passion? There will appeared as what properly sustains and dominates, being synonymous with mastery itself. Is it now to be reduced to a feeling of pleasure that merely accompanies something else?

From such passages we see clearly how unconcerned Nietzsche is about a unified, solidly grounded presentation of his teaching. We realize that he is only getting under way, that he is resolutely open. His task is not a matter of indifference to him; neither is it of only supplemental interest. He knows, as only a creator can, that what from the outside looks like a summary presentation is actually the configuration of the real issue, where things collide against one another in such a way that they expose their proper essence. Nevertheless, Nietzsche remains under way, and the immediate casting of what he wants to say always forces itself upon him. In such a position he speaks directly the language of his times and of the contemporary "science." When he does so he does not shy from conscious exaggeration and one-sided formulations of his thoughts, believing that in this way he can most clearly set in relief what in his vision and in his inquiry is different from the run-of-the-mill. Yet when he proceeds in such a manner he is always able to keep his eye on the whole; he can make do, as it were, with one-sidedness. The results are fatal when others, his readers, latch onto such statements in a superficial way and, depending on what Nietzsche just then is offering them, either declare it his sole opinion on the matter or, on the grounds of any given particular utterances, all too facilely refute him.

If it is true that will to power constitutes the basic character of all beings, and if Nietzsche now defines will as an accompanying feeling of pleasure, these two conceptions of will are not automatically compatible. Nor will one ascribe to Nietzsche the view that Being simply accompanies something else as a feeling of pleasure—that "something else" being yet another entity whose Being would have to be determined. The only way out is to assume that the definition of will as an accompanying feeling of pleasure, which is at first so foreign to what was presented earlier, is neither *the* essential definition of will nor one such definition among others. It is much more the case that it refers to something altogether proper to the full essence of will. But if this is the case, and if in our earlier remarks we have sketched an outline of the essential structure of will, then the definition just mentioned must somehow fit into the general pattern we have presented.

"Willing: a compelling feeling, quite pleasant!" A feeling is the way we find ourselves in relationship to beings, and thereby at the same time to ourselves. It is the way we find ourselves particularly attuned to beings which we are not and to the being we ourselves are. In feeling, a state opens up, and stays open, in which we stand related to things, to ourselves, and to the people around us, always simultaneously. Feeling is the very state, open to itself, in which our Dasein hovers. Man is not a rational creature who also wills, and in addition to thinking and willing is equipped with feelings, whether these make him admirable or despicable; rather, the state of feeling is original, although in such a way that thinking and willing belong together with it. Now the only important matter that remains for us to see is that feeling has the character of opening up and keeping open, and therefore also, depending on the kind of feeling it is, the character of closing off.

But if will is willing out beyond itself, the "out beyond" does not imply that will simply wanders away from itself; rather, will gathers itself together in willing. That the one who wills, wills himself into his will, means that such willing itself, and in unity with it he who wills and what is willed, become manifest in the willing. In the essence of will, in resolute openness, will discloses itself to itself, not merely by means of some further act appended to it, some sort of observation of the willing process and reflection on it; on the contrary, it is will itself that has the character of opening up and keeping open. No self-observation or self-analysis which we might undertake, no matter how penetrating, brings to light our self, and how it is with our self. In contrast, in willing and, correspondingly, in not willing, we bring ourselves to light; it is a light kindled only by willing. Willing always brings the self to itself; it thereby finds itself out beyond itself. It maintains itself within the thrust away from one thing toward something else. Will therefore has the character of feeling, of keeping open our very state of being, a state that in the case of will—being out beyond itself—is a pulsion. Will can thus be grasped as a "compelling feeling." It is not only a feeling of something that prods us, but is itself a prodding, indeed of a sort that is "quite pleasant." What opens up in the will— willing itself as resolute openness—is agreeable to the one for whom it is so opened, the one who wills. In willing we come toward ourselves, as the ones we properly are. Only in will do we capture ourselves in our most proper essential being. He who wills is, as such, one who wills out beyond himself; in willing we know ourselves as out beyond ourselves; we sense a mastery over . . . , somehow achieved; a thrill of pleasure announces to us the power attained, a power that enhances itself. For that reason Nietzsche speaks of a "consciousness of difference."

If feeling and will are grasped here as "consciousness" or "knowl-edge," it is to exhibit most clearly that moment of the opening up of something in will itself. But such opening is not an observing; it is feeling. This suggests that willing is itself a kind of state, that it is open in and to itself. Willing is feeling (state of attunement). Now since the will possesses that manifold character of willing out beyond itself, as we have suggested, and since all this becomes manifest as a whole, we can conclude that a multiplicity of feelings haunts our willing. Thus in *Beyond Good and Evil* (VII, 28–29) Nietzsche says:

> . . . in every willing there is in the first place a multiplicity of feelings, namely, the feeling of the state *away from* which, the feeling of the state *toward* which, the feeling of this very "away" and "toward"; then there is also an accompanying feeling in the musculature that comes into play by force of habit as soon as we "will," even if we do not set "arms and legs" in motion.

That Nietzsche designates will now as affect, now as passion, now as feeling should suggest that he sees something more unified, more original, and even more fertile behind that single rude word, "will." If he calls will an affect, it is not a mere equation, but a designation of will with regard to what distinguishes the affect as such. The same is true for the concepts of passion and feeling. We have to go even further and reverse the state of affairs. What we otherwise recognize as affect, passion, and feeling, Nietzsche recognizes in its essential roots as will to power. Thus he grasps "joy" (normally an affect) as a "feeling-stronger," as a feeling of being out beyond oneself and of being capable of being so (WM, 917):

> To feel stronger—or, to express it differently, joy—always presupposes comparison (but *not* necessarily with others; rather, with oneself, within a state of growth, and without first knowing to what extent one is comparing—).

This is a reference to that "consciousness of difference" which is not knowledge in the sense of mere representation and cognition.

Joy does not simply presuppose an unwitting comparison. It is rather something that brings us to ourselves, not by way of knowledge but by way of feeling, by way of an away-beyond-us. Comparison is not presupposed. Rather, the disparity implied in being out beyond ourselves is first opened up and given form by joy.

If we examine all this from the outside rather than the inside, if we judge it by the standards of customary theories of knowledge and consciousness, whether idealistic or realistic, we proceed to declare that Nietzsche's concept of will is an emotional one, conceived in terms of our emotional lives, our feelings, and that it is therefore ultimately a biological notion. All well and good. But such explanations pigeonhole Nietzsche in that representational docket which he would like to escape. That is also true of the interpretation that tries to distinguish Nietzsche's "emotional" concept of will from the "idealistic" one.

9. The Idealistic Interpretation of Nietzsche's Doctrine of Will

We have now arrived at the second of the questions posed above [p. 43], which asks: if we believe we have found that the idealistic concept of will has nothing to do with Nietzsche's, how are we understanding "Idealism"?

Generally we can call "idealistic" that mode of observation which looks to ideas. Here "idea" means as much as representation. To represent means to envisage in the widest sense: *idein*. To what extent can an elucidation of the essence of will see in will a trait of representation?

Willing is a kind of desiring and striving. The Greeks call it *orexis*. In the Middle Ages and in modern times it is called *appetitus* and *inclinatio*. Hunger, for example, is sheer compulsion and striving, a compulsion toward food for the sake of nourishment. In the case of animals the compulsion itself as such does not have explicitly in view what it is being compelled toward; animals do not represent food as such and do not strive for it as nourishment. Such striving does not know what it will have, since it does not will at all; yet it goes after what is striven for, though never going after it *as* such. But will, as striving, is not blind compulsion. What is desired and striven for is represented as such along with the compulsion; it too is taken up into view and co-apprehended.

To bring something forward and to contemplate it is called in Greek *noein*. What is striven for, *orekton*, in the willing is at the same time something represented, *noēton*. But that does not at all mean that willing is actually representation of such a kind that a striving tags along after what is represented. The reverse is the case. We shall offer as unequivocal proof a passage from Aristotle's treatise *Peri psychēs,* "On the Soul."

When we translate the Greek *psyche* as "soul" we dare not think of it in the sense of "life experiences," nor may we think of what we know in the consciousness of our *ego cogito,* nor finally may we think of the "unconscious." For Aristotle *psyche* means the principle of living creatures as such, whatever it is that makes living things to be alive, what pervades their very essence. The treatise just mentioned discusses the essence of life and the hierarchy of living creatures.

The treatise contains no psychology, and no biology either. It is a metaphysics of living creatures, among which man too belongs. What lives moves itself by itself. Movement here means not only change of place but every mode of behavior and self-alteration. Man is the highest form of living creature. The basic type of self-movement for him is action, *praxis.* So the question arises: what is the determining ground, the *archē,* of action, i.e., of proceeding in a considered fashion and establishing something? What is determinative here, the represented as such or what is sought? Is the representing-striving determined by representation or desire? To ask it another way: is will a representing, and is it therefore determined by ideas, or not? If what is taught is that will is in essence a representing, then such a doctrine of will is "idealistic."

What does Aristotle teach concerning will? The tenth chapter of Book III deals with *orexis,* desiring. Here Aristotle says (433a 15 ff.):

Kai hē orexis heneka tou pasa · hou gar hē orexis, hautē archē tou praktikou nou · to d' eschaton archē tēs praxeōs. Hoste eulogōs dyo tauta phainetai ta kinounta, orexis kai dianoia praktikē · to orekton gar kinei, kai dia touto hē dianoia kinei, hoti archē autēs esti to orekton.

And every desire has that on account of which it is desire [what the desire aims at]; it is that on the basis of which the *considering* intellect *as such*

determines itself; the terminal point is that by which the action is determined. Therefore these two, desiring and the considering intellect, show
themselves with good grounds to be what moves; for what is desired in the
desiring moves, and the intellect, representation, moves only because it
represents to itself what is desired in the desiring.

Aristotle's conception of the will becomes definitive for all Western
thought; it is still today the common conception. In the Middle Ages
voluntas is interpreted as *appetitus intellectualis,* i.e., *orexis dianoētikē,*
the desiring which is proper to intellectual representation. For Leibniz
agere, doing, is *perceptio* and *appetitus* in one; *perceptio* is *idea,*
representation. For Kant the will is that faculty of desire which works
according to concepts, which is to say, in such a way that what is willed,
as something represented in general, is itself determinative of action.
Although representation sets in relief the will as a faculty of desire over
against sheer blind striving, it does not serve as the proper moving and
willing force in will. Only a conception of will that would ascribe to
representation or the *idea* such an unjustified preeminence could be
classified as idealistic in the strict sense. Indeed we do find such conceptions. In the Middle Ages, Thomas Aquinas inclines toward such an
interpretation of the will, although even with him the question is not
decided so unequivocally. Viewed as a whole, the great thinkers have
never assigned to representation the highest rank in their conceptions
of the will.

If by an "idealistic interpretation of the will" we understand every
conception that in any way emphasizes representation, thought, knowledge, and concept as essential components of will, then Aristotle's
interpretation of will is undoubtedly idealistic. So in the same way are
those of Leibniz and Kant; but then so too is that of Nietzsche. Proof
for this assertion is quite easy to come by: we need only read a bit
farther into that passage where Nietzsche says that will consists of a
multiplicity of feelings.

Therefore, just as we must acknowledge feeling, and indeed many types of
feelings, as ingredients of the will, so must we also in the second place

acknowledge thinking: in every act of the will there is a commandeering thought; —and one should not think that he can sever this thought from the "willing," as though will would be what were left over! (VII, 29).

That is spoken clearly enough, not only against Schopenhauer, but against all those who want to appeal to Nietzsche when they defy thinking and the power of the concept.

In the light of these clear statements by Nietzsche, an outright rejection of the idealistic interpretation of his doctrine of will seems futile. But perhaps one might argue that Nietzsche's conception of will differs from that of German Idealism. There too, however, the Kantian and Aristotelian concept of will is adopted. For Hegel, knowing and willing are the same, which is to say, true knowledge is also already action and action is only in knowledge. Schelling even says that what actually wills in the will is the intellect. Is that not unclouded Idealism, if one understands by that a tracing of will back to representation? But by his extravagant turn of phrase Schelling wants to emphasize nothing else than what Nietzsche singles out in the will when he says that will is command. For when Schelling says "intellect," and when German Idealism speaks of knowing, they do not mean a faculty of representation as the discipline of psychology would think it; they do not mean the kind of behavior that merely accompanies and observes the other processes of psychic life. Knowing means opening upon Being, which is a willing—in Nietzsche's language, an "affect." Nietzsche himself says, *"To will is to command:* but commanding is a particular *affect* (this affect is a sudden explosion of energy)—intent, clear, having one thing exclusively in view, innermost conviction of its superiority, certain that it will be obeyed—" (XIII, 264). To have one thing clearly, intently, exclusively in view: what else is that than, in the strict sense of the word, holding one thing before oneself, presenting it before oneself? But *intellect,* Kant says, is the faculty of representation.

No designation of will is more common in Nietzsche than the one just cited: to will is to command; in the will lies a commandeering thought. But at the same time no other conception of will emphasizes more decisively than this one the essential role of knowledge and representation, the role of intellect, in the will.

Hence, if we want to get as close as we can to Nietzsche's conception of the will, and stay close to it, then we are well advised to hold all the usual terminology at a distance. Whether we call his conception idealistic or nonidealistic, emotional or biological, rational or irrational—in each case it is a falsification.

10. Will and Power. The Essence of Power

Now we can—indeed it seems we must—gather together the series of determinations of the essence of will which we have elaborated and conjoin them in a single definition: will as mastery over something, reaching out beyond itself; will as affect (the agitating seizure); will as passion (the expansive plunge into the breadth of beings); will as feeling (being the state of having a stance-toward-oneself); and will as command. With some effort we certainly could produce a formally proper "definition" bristling with all these attributes. All the same, we will forego that. Not as though we laid no value on strict and univocal concepts—on the contrary, we are searching for them. But a notion is not a concept, not in philosophy at any rate, if it is not founded and grounded in such a way as to allow what it is grasping to become its standard and the pathway of its interrogation, instead of camouflaging it under the net of a mere formula. But what the concept "will," as the basic character of beings, is to grasp, i.e., Being, is not yet in our vicinity; better, *we* are not close enough to *it*. To be cognizant, to know, is not mere familiarity with concepts. Rather, it is to grasp what the concept itself catches hold of. To grasp Being means to remain knowingly exposed to its sudden advance, its presencing. If we consider what the word "will" is to name, the essence of beings themselves, then we shall comprehend how powerless such a solitary word must remain, even when a definition is appended to it. Hence Nietzsche can say, "Will: that is a supposition which clarifies nothing else for me. For those who know, there is no willing" (XII, 303). From such statements we should not conclude that the whole effort to capture the essence of will is without prospect, nothing worth, and that therefore it is a matter of indifference and arbitrariness what words or concepts we use when speaking of "will." On the contrary, we have to question, right from the start and continually, on the basis of the matter itself. Only in that way do we arrive at the concept and at the proper use of the word.

Now, in order from the outset to avoid the vacuity of the word "will," Nietzsche says "will to power." Every willing is a willing to be more. Power itself only *is* inasmuch as, and so long as, it remains a willing to be more power. As soon as such will disappears, power is no longer power, even if it still holds in subjection what it has overmastered. In will, as willing to be more, as will to power, enhancement and heightening are essentially implied. For only by means of perpetual heightening can what is elevated be held aloft. Only a more powerful heightening can counter the tendency to sink back; simply holding onto the position already attained will not do, because the inevitable consequence is ultimate exhaustion. In *The Will to Power* Nietzsche says (WM, 702):

> —what man wants, what every smallest part of a living organism wants, is an *increase of power*.... Let us take the simplest case, that of primitive nourishment: the protoplasm stretches its pseudopodia in order to search for something that resists it—not from hunger but from will to power. It then attempts to overcome this thing, to appropriate it, to incorporate it. What we call "nourishment" is merely a derivative appearance, a practical application of that original will to become *stronger*.*

To will is to want to become stronger. Here too Nietzsche speaks by way of reversal and at the same time by way of defense against a contemporary trend, namely, Darwinism. Let us clarify this matter briefly. Life not only exhibits the drive to maintain itself, as Darwin

---

*Walter Kaufmann notes that all editions omit a sentence from this note. It should be inserted after the phrase "not from hunger but from will to power." In translation it reads: "Duality as the consequence of too weak a unity." See Kaufmann's edition of *The Will to Power,* p. 373, n. 80.

thinks, but also is self-assertion. The will to maintain merely clings to what is already at hand, stubbornly insists upon it, loses itself in it, and so becomes blind to its proper essence. Self-assertion, which wants to be ahead of things, to stay on top of things, is always a going back into its essence, into the origin. *Self-assertion is original assertion of essence.*

Will to power is never the willing of a particular actual entity. It involves the Being and essence of beings; it is this itself. Therefore we can say that will to power is always essential will. Although Nietzsche does not formulate it expressly in this way, at bottom that is what he means. Otherwise we could not understand what he always refers to in connection with his emphasis on the character of enhancement in will, of the "increase of power," namely, the fact that will to power is something creative. That designation too remains deceptive; it often seems to suggest that in and through will to power something is to be produced. What is decisive is not production in the sense of manufacturing but taking up and transforming, making something other than. . . , other in an essential way. For that reason the need to destroy belongs essentially to creation. In destruction, the contrary, the ugly, and the evil are posited; they are of necessity proper to creation, i.e., will to power, and thus to Being itself. To the essence of Being nullity belongs, not as sheer vacuous nothingness, but as the empowering "no."

We know that German Idealism thought Being as will. That philosophy also dared to think the negative as proper to Being. It suffices to refer to a passage in the Preface to Hegel's *Phenomenology of Spirit.* Here Hegel avers that the "monstrous power of the negative" is the "energy of thinking, of the pure ego." He continues:

> Death, if we want to name that unreality so, is the most frightful thing, and to hold fast to what is dead requires the greatest force. Beauty without force hates the intellect because intellect demands of her something of which she is incapable. But the life of Spirit is not one that shies from death and merely preserves itself from corruption; it is rather the life that endures death and maintains itself in death. Spirit achieves its truth only inasmuch as it finds itself in absolute abscission. It is not this power as something positive that

averts its glance from everything negative, as when we say of something that it is nothing, or false, and that now we are done with it and can leave it behind and go on to something else; rather, it is this power only insofar as it looks the negative in the eye and lingers with it.*

Thus German Idealism *too* dares to think evil as proper to the essence of Being. The greatest attempt in this direction we possess in Schelling's treatise *On the Essence of Human Freedom*. Nietzsche had a much too original and mature relation to the history of German metaphysics to have overlooked the might of thoughtful will in German Idealism. Hence at one point he writes (WM, 416):

> The significance of German philosophy (Hegel): to elaborate a pantheism in which evil, error, and suffering are *not* felt to be arguments against divinity. *This grandiose initiative* has been misused by the existing powers (the state, etc.), as though it sanctioned the rationality of those who happened to be ruling.
>
> In contrast, Schopenhauer appears as the stubborn moral-man who in order to retain his moral estimation finally becomes a *world-denier,* ultimately a "mystic."

This passage also reveals clearly that Nietzsche was by no means willing to join in the belittling, denegrating, and berating of German Idealism which became common with Schopenhauer and others in the middle of the nineteenth century. Schopenhauer's philosophy, which had been available in its finished form since 1818, began to reach a broader public by mid-century. Richard Wagner and the young Nietzsche were also caught up in the movement. We obtain a vivid picture of the enthusiasm for Schopenhauer which moved young people at that time from the letters of the youthful Baron Carl von Gersdorff to Nietzsche. They were friends since their high school days at Schulpforta. Especially important are the letters Gersdorff wrote to Nietzsche while at the front in 1870–71. (See *Die Briefe des Freiherrn Carl von Gersdorff an Friedrich Nietzsche,* edited by Karl Schlechta, first part: 1864–71, Weimar, 1934; second part: 1871–74, Weimar, 1935.)

---

*G. W. F. Hegel, *Phänomenologie des Geistes* (Hamburg: F. Meiner, 1952), pp. 29–30.

Schopenhauer interpreted the state of affairs—that he was suddenly now being read by the educated classes—as a philosophical victory over German Idealism. But Schopenhauer advanced to the forefront of philosophy at that time not because his philosophy conquered German Idealism philosophically, but because the Germans lay prostrate before German Idealism and were no longer equal to its heights. Its decline made Schopenhauer a great man. The consequence was that the philosophy of German Idealism, seen from the point of view of Schopenhauer's commonplaces, became something foreign, an oddity. It fell into oblivion. Only by detours and byways do we find our way back into that era of the German spirit; we are far removed from a truly historical relation to our history. Nietzsche sensed that here a "grandiose initiative" of metaphysical thought was at work. Yet for him it remained, had to remain, a mere glimmer. For the one decade of creative labor on his major work did not grant him the time and tranquillity to linger in the vast halls of Hegel's and Schelling's works.

Will is in itself simultaneously creative and destructive. Being master out beyond oneself is always also annihilation. All the designated moments of will—the out-beyond-itself, enhancement, the character of command, creation, self-assertion—speak clearly enough for us to know that will in itself is already will to power. Power says nothing else than the actuality of will.

Prior to our general description of Nietzsche's concept of will we made brief reference to the metaphysical tradition, in order to suggest that the conception of Being as will is not in itself peculiar. But the same is true also of the designation of Being as power. No matter how decisively the interpretation of Being as will to power remains Nietzsche's own, and no matter how little Nietzsche explicitly knew in what historical context the very concept of power as a determination of Being stood, it is certain that with this interpretation of the Being of beings Nietzsche advances into the innermost yet broadest circle of Western thought.

Ignoring for a moment the fact that for Nietzsche power means the same as will, we note that the essence of power is just as intricate as the essence of will. We could clarify the state of affairs by proceeding as we did when we listed the particular definitions of will that Nietzsche gives. But we will now emphasize only two moments within the essence of power.

Nietzsche often identifies power with force, without defining the latter more closely. Force, the capacity to be gathered in itself and prepared to work effects, to be in a position to do something, is what the Greeks (above all, Aristotle) denoted as *dynamis*. But power is every bit as much a being empowered, in the sense of the process of dominance, the being-at-work of force, in Greek, *energeia*. Power is will as willing out beyond itself, precisely in that way to come to itself, to find and assert itself in the circumscribed simplicity of its essence, in Greek, *entelecheia*. For Nietzsche power means all this at once: *dynamis, energeia, entelecheia*.

In the collection of treatises by Aristotle which we know under the title *Metaphysics* there is one, Book Theta (IX), that deals with *dynamis, energeia,* and *entelecheia,* as the highest determinations of Being.*

What Aristotle, still on the pathway of an original philosophy, but also already at its end, here thinks, i.e., asks, about Being, later is transformed into the doctrine of *potentia* and *actus* in Scholastic philosophy. Since the beginning of modern times philosophy entrenches itself in the effort to grasp Being by means of thinking. In that way the determinations of Being, *potentia* and *actus,* slip into the vicinity of the basic forms of thought or judgment. Possibility, actuality, and necessity along with them become modalities of Being and of thinking. Since then the doctrine of modalities becomes a component part of every doctrine of categories.

What contemporary academic philosophy makes of all this is a matter of scholarship and an exercise in intellectual acuity. What we find

---

*Heidegger had lectured in the summer of 1931 on Aristotle, *Metaphysics IX.* (The text of that course is to appear as vol. 33 of the *Gesamtausgabe.*) On the question of *alētheia* and Being in chapter 10 of *Metaphysics IX,* see Martin Heidegger, *Logik: Die Frage nach der Wahrheit* (Frankfurt/Main: V. Klostermann, 1976), pp. 170–82, the text of his 1925–26 lecture course. Cf. the review of this volume in *Research in Phenomenology,* VI (1976), 151–66.

in Aristotle, as knowledge of *dynamis, energeia, entelecheia,* is still philosophy; that is to say, the book of Aristotle's *Metaphysics* which we have referred to is the most worthy of question of all the books in the entire Aristotelian corpus. Although Nietzsche does not appreciate the concealed and vital connection between his concept of power, as a concept of Being, and Aristotle's doctrine, and although that connection remains apparently quite loose and undetermined, we may say that the Aristotelian doctrine has more to do with Nietzsche's doctrine of will to power than with any doctrine of categories and modalities in academic philosophy. But the Aristotelian doctrine itself devolves from a tradition that determines its direction; it is a first denouement of the first beginnings of Western philosophy in Anaximander, Heraclitus, and Parmenides.

However, we should not understand the reference to the inner relation of Nietzsche's will to power to *dynamis, energeia,* and *entelecheia* in Aristotle as asserting that Nietzsche's doctrine of Being can be interpreted immediately with the help of the Aristotelian teaching. Both must be conjoined in a more original context of questions. That is especially true of Aristotle's doctrine. It is no exaggeration to say that we today simply no longer understand or appreciate anything about Aristotle's teaching. The reason is simple: we interpret his doctrine right from the start with the help of corresponding doctrines from the Middle Ages and modern times, which on their part are only a transformation of and a decline from Aristotelian doctrine, and which therefore are hardly suited to provide a basis for our understanding.

Thus when we examine various aspects of the essence of will to power as powerfulness of will, we recognize how that interpretation of beings stands within the basic movement of Western thought. We discern how solely for that reason it is able to bring an essential thrust to the task of thinking in the twentieth century.

But of course we will never comprehend the innermost historicity of Nietzschean thought, by virtue of which it spans the breadth of centuries, if we only hunt for reminiscences, borrowings, and divergences in an extrinsic manner. We must grasp what it was that Nietzsche properly wanted to think. It would be no great trick—better, it would be precisely that, a mere trick—if, armed with a readymade conceptual apparatus, we proceeded to flush out particular disagreements, contradictions, oversights, and overhasty and often superficial and contingent remarks in Nietzsche's presentations. *As opposed to that, we are searching for the realm of his genuine questioning.*

In the final year of his creative life Nietzsche was wont to designate his manner of thinking as "philosophizing with the hammer." The expression has more than one meaning, in accordance with Nietzsche's own viewpoint. Least of all does it mean to go in swinging, wrecking everything. It means to hammer out a content and an essence, to sculpt a figure out of stone. Above all it means to tap all things with the hammer to hear whether or not they yield that familiar hollow sound, to ask whether there is still solidity and weight in things or whether every possible center of gravity has vanished from them. That is what Nietzsche's thought wants to achieve: it wants to give things weight and importance again.

Even if in the execution much remained unaccomplished and only projected, we should not conclude from the manner of Nietzsche's speech that the rigor and truth of the concept, the relentless effort to ground things by inquiring into them, was of secondary importance for his philosophical exertions. Whatever is a need in Nietzsche, and therefore a right, does not apply to anyone else; for Nietzsche is who he is, and he is unique. Yet such singularity takes on definition and first becomes fruitful when seen within the basic movement of Western thought.

11. The Grounding Question and the Guiding Question of Philosophy

We provided a general characterization of the will as will to power in order to illuminate to some extent the region we must now investigate.

We will begin the interpretation of Book III, "Principle of a New Valuation," with the fourth and final chapter, "Will to Power as Art." As we make clear in rough outline how Nietzsche grasps art and how he approaches the question of art, it will become clear at the same time *why an interpretation of the nucleus of will to power must begin precisely here, with art.*

Of course, it is decisive that the basic philosophical intention of the interpretation be held fast. Let us try to sharpen that intention further. The inquiry goes in the direction of asking what the being is. This traditional "chief question" of Western philosophy we call the guiding question. But it is only the *penultimate* question. The *ultimate,* i.e., *first* question is: what is Being itself? This question, the one which above all is to be unfolded and grounded, we call the grounding question of philosophy, because in it philosophy first inquires into the ground of beings *as ground,* inquiring at the same time into its own ground and in that way grounding itself. Before the question is posed explicitly, philosophy must, if it wants to ground itself, get a firm foothold on the path of an epistemology or doctrine of consciousness; but in so doing it remains forever on a path that leads only to the anteroom of philosophy, as it were, and does not penetrate to the very center of philosophy. The grounding question remains as foreign to Nietzsche as it does to the history of thought prior to him.

But when the guiding question (What is the being?) and the grounding question (What is Being?) are asked, we are asking: What is . . . ? The opening up of beings as a whole and of Being is the target for thought. Beings are to be brought into the open region of Being itself, and Being is to be conducted into the open region of its essence. The openness of beings we call unconcealment—*alētheia*, truth. The guiding and the grounding questions of philosophy ask what beings and Being in truth are. With the question of the essence of Being we are inquiring in such a way that nothing remains outside the question, not even nothingness. Therefore the question of what Being in truth is must at the same time ask what the truth in which Being is to be illumined itself is. Truth stands with Being in the realm of the grounding question, not because the possibility of truth is cast in doubt epistemologically, but because it already belongs to the essence of the grounding question in a distinctive sense, as its "space." In the grounding and guiding questions concerning Being and beings, we are also asking simultaneously and inherently about the essence of truth. "Also" about truth, we say, speaking altogether extrinsically. For truth cannot be what "also" comes forward somewhere in proximity to Being. Rather, the questions will arise as to how both are united in essence and yet are foreign to one another, and "where," in what domain, they somehow come together, and what that domain itself "is." Those are indeed questions that inquire beyond Nietzsche. But they alone provide the guarantee that we will bring his thought out into the open and make it fruitful, and also that we will come to experience and know the essential borders between us, recognizing what is different in him.

But if will to power determines beings as such, which is to say, in their truth, then the question concerning truth, i.e., the question of the essence of truth, must always be inserted into the interpretation of beings as will to power. And if for Nietzsche *art* attains an exceptional position within the task of a general interpretation of all occurrence, which is understood as will to power, then the question of *truth* must play a leading role precisely here.

12. Five Statements on Art

We shall now attempt a first characterization of Nietzsche's total conception of the essence of art. We will do this by exhibiting a sequence of five statements on art which provide weighty evidence.

Why is art of decisive importance for the task of grounding the principle of the new valuation? The immediate answer is found in number 797 of *The Will to Power,* which really ought to stand in the position of number 794* : "The phenomenon 'artist' is still the most *perspicuous*—." At first we will read no further, but consider only this statement. "The most perspicuous," that is, what for us is most accessible in its essence, is the phenomenon "artist"—the being of an artist. With this being, the artist, Being lights up for us most immediately and brightly. Why? Nietzsche does not explicitly say why; yet we can easily discover the reason. To be an artist is to be able to bring something forth. But to bring forth means to establish in Being something that does not yet exist. It is as though in bringing-forth we dwelled upon the coming to be of beings and could see there with utter clarity their essence. Because it is a matter of illuminating will to power as the basic character of beings, the task must begin where what is in question shows itself most brightly. For all clarifying must proceed from what is clear to what is obscure, not the other way round.

Being an artist is a way of *life.* What does Nietzsche say about life in general? He calls life "the form of Being most familiar to us" (WM, 689). For him "Being" itself serves only "as a generalization of the

---

*I.e., as the *first* of all the aphorisms and notes gathered under the title "Will to Power as Art."

concept 'life' (breathing), 'being besouled,' 'willing, effecting,' 'becoming' " (WM, 581). " 'Being'—we have no other way to represent it than as *'living.'* How then can something dead 'be'?" (WM, 582). "If the innermost essence of Being is will to power . . ." (WM, 693).

With these somewhat formula-like references we have already taken measure of the framework within which the "artist phenomenon" is to be conceived, the framework that is to be maintained throughout the coming considerations. We repeat: the being of an artist is the most perspicuous mode of life. Life is for us the most familiar form of Being. The innermost essence of Being is will to power. In the being of the artist we encounter the most perspicuous and most familiar mode of will to power. Since it is a matter of illuminating the Being of beings, meditation on art has in this regard decisive priority.

However, here Nietzsche speaks only of the "artist phenomenon," not about art. Although it is difficult to say what art "as such" is, and how it is, still it is clear that works of art too belong to the reality of art, and furthermore so do those who, as we say, "experience" such works. The artist is but one of those things that together make up the actuality of art as a whole. Certainly, but this is precisely what is decisive in Nietzsche's conception of art, that he sees it in its essential entirety in terms of the *artist;* this he does consciously and in explicit opposition to that conception of art which represents it in terms of those who "enjoy" and "experience" it.

That is a guiding principle of Nietzsche's teaching on art: art must be grasped in terms of creators and producers, not recipients. Nietzsche expresses it unequivocally in the following words (WM, 811): "Our aesthetics heretofore has been a woman's aesthetics, inasmuch as only the recipients of art have formulated their experiences of 'what is beautiful.' In all philosophy to date the artist is missing. . . ." Philosophy of art means "aesthetics" for Nietzsche too—but masculine aesthetics, not feminine aesthetics. The question of art is the question of the artist as the productive, creative one; *his* experiences of what is beautiful must provide the standard.

We now go back to number 797: "The phenomenon 'artist' is still the most *perspicuous*—." If we take the assertion in the guiding context of the question of will to power, with a view to the essence of art, then we derive at once two essential statements about art:

1. Art is the most perspicuous and familiar configuration of will to power;
2. Art must be grasped in terms of the artist.

And now let us read further (WM, 797): "... from that position to scan the *basic instincts of power,* of nature, etc.! Also of religion and morals!" Here Nietzsche says explicitly that with a view toward the essence of the artist the other configurations of will to power also— nature, religion, morals, and we might add, society and individual, knowledge, science, and philosophy—are to be observed. These kinds of beings hence correspond in a certain way to the being of the artist, to artistic creativity, and to being created. The remaining beings, which the artist does not expressly bring forth, have the mode of Being that corresponds to what the artist creates, the work of art. Evidence for such a thought we find in the aphorism immediately preceding (WM, 796): "The work of art, where it appears *without* artist, e.g., as body, as organization (the Prussian officer corps, the Jesuit order). To what extent the artist is only a preliminary stage. The world as a work of art that gives birth to itself—." Here the concept of art and of the work of art is obviously extended to every ability to bring forth and to everything that is essentially brought forth. To a certain extent that also corresponds to a usage that was common until the outset of the nine-teenth century. Up to that time art meant every kind of ability to bring forth. Craftsmen, statesmen, and educators, as men who brought some-thing forth, were artists. Nature too was an artist, a female artist. At that time art did not mean the current, narrow concept, as applied to "fine art," which brings forth something beautiful in its work.

However, Nietzsche now interprets that earlier, extended usage of art, in which fine art is only one type among others, in such a way that all bringing-forth is conceived as corresponding to fine art and to the artist devoted to it. "The artist is only a preliminary stage" means the artist in the narrower sense, one who brings forth works of fine art. On that basis we can exhibit a third statement about art:

3. According to the expanded concept of artist, art is the basic occurrence of all beings; to the extent that they are, beings are self-creating, created.

But we know that will to power is essentially a creating and destroying. That the basic occurrence of beings is "art" suggests nothing else than that it is will to power.

Long before Nietzsche grasps the essence of art explicitly as a configuration of will to power, in his very first writing, *The Birth of Tragedy from the Spirit of Music,* he sees art as the basic character of beings. Thus we can understand why during the time of his work on *The Will to Power* Nietzsche returns to the position he maintained on art in *The Birth of Tragedy.* An observation that is pertinent here is taken up into *The Will to Power* (WM, 853, Section IV). The final paragraph of the section reads: "Already in the Foreword [i.e., to the book *The Birth of Tragedy*], where Richard Wagner is invited, as it were, to a dialogue, this confession of faith, this artists' gospel, appears: 'art as the proper task of life, art as its *metaphysical* activity. . . .' " "Life" is not only meant in the narrow sense of human life but is identified with "world" in the Schopenhauerian sense. The statement is reminiscent of Schopenhauer, but it is already speaking against him.

Art, thought in the broadest sense as the creative, constitutes the basic character of beings. Accordingly, art in the narrower sense is that activity in which creation emerges for itself and becomes most perspicuous; it is not merely one configuration of will to power among others but the *supreme* configuration. Will to power becomes genuinely visible in terms of art and as art. But will to power is the ground upon which all valuation in the future is to stand. It is the principle of the new valuation, as opposed to the prior one which was dominated by religion, morality, and philosophy. If will to power therefore finds its supreme configuration in art, the positing of the new relation of will to power must proceed from art. Since the new valuation is a revaluation of the prior one, however, opposition and upheaval arise from art. That is averred in *The Will to Power,* no. 794:

Our religion, morality, and philosophy are *decadence*-forms of humanity.
—The *countermovement: art.*

According to Nietzsche's interpretation the very first principle of morality, of Christian religion, and of the philosophy determined by Plato reads as follows: This world is worth nothing; there must be a "better" world than this one, enmeshed as it is in sensuality; there must be a "true world" beyond, a supersensuous world; the world of the senses is but a world of appearances.

In such manner this world and this life are at bottom negated. If a "yes" apparently is uttered to the world, it is ultimately only in order to deny the world all the more decisively. But Nietzsche says that the "true world" of morality is a world of lies, that the true, the supersensuous, is an error. The sensuous world—which in Platonism means the world of semblance and errancy, the realm of error—is the true world. But the sensuous, the sense-semblant, is the very element of art. So it is that art affirms what the supposition of the ostensibly true world denies. Nietzsche therefore says (WM, 853, section II): "Art as the single superior counterforce against all will to negation of life, art as the anti-Christian, anti-Buddhist, anti-Nihilist *par excellence.*" With that we attain a fourth statement about the essence of art:

4. Art is the distinctive countermovement to nihilism.

The artistic creates and gives form. If the artistic constitutes metaphysical activity pure and simple, then every deed, especially the highest deed and thus the thinking of philosophy too, must be determined by it. The concept of philosophy may no longer be defined according to the pattern of the teacher of morality who posits another higher world in opposition to this presumably worthless one. Against the nihilistic philosopher of morality (Schopenhauer hovers before Nietzsche as the most recent example of this type) must be deployed the philosopher who goes counter, who emerges from a countermovement, the "artist-philosopher." Such a philosopher is an artist in that he gives form to beings as a whole, beginning there where they reveal themselves, i.e., in man. It is with this thought in mind that we are to read number 795 of *The Will to Power:*

> The *artist*-philosopher. Higher concept of *art.* Whether a man can remove himself far enough from other men, in order to *give them form?* (—Prelimi-

nary exercises: 1. the one who gives himself form, the hermit; 2. the artist *hitherto,* as the insignificant perfecter of a piece of raw material.)

Art, particularly in the narrow sense, is yes-saying to the sensuous, to semblance, to what is not "the true world," or as Nietzsche says succinctly, to what is not "the truth."

In art a decision is made about what truth is, and for Nietzsche that always means true beings, i.e., beings proper. This corresponds to the necessary connection between the guiding question and the grounding question of philosophy, on the one hand, and to the question of what truth is, on the other. Art is the will to semblance as the sensuous. But concerning such will Nietzsche says (XIV, 369): "The will to *semblance,* to illusion, to deception, to Becoming and change is deeper, more 'metaphysical,' than the will to *truth,* to reality, to Being." The true is meant here in Plato's sense, as being in itself, the Ideas, the supersensuous. The will to the sensuous world and to its richness is for Nietzsche, on the contrary, the will to what "metaphysics" seeks. Hence the will to the sensuous is metaphysical. That metaphysical will is actual in art.

Nietzsche says (XIV, 368):

Very early in my life I took the question of the relation of *art* to *truth* seriously: even now I stand in holy dread in the face of this discordance. My first book was devoted to it. *The Birth of Tragedy* believes in art on the background of another belief—that it *is not possible to live with truth,* that the "will to truth" is already a symptom of degeneration.

The statement sounds perverse. But it loses its foreignness, though not its importance, as soon as we read it in the right way. "Will to truth" here (and with Nietzsche always) means the will to the "true world" in the sense of Plato and Christianity, the will to supersensuousness, to being in itself. The will to such "true beings" is in truth a no-saying to our present world, precisely the one in which art is at home. Because this world is the genuinely real and only true world, Nietzsche can declare with respect to the relation of art and truth that "art is *worth more* than truth" (WM, 853, section IV). That is to say, the sensuous stands in a higher place and *is* more genuinely than the supersensuous.

In that regard Nietzsche says, "We have *art* in order *not to perish from the truth*" (WM, 822). Again "truth" means the "true world" of the supersensuous, which conceals in itself the danger that life may perish, "life" in Nietzsche's sense always meaning "life which is on the ascent." The supersensuous lures life away from invigorating sensuality, drains life's forces, weakens it. When we aim at the supersensuous, submission, capitulation, pity, mortification, and abasement become positive "virtues." "The simpletons of this world," the abject, the wretched, become "children of God." They are the true beings. It is the lowly ones who belong "up above" and who are to say what is "lofty," that is, what reaches their own height. For them all creative heightening and all pride in self-subsistent life amount to rebellion, delusion, and sin. But we have art so that we do not perish from such supersensuous "truth," so that the supersensuous does not vitiate life to the point of general debility and ultimate collapse. With regard to the essential relation of art and truth yet another statement about art, the final one in our series, results:

5. Art is worth more than "the truth."

Let us review the preceding statements:

1. Art is the most perspicuous and familiar configuration of will to power;
2. Art must be grasped in terms of the artist;
3. According to the expanded concept of artist, art is the basic occurrence of all beings; to the extent that they are, beings are self-creating, created;
4. Art is the distinctive countermovement to nihilism.

At the instigation of the five statements on art, we should now recall an utterance of Nietzsche's on the same subject cited earlier: ". . . we find it to be the greatest *stimulans* of life—" (WM, 808). Earlier the statement served only as an example of Nietzsche's procedure of reversal (in this case the reversal of Schopenhauer's sedative). Now we must grasp the statement in terms of its most proper content. On the basis of all the intervening material we can easily see that this definition of art as the stimulant of life means nothing else than that art is a configuration of will to power. For a "stimulant" is what propels and advances, what lifts a thing beyond itself; it is increase of power and thus power pure and simple, which is to say, will to power. Hence we cannot merely append to the five previous statements the one about art as the greatest stimulant of life. On the contrary, it is Nietzsche's *major statement on art.* Those five statements enlarge upon it.

On the cursory view, we are already at the end of our task. We were to indicate art as a configuration of will to power. Such is Nietzsche's intention. But with a view to Nietzsche we are searching for something else. We are asking, first, what does this conception of art achieve for the essential definition of will to power and thereby for that of beings as a whole? We can come to know that only if beforehand we ask, second, what is the significance of this interpretation for our knowledge of art and for our position with respect to it?

13. Six Basic Developments in the History of Aesthetics

We shall begin with the second question. In order to come to terms with it we must characterize Nietzsche's procedure for defining the essence of art with greater penetration and must place it in the context of previous efforts to gain knowledge of art.

With the five statements on art that we brought forward the essential aspects of Nietzsche's interrogation of art have been established. From them one thing is clear: Nietzsche does not inquire into art in order to describe it as a cultural phenomenon or as a monument to civilization. Rather, by means of art and a characterization of the essence of art, he wants to show what will to power is. Nevertheless, Nietzsche's meditation on art keeps to the traditional path. The path is defined in its peculiarity by the term "aesthetics." True, Nietzsche speaks against feminine aesthetics. But in so doing he speaks for masculine aesthetics, hence for aesthetics. In that way Nietzsche's interrogation of art is aesthetics driven to the extreme, an aesthetics, so to speak, that somersaults beyond itself. But what else should inquiry into art and knowledge of it be than "aesthetics"? What does "aesthetics" mean?

The term "aesthetics" is formed in the same manner as "logic" and "ethics." The word *epistēmē,* knowledge, must always complete these terms. Logic: *logikē epistēmē:* knowledge of *logos,* that is, the doctrine of assertion or judgment as the basic form of thought. Logic is knowledge of thinking, of the forms and rules of thought. Ethics: *ēthikē epistēmē:* knowledge of *ēthos,* of the inner character of man and of the way it determines his behavior. Logic and ethics both refer to human behavior and its lawfulness.

The word "aesthetics" is formed in the corresponding way: *aisthētikē epistēmē:* knowledge of human behavior with regard to sense, sensation, and feeling, and knowledge of how these are determined.

What determines thinking, hence logic, and what thinking comports itself toward, is the true. What determines the character and behavior of man, hence ethics, and what human character and behavior comport themselves toward, is the good. What determines man's feeling, hence aesthetics, and what feeling comports itself toward, is the beautiful. The true, the good, and the beautiful are the objects of logic, ethics, and aesthetics.

Accordingly, aesthetics is consideration of man's state of feeling in its relation to the beautiful; it is consideration of the beautiful to the extent that it stands in relation to man's state of feeling. The beautiful itself is nothing other than what in its self-showing brings forth that state. But the beautiful can pertain to either nature or art. Because art in its way brings forth the beautiful, inasmuch as it is "fine" art, meditation on art becomes aesthetics. With relation to knowledge of art and inquiry into it, therefore, aesthetics is that kind of meditation on art in which man's affinity to the beautiful represented in art sets the standard for all definitions and explanations, man's state of feeling remaining the point of departure and the goal of the meditation. The relation of feeling toward art and its bringing-forth can be one of production or of reception and enjoyment.

Now, since in the aesthetic consideration of art the artwork is defined as the beautiful which has been brought forth in art, the work is represented as the bearer and provoker of the beautiful with relation to our state of feeling. The artwork is posited as the "object" for a "subject"; definitive for aesthetic consideration is the subject-object relation, indeed as a relation of feeling. The work becomes an object in terms of that surface which is accessible to "lived experience."

Just as we say that a judgment that satisfies the laws of thought promulgated in logic is "logical," so do we apply the designation "aesthetic," which really only means a kind of observation and investigation with regard to a relation of feeling, to this sort of behavior itself. We speak of aesthetic feeling and an aesthetic state. Strictly speaking, a state of feeling is not "aesthetic." It is rather something that can become the object of aesthetic consideration. Such consideration is called "aesthetic" because it observes from the outset the state of feeling aroused by the beautiful, relates everything to that state, and defines all else in terms of it.

The name "aesthetics," meaning meditation on art and the beautiful, is recent. It arises in the eighteenth century. But the matter which the word so aptly names, the manner of inquiry into art and the beautiful on the basis of the state of feeling in enjoyers and producers, is old, as old as meditation on art and the beautiful in Western thought. Philosophical meditation on the essence of art and the beautiful even *begins* as aesthetics.

In recent decades we have often heard the complaint that the innumerable aesthetic considerations of and investigations into art and the beautiful have achieved nothing, that they have not helped anyone to gain access to art, that they have contributed virtually nothing to artistic creativity and to a sound appreciation of art. That is certainly true, especially with regard to the kind of thing bandied about today under the name "aesthetics." But we dare not derive our standards for judging aesthetics and its relation to art from such contemporary work. For, in truth, the fact whether and how an era is committed to an aesthetics, whether and how it adopts a stance toward art of an aesthetic character, is decisive for the way art shapes the history of that era—or remains irrelevant for it.

Because what stands in question for us is art as a configuration of will to power, which is to say, as a configuration of Being in general, indeed the distinctive one, the question of aesthetics as the basic sort of meditation on art and the knowledge of it can be treated only with respect to fundamentals. Only with the help of a reflection on the essence of aesthetics developed in this way can we get to the point where we can grasp Nietzsche's interpretation of the essence of art; only with the help of such a reflection can we at the same time take a position with regard to Nietzsche's interpretation, so that on this basis a *confrontation* can flourish.

In order to characterize the essence of aesthetics, its role in Western

thought, and its relation to the history of Western art, we shall introduce six basic developments for consideration. Such consideration,
of course, can only be by way of brief reference.

1. The magnificent art of Greece remains without a corresponding
cognitive-conceptual meditation on it, such meditation not having to
be identical with aesthetics. The lack of such a simultaneous reflection
or meditation on great art does not imply that Greek art was only
"lived," that the Greeks wallowed in a murky brew of "experiences"
braced by neither concepts nor knowledge. It was their good fortune
that the Greeks had no "lived experiences." On the contrary, they had
such an originally mature and luminous knowledge, such a passion for
knowledge, that in their luminous state of knowing they had no need
of "aesthetics."

2. Aesthetics begins with the Greeks only at that moment when
their great art and also the great philosophy that flourished along with
it comes to an end. At that time, during the age of Plato and Aristotle,
in connection with the organization of philosophy as a whole, those
basic concepts are formed which mark off the boundaries for all future
inquiry into art. One of those basic notions is the conceptual pair
hylē-morphē, materia-forma, matter-form. The distinction has its origin in the conception of beings founded by Plato, the conception of
beings with regard to their outer appearance: *eidos, idea.* Where beings
are apprehended as beings, and distinguished from other beings, in
view of their outer appearance, the demarcation and arrangement of
beings in terms of outer and inner limits enters on the scene. But what
limits is form, what is limited is matter. Whatever comes into view as
soon as the work of art is experienced as a self-showing according to
its *eidos,* as *phainesthai,* is now subsumed under these definitions. The
ekphanestaton, what properly shows itself and is most radiant of all, is
the beautiful. By way of the *idea,* the work of art comes to appear in
the designation of the beautiful as *ekphanestaton.*

With the distinction of *hylē-morphē,* which pertains to beings as
such, a second concept is coupled which comes to guide all inquiry into
art: art is *technē.* We have long known that the Greeks name art as
well as handicraft with the same word, *technē,* and name correspond-

ingly both the craftsman and the artist *technitēs*. In accordance with the later "technical" use of the word *technē*, where it designates (in a way utterly foreign to the Greeks) a mode of production, we seek even in the original and genuine significance of the word such later content: we aver that *technē* means hand manufacture. But because what we call fine art is also designated by the Greeks as *technē*, we believe that this implies a glorification of handicraft, or else that the exercise of art is degraded to the level of a handicraft.

However illuminating the common belief may be, it is not adequate to the actual state of affairs; that is to say, it does not penetrate to the basic position from which the Greeks define art and the work of art. But this will become clear when we examine the fundamental word *technē*. In order to catch hold of its true significance, it is advisable to establish the concept that properly counters it. The latter is named in the word *physis*. We translate it with "nature," and think little enough about it. For the Greeks, *physis* is the first and the essential name for beings themselves and as a whole. For them the being is what flourishes on its own, in no way compelled, what rises and comes forward, and what goes back into itself and passes away. It is the rule that rises and resides in itself.

If man tries to win a foothold and establish himself among the beings (*physis*) to which he is exposed, if he proceeds to master beings in this or that way, then his advance against beings is borne and guided by a knowledge of them. Such *knowledge* is called *technē*. From the very outset the word is not, and never is, the designation of a "making" and a producing; rather, it designates that knowledge which supports and conducts every human irruption into the midst of beings. For that reason *technē* is often the word for human knowledge without qualification. The kind of knowledge that guides and grounds confrontation with and mastery over beings, in which new and other beings are expressly produced and generated in addition to and on the basis of the beings that have already come to be (*physis*), in other words, the kind of knowledge that produces utensils and works of art, is then specially designated by the word *technē*. But even here, *technē* never means making or manufacturing as such; it always means knowledge, the disclosing of beings as such, in the manner of a knowing guidance of bringing-forth. Now, since the manufacture of utensils and the creation of artworks each in its way inheres in the immediacy of everyday existence, the knowledge that guides such procedures and modes of bringing-forth is called *technē* in an exceptional sense. The artist is a *technitēs,* not because he too is a handworker, but because the bringing-forth of artworks as well as utensils is an irruption by the man who knows and who goes forward in the midst of *physis* and upon its basis. Nevertheless, such "going forward," thought in Greek fashion, is no kind of attack: it lets what is already coming to presence arrive.

With the emergence of the distinction between matter and form, the essence of *technē* undergoes an interpretation in a particular direction; it loses the force of its original, broad significance. In Aristotle *technē* is still a mode of knowing, if only one among others (see the *Nicomachean Ethics,* Bk. VI). If we understand the word "art" quite generally to mean every sort of human capacity to bring forth, and if in addition we grasp the capacity and ability more originally as a knowing, then the word "art" corresponds to the Greek concept of *technē* also in its broad significance. But to the extent that *technē* is then brought expressly into relation with the production of beautiful things, or their representation, meditation on art is diverted by way of the beautiful into the realm of aesthetics. What in truth is decided in the apparently extrinsic and, according to the usual view, even misguided designation of art as *technē* never comes to light, neither with the Greeks nor in later times.

But here we cannot show how the conceptual pair "matter and form" came to be the really principal schema for all inquiry into art and all further definition of the work of art. Nor can we show how the distinction of "form and content" ultimately came to be a concept applicable to everything under the sun, a concept under which anything and everything was to be subsumed. It suffices to know that the distinction of "matter and form" sprang from the area of manufacture of tools or utensils, that it was not originally acquired in the realm of art in the narrower sense, i.e., fine art and works of art, but that it was merely transferred and applied to this realm. Which is reason enough to be dominated by a deep and abiding doubt concerning the trenchancy of these concepts when it comes to discussions about art and works of art.

3. The third basic development for the history of knowledge about art, and that now means the origin and formation of aesthetics, is once again a happenstance that does not flow immediately from art or from meditation on it. On the contrary, it is an occurrence that involves our entire history. It is the beginning of the modern age. Man and his unconstrained knowledge of himself, as of his position among beings, become the arena where the decision falls as to how beings are to be experienced, defined, and shaped. Falling back upon the state and condition of man, upon the way man stands before himself and before things, implies that now the very way man freely takes a position toward things, the way he finds and feels them to be, in short, his "taste," becomes the court of judicature over beings. In metaphysics that becomes manifest in the way in which certitude of all Being and all truth is grounded in the self-consciousness of the individual ego: *ego cogito ergo sum.* Such finding ourselves before ourselves in our own state and condition, the *cogito me cogitare,* also provides the first "object" which is secured in its Being. I myself, and my states, are the primary and genuine beings. Everything else that may be said to be is measured against the standard of this quite certain being. My having various states—the ways I find myself to be with something—participates essentially in defining how I find the things themselves and everything I encounter to be.

Meditation on the beautiful in art now slips markedly, even exclusively, into the relationship of man's state of feeling, *aisthēsis.* No wonder that in recent centuries aesthetics as such has been grounded and conscientiously pursued. That also explains why the name only now comes into use as a mode of observation for which the way had long been paved: "aesthetics" is to be in the field of sensuousness and feeling precisely what logic is in the area of thinking—which is why it is also called "logic of sensuousness."

Parallel to the formation of aesthetics and to the effort to clarify and ground the aesthetic state, another decisive process unfolds within the history of art. Great art and its works are great in their historical emergence and Being because in man's historical existence they accomplish a decisive task: they make manifest, in the way appropriate to works, what beings as a whole are, preserving such manifestation in the work. Art and its works are necessary only as an itinerary and sojourn for man in which the truth of beings as a whole, i.e., the unconditioned, the absolute, opens itself up to him. What makes art great is not only and not in the first place the high quality of what is created. Rather, art is great because it is an "absolute need." Because it is that, and to the extent it is that, it also can and must be great in rank. For only on the basis of the magnitude of its essential character does it also create a dimension of magnitude for the rank and stature of what is brought forth.

Concurrent with the formation of a dominant aesthetics and of the aesthetic relation to art in modern times is the decline of great art, great in the designated sense. Such decline does not result from the fact that the "quality" is poorer and the style less imposing; it is rather that art forfeits its essence, loses its immediate relation to the basic task of representing the absolute, i.e., of establishing the absolute definitively as such in the realm of historical man. From this vantage point we can grasp the fourth basic development.

4. At the historical moment when aesthetics achieves its greatest possible height, breadth, and rigor of form, great art comes to an end. The achievement of aesthetics derives its greatness from the fact that it recognizes and gives utterance to the end of great art as such. The final and greatest aesthetics in the Western tradition is that of Hegel. It is recorded in his *Lectures on Aesthetics,* held for the last time at the University of Berlin in 1828–29 (see Hegel's *Works,* vol. X, parts 1, 2 and 3). Here the following statements appear:

> . . . yet in this regard there is at least no absolute need at hand for it [the matter] to be brought to representation by *art* (X, 2, p. 233).

> In all these relations art is and remains for us, with regard to its highest determination, something past (X, 1, p. 16).

> The magnificent days of Greek art, like the golden era of the later Middle Ages, are gone (X, 1, pp. 15–16).

One cannot refute these statements and overcome all the history and happenings that stand behind them by objecting against Hegel that since 1830 we have had many considerable works of art which we might point to. Hegel never wished to deny the possibility that also in the future individual works of art would originate and be esteemed. The fact of such individual works, which exist as works only for the enjoyment of a few sectors of the population, does not speak against Hegel but for him. It is proof that art has lost its power to be the absolute, has lost its absolute power. On the basis of such loss the position of art and the kind of knowledge concerning it are defined for the nineteenth century. This we can demonstrate briefly in a fifth point.

5. Catching a glimpse of the decline of art from its essence, the nineteenth century once more dares to attempt the "collective artwork." That effort is associated with the name Richard Wagner. It is no accident that his effort does not limit itself to the creation of works that might serve such an end. His effort is accompanied and undergirded by reflections on the principles of such works, and by corresponding treatises, the most important of which are *Art and Revolution* (1849), *The Artwork of the Future* (1850), *Opera and Drama* (1851), *German Art and German Politics* (1865). It is not possible here to clarify to any great extent the complicated and confused historical and intellectual milieu of the mid-nineteenth century. In the decade 1850–1860 two streams interpenetrate in a remarkable fashion, the genuine and well-preserved tradition of the great age of the German movement, and the slowly expanding wasteland, the uprooting of human existence, which comes to light fully during the Gilded Age. One can never understand this most ambiguous century by describing the sequence of its periods. It must be demarcated simultaneously from both ends, i.e., from the last third of the eighteenth century and the first third of the twentieth.

Here we have to be satisfied with one indication, delineated by our guiding area of inquiry. With reference to the historical position of art, the effort to produce the "collective artwork" remains essential. The very name is demonstrative. For one thing, it means that the arts should no longer be realized apart from one another, that they should be conjoined in *one* work. But beyond such sheer quantitative unification, the artwork should be a celebration of the national community, it should be *the* religion. In that respect the definitive arts are literary and musical. Theoretically, music is to be a means for achieving effective drama; in reality, however, music in the form of opera becomes the authentic art. Drama possesses its importance and essential character, not in poetic originality, i.e., not in the well-wrought truth of the linguistic work, but in things pertaining to the stage, theatrical arrangements and gala productions. Architecture serves merely for theater construction, painting provides the backdrops, sculpture portrays the gestures of actors. Literary creation and language remain without the essential and decisive shaping force of genuine knowledge. What is wanted is the domination of art as music, and thereby the domination of the pure state of feeling—the tumult and delirium of the senses, tremendous contraction, the felicitous distress that swoons in enjoyment, absorption in "the bottomless sea of harmonies," the plunge into frenzy and the disintegration into sheer feeling as redemptive. The "lived experience" as such becomes decisive. The work is merely what arouses such experience. All portrayal is to work its effects as foreground and superficies, aiming toward the impression, the effect, wanting to work on and arouse the audience: theatrics. Theater and orchestra determine art. Of the orchestra Wagner says:

> The orchestra is, so to speak, the basis of infinite, universally common feeling, from which the individual feeling of the particular artist can blossom to the greatest fullness: it dissolves to a certain extent the static, motionless basis of the scene of reality into a liquid-soft, flexible, impressionable, ethereal surface, the immeasurable ground of which is the sea of feeling itself. (*The Artwork of the Future,* in *Gesammelte Schriften und Dichtungen,* 2nd ed., 1887, p. 157.)

To this we should compare what Nietzsche says in *The Will to Power* (WM, 839) about Wagner's "means of achieving effects":

> Consider the means of achieving effects to which Wagner most likes to turn (and which for the most part he had to invent): to an astonishing extent they resemble the means by which the hypnotist achieves his effect (his selection

of tempi and tonal hues for his orchestra; a repulsive avoidance of the logic and intervals of rhythm; the lingering, soothing, mysterious, hysterical quality of his "endless melody"). And is the state to which the prelude to *Lohengrin* reduces its listeners, especially the lady listeners, essentially different from that of a somnambulistic trance?—I heard an Italian woman who had just listened to that prelude say, flashing those lovely mesmerized eyes that Wagneriennes know how to affect, "Come si *dorme* con questa musica!"

Here the essential character of the conception "collective artwork" comes to unequivocal expression: the dissolution of everything solid into a fluid, flexible, malleable state, into a swimming and floundering; the unmeasured, without laws or borders, clarity or definiteness; the boundless night of sheer submergence. In other words, art is once again to become an absolute need. But now the absolute is experienced as sheer indeterminacy, total dissolution into sheer feeling, a hovering that gradually sinks into nothingness. No wonder Wagner found the metaphysical confirmation and explanation of his art in Schopenhauer's main work, which he studied diligently four different times.

However persistently Wagner's will to the "collective artwork" in its results and influence became the very opposite of great art, the will itself remains singular for his time. It raises Wagner—in spite of his theatricality and recklessness—above the level of other efforts focusing on art and its essential role in existence. In that regard Nietzsche writes (XIV, 150–51):

> Without any doubt, Wagner gave the Germans of this era the most considerable indication of what an artist *could* be: reverence for "the artist" suddenly grew to great heights; he awakened on all sides new evaluations, new desires, new hopes; and this perhaps not least of all because of the merely preparatory, incomplete, imperfect nature of his artistic products. Who has not *learned* from him!

That Richard Wagner's attempt had to fail does not result merely from the predominance of music with respect to the other arts in his work. Rather, that the music could assume such preeminence at all has its grounds in the increasingly aesthetic posture taken toward art as a whole—it is the conception and estimation of art in terms of the unalloyed state of feeling and the growing barbarization of the very state to the point where it becomes the sheer bubbling and boiling of feeling abandoned to itself.

And yet such arousal of frenzied feeling and unchaining of "affects" could be taken as a rescue of "life," especially in view of the growing impoverishment and deterioration of existence occasioned by industry, technology, and finance, in connection with the enervation and depletion of the constructive forces of knowledge and tradition, to say nothing of the lack of every establishment of goals for human existence. Rising on swells of feeling would have to substitute for a solidly grounded and articulated position in the midst of beings, the kind of thing that only great poetry and thought can create.

It was the frenzied plunge into the whole of things in Richard Wagner's person and work that captivated the young Nietzsche; yet his captivation was possible only because something correlative came from him, what he then called the Dionysian. But since Wagner sought sheer upsurgence of the Dionysian upon which one might ride, while Nietzsche sought to leash its force and give it form, the breach between the two was already predetermined.

Without getting into the history of the friendship between Wagner and Nietzsche here, we shall indicate briefly the proper root of the conflict that developed early on, slowly, but ever more markedly and decisively. On Wagner's part, the reason for the breach was personal in the widest sense: Wagner did not belong to that group of men for whom their own followers are the greatest source of revulsion. Wagner required Wagnerians and Wagneriennes. So far as the personal aspect is concerned, Nietzsche loved and respected Wagner all his life. His struggle with Wagner was an essential one, involving real issues. Nietzsche waited for many years, hoping for the possibility of a fruitful confrontation with Wagner. His opposition to Wagner involved two things. First, Wagner's neglect of inner feeling and proper style. Nietzsche expressed it once this way: with Wagner it is all "floating and swimming" instead of "striding and dancing," which is to say, it is a floundering devoid of measure and pace. Second, Wagner's deviation into an insincere, moralizing Christianity mixed with delirium and tumult. (See *Nietzsche contra Wagner,* 1888; on the relationship of Wagner and Nietzsche, cf. Kurt Hildebrandt, *Wagner und Nietzsche: ihr Kampf gegen das 19. Jahrhundert,* Breslau, 1924).

We hardly need to note explicitly that in the nineteenth century there were sundry essential works in the various artistic genres besides those of Wagner's and even opposed to his. We know, for example, in what high esteem Nietzsche held such a work as Adalbert Stifter's *Late Summer,* whose world is well-nigh the perfect antithesis to that of Wagner.

But what matters is the question of whether and how art is still known and willed as the definitive formation and preservation of beings as a whole. The question is answered by the reference to the attempt to develop a collective artwork on the basis of music and to its inevitable demise. Corresponding to the growing incapacity for metaphysical knowledge, knowledge of art in the nineteenth century is transformed into discovery and investigation of mere developments in art history. What in the age of Herder and Winckelmann stood in service to a magnificent self-meditation on historical existence is now carried on for its own sake, i.e., as an academic discipline. Research into the history of art as such begins. (Of course, figures like Jacob Burckhardt and Hippolyte Taine, as different from one another as they may be, cannot be measured according to such academic standards.) Examination of literary works now enters the realm of philology; "it developed in its sense for the minuscule, for genuine philology" (Wilhelm Dilthey, *Gesammelte Schriften,* XI, 216). Aesthetics becomes a psychology that proceeds in the manner of the natural sciences: states of feeling are taken to be facts that come forward of themselves and may be subjected to experiments, observation, and measurement. (Here Friedrich Theodor Vischer and Wilhelm Dilthey are also exceptions, supported and guided by the tradition of Hegel and Schiller.) The history of literature and creative art is ostensibly of such a nature that there can be a science of art and literature that brings to light important insights and at the same time keeps alive the cultivation of thought. Pursuit of such science is taken to be the proper actuality of the "spirit." Science itself is, like art, a cultural phenomenon and an area of cultural activity. But wherever the "aesthetic" does not become an object of research but determines the character of man, the aesthetic state becomes one among other possible states, e.g., the political or the scientific. The "aesthetic man" is a nineteenth-century hybrid.

> The aesthetic man seeks to realize balance and harmony of feelings in himself and in others. On the basis of this need he forms his feeling for life and his intuitions of the world. His estimation of reality depends on the extent to which reality guarantees the conditions for such an existence. (Dilthey, in commemoration of the literary historian Julian Schmidt, 1887; *Gesammelte Schriften,* XI, 232.)

But there must be culture, because man must progress—whither, no one knows, and no one is seriously asking anymore. Besides, one still has his "Christianity" at the ready, and his Church; these are already becoming essentially more political than religious institutions.

The world is examined and evaluated on the basis of its capacity to produce the aesthetic state. The aesthetic man believes that he is protected and vindicated by the whole of a culture. In all of that there is still a good bit of ambition and labor, and at times even good taste and genuine challenge. Nevertheless, it remains the mere foreground of that occurrence which Nietzsche is the first to recognize and proclaim with full clarity: nihilism. With that we come to the final development to be mentioned. We already know its contents, but they now require explicit definition.

6. What Hegel asserted concerning art—that it had lost its power to be the definite fashioner and preserver of the absolute—Nietzsche recognized to be the case with the "highest values," religion, morality, and philosophy: the lack of creative force and cohesion in grounding man's historical existence upon beings as a whole.

Whereas for Hegel it was art—in contrast to religion, morality, and philosophy—that fell victim to nihilism and became a thing of the past, something nonactual, for Nietzsche art is to be pursued as the countermovement. In spite of Nietzsche's essential departure from Wagner, we see in this an outgrowth of the Wagnerian will to the "collective artwork." Whereas for Hegel art as a thing of the past became an object of the highest speculative knowledge, so that Hegel's aesthetics assumed the shape of a metaphysics of spirit, Nietzsche's meditation on art becomes a "physiology of art."

In the brief work *Nietzsche contra Wagner* (1888) Nietzsche says (VIII, 187): "Of course, aesthetics is nothing else than applied physiology." It is therefore no longer even "psychology," as it usually is in the nineteenth century, but investigation of bodily states and processes and their activating causes by methods of natural science.

We must keep the state of affairs quite clearly in view: on the one hand, art in its historical determination as the countermovement to nihilism; on the other, knowledge of art as "physiology"; art is delivered over to explanation in terms of natural science, relegated to an area of the science of facts. Here indeed the aesthetic inquiry into art in its ultimate consequences is thought to an end. The state of feeling is to be traced back to excitations of the nervous system, to bodily conditions.

With that we have defined more closely both Nietzsche's basic position toward art as historical actuality and the way in which he knows and wants to know about art: aesthetics as applied physiology. But at the same time we have assigned places to both in the broad context of the history of art, in terms of the relation of that history to the knowledge of art prevailing at a given time.

14. Rapture as Aesthetic State*

But our genuine intention is to conceive of art as a configuration of will to power, indeed as its distinctive form. This means that on the basis of Nietzsche's conception of art and by means of that very conception we want to grasp will to power itself in its essence, and thereby being as a whole with regard to its basic character. To do that we must now try to grasp Nietzsche's conception of art in a unified way, which is to say, to conjoin in thought things that at first blush seem to run wholly contrary ways. On the one hand, art is to be the countermovement to nihilism, that is, the establishment of the new supreme values; it is to prepare and ground standards and laws for historical, intellectual existence. On the other hand, art is at the same time to be properly grasped by way of physiology and with its means.

Viewed extrinsically, it seems easy to designate Nietzsche's position toward art as senseless, nonsensical, and therefore nihilistic. For if art is just a matter of physiology, then the essence and reality of art dissolve into nervous states, into processes in the nerve cells. Where in such

---

*Der Rausch als ästhetischer Zustand. Rausch is commonly rendered as "frenzy" in translations of Nietzsche's writings, but "rapture," from the past participle of rapere, to seize, seems in some respects a better alternative. No single English word—rapture, frenzy, ecstasy, transport, intoxication, delirium—can capture all the senses of Rausch. Our word "rush" is related to it: something "rushes over" us and sweeps us away. In modern German Rausch most often refers to drunken frenzy or narcotic intoxication, as Heidegger will indicate below; but Nietzsche's sense for the Dionysian is both more variegated and more subtle than that, and I have chosen the word "rapture" because of its complex erotic and religious background. But Rausch is more than a problem of translation. The reader is well advised to examine Nietzsche's analyses of Rausch in the works Heidegger cites in this section, especially Die Geburt der Tragödie and Götzen-Dämmerung.

blind transactions are we to find something that could of itself determine meaning, posit values, and erect standards?

In the realm of natural processes, conceived scientifically, where the only law that prevails is that of the sequence and commensurability (or incommensurability) of cause-effect relations, every result is equally essential and inessential. In this area there is no establishment of rank or positing of standards. Everything is the way it is, and remains what it is, having its right simply in the fact that it is. Physiology knows no arena in which something could be set up for decision and choice. To deliver art over to physiology seems tantamount to reducing art to the functional level of the gastric juices. Then how could art also ground and determine the genuine and decisive valuation? Art as the countermovement to nihilism and art as the object of physiology—that's like trying to mix fire and water. If a unification is at all possible here, it can only occur in such a way that art, as an object of physiology, is declared the utter apotheosis of nihilism—and not at all the countermovement to it.

And yet in the innermost will of Nietzsche's thought the situation is altogether different. True, there is a perpetual discordance prevailing in what he achieves, an instability, an oscillation between these opposite poles which, perceived from the outside, can only confuse. In what follows we will confront the discordancy again and again. But above all else we must try to see what it is that is "altogether different" here.

All the same, in so trying we may not close our eyes to what Nietzsche's aesthetics-as-physiology says about art and how it says it. To be sure, a conclusive presentation of that aesthetics is seriously impaired by the fact that Nietzsche left behind only undetailed observations, references, plans, and claims. We do not even possess an intrinsic, carefully projected outline of his aesthetics. True, among the plans for *The Will to Power* we find one of Nietzsche's own sketches with the title "Toward the Physiology of Art" (XVI, 432–34). But it is only a list of seventeen items, not arranged according to any visible guiding thought. We will present in full this collection of headings of investigations that remained to be carried out, because in terms of pure content it offers an immediate overview of what such an aesthetics was to treat.

TOWARD THE PHYSIOLOGY OF ART

1. Rapture as presupposition: causes of rapture.
2. Typical symptoms of rapture.
3. The *feeling* of force and plenitude in rapture: its *idealizing* effect.
4. The factual *increase* of *force:* its factual beautification. (The increase of force, e.g., in the *dance* of the sexes.) The pathological element in rapture: the physiological danger of art—. For consideration: the extent to which our value "beautiful" is completely *anthropocentric:* based on biological presuppositions concerning growth and progress—.
5. The Apollonian, the Dionysian: basic types. In broader terms, compared with our specialized arts.
6. Question: where architecture belongs.
7. The part artistic capacities play in normal life, the tonic effect of their exercise: as opposed to the ugly.
8. The question of epidemic and contagion.
9. Problem of "health" and "hysteria": genius = neurosis.
10. Art as suggestion, as means of communication, as the realm of invention of the *induction psycho-motrice.*
11. The inartistic states: objectivity, the mania to mirror everything, neutrality. The impoverished *will;* loss of capital.
12. The inartistic states: abstractness. The impoverished *senses.*
13. The inartistic states: vitiation, impoverishment, depletion—will to nothingness (Christian, Buddhist, nihilist). The impoverished *body.*
14. The inartistic states: the *moral* idiosyncrasy. The fear that characterizes the weak, the mediocre, before the senses, power, rapture (instinct of those whom life has defeated).
15. How is *tragic* art possible?
16. The romantic type: ambiguous. Its consequence is "naturalism."
17. Problem of the *actor.* The "dishonesty," the typical ability to metamorphose as a *flaw in character.* . . . Lack of shame, the Hanswurst, the satyr, the buffo, the Gil Blas, the actor who plays the artist. . . .*

---

*The new historical-critical edition of Nietzsche's works (CM VIII, 3, p. 328) lists an eighteenth note, printed in none of the earlier editions.

18. Die Kunst als *Rausch,* medizinisch: Amnestie. tonicum ganze und partielle Impotenz.

The meaning of the passage is anything but obvious; it is easy to understand why previous editors let it fall. An attempt at translation:

18. Art as *rapture,* medically: tonic oblivion, complete and partial impotence.

A multiplicity of different points of inquiry lies before us here, but no blueprint or outline of a structure, not even a preliminary mapping out of the space in which all this is to be joined. Yet at bottom the same is the case with those fragments assembled between numbers 794 and 853 in *The Will to Power*, except that these go beyond mere catchwords and headlines in providing greater detail. The same is also true of the pieces taken up into volume XIV, pp. 131–201, which belong here thematically. We must therefore try all the harder to bring a higher determination and an essential coherence to the materials that lie before us. To that end we will follow a twofold guideline: for one thing, we will try to keep in view the whole of the doctrine of will to power; for another, we will recall the major doctrines of traditional aesthetics.

But on our way we do not want merely to become cognizant of Nietzsche's teachings on aesthetics. Rather, we want to conceive how the apparently antithetical directions of his basic position with respect to art can be reconciled: art as countermovement to nihilism and art as object of physiology. If a unity prevails here, eventuating from the essence of art itself as Nietzsche sees it, and if art is a configuration of will to power, then insight into the possibility of unity between the antithetical determinations should provide us with a higher concept of the essence of will to power. That is the goal of our presentation of the major teachings of Nietzsche's aesthetics.

At the outset we must refer to a general peculiarity of most of the larger fragments: Nietzsche begins his reflections from various points of inquiry within the field of aesthetics, but he manages at once to touch upon the general context. So it is that many fragments treat the same thing, the only difference being in the order of the material and the distribution of weight or importance. In what follows we shall forego discussion of those sections that are easy to comprehend on the basis of ordinary experience.

Nietzsche's inquiry into art is aesthetics. According to the definitions provided earlier, art in aesthetics is experienced and defined by falling back upon the state of feeling in man that corresponds and pertains to the bringing-forth and the enjoyment of the beautiful. Nietzsche himself uses the expression "aesthetic state" (WM, 801) and speaks of "aesthetic doing and observing" (VIII, 122). But this aesthetics is to be "physiology." That suggests that states of feeling, taken to be purely psychical, are to be traced back to the bodily condition proper to them. Seen as a whole, it is precisely the unbroken and indissoluble unity of the corporeal-psychical, the living, that is posited as the realm of the aesthetic state: the living "nature" of man.

When Nietzsche says "physiology" he does mean to emphasize the bodily state; but the latter is in itself always already something psychical, and therefore also a matter for "psychology." The bodily state of an animal and even of man is essentially different from the property of a "natural body," for example, a stone. Every body is also a natural body, but the reverse does not hold. On the other hand, when Nietzsche says "psychology" he always means what also pertains to bodily states (the physiological). Instead of "aesthetic" Nietzsche often speaks more correctly of "artistic" or "inartistic" states. Although he sees art from the point of view of the artist, and demands that it be seen that way, Nietzsche does not mean the expression "artistic" only with reference to the artist. Rather, artistic and inartistic states are those that support and advance—or hamper and preclude—a relation to art of a creative or receptive sort.

The basic question of an aesthetics as physiology of art, and that means of the artist, must above all aim to reveal those special states in the essence of the corporeal-psychical, i.e., living nature of man in which artistic doing and observing occur, as it were, in conformity with and confinement to nature. In defining the basic aesthetic state we shall at first not refer to the text of *The Will to Power* but restrict ourselves to what Nietzsche says in the last writing he himself published (*Twilight of the Idols*, 1888; VIII, 122–23). The passage reads:

> *Toward the psychology of the artist.* — If there is to be art, if there is to be any aesthetic doing and observing, one physiological precondition is indispensable: *rapture.* Rapture must first have augmented the excitability of the entire machine: else it does not come to art. All the variously conditioned forms of rapture have the requisite force: above all, the rapture of sexual arousal, the oldest and most original form of rapture. In addition, the rapture that comes as a consequence of all great desires, all strong affects;

the rapture of the feast, contest, feat of daring, victory; all extreme movement; the rapture of cruelty; rapture in destruction; rapture under certain meteorological influences, for example, the rapture of springtime; or under the influence of narcotics; finally, the rapture of will, of an overfull, teeming will.

We can summarize these remarks with the general statement that rapture is the basic aesthetic state, a rapture which for its part is variously conditioned, released, and increased. The passage cited was not chosen simply because Nietzsche published it but because it achieves the greatest clarity and unity of all the Nietzschean definitions of the aesthetic state. We can readily discern what remains unresolved throughout the final period of Nietzsche's creative life, although in terms of the matter itself it does not deviate essentially from what has gone before, when we compare to this passage number 798 (and the beginning of 799) of *The Will to Power*. Here Nietzsche speaks of "two states in which art itself emerges as a force of nature in man." According to the aphorism's title, the two states meant are the "Apollonian" and the "Dionysian." Nietzsche developed the distinction and opposition in his first writing, *The Birth of Tragedy from the Spirit of Music* (1872). Even here, at the very beginning of his distinguishing between the Apollonian and the Dionysian, the "physiological symptoms" of "dream" and "rapture" were brought into respective relation. We still find this connection in *The Will to Power*, number 798 (from the year 1888!): "Both states are rehearsed in normal life as well, only more weakly: in dreams and in rapture." Here, as earlier, rapture is but one of the two aesthetic states, juxtaposed to the dream. But from the passage in *Twilight of the Idols* we gather that rapture is the basic aesthetic state without qualification. Nonetheless, in terms of the genuine issue the same conception prevails also in *The Will to Power*. The first sentence of the following aphorism (WM, 799) reads: "In Dionysian rapture there is sexuality and voluptuousness: in the Apollonian they are not lacking." According to *The Birth of Tragedy*, to the remarks in *The Will to Power*, number 798, and elsewhere, the Dionysian alone is the rapturous and the Apollonian the dreamlike; now, in *Twilight of the Idols*, the Dionysian and the Apollonian are two kinds of rapture, rapture itself being the basic state. Nietzsche's ultimate doctrine must be grasped according to this apparently insignificant but really quite essential clarification. We must read a second passage from *Twilight of the Idols* in company with the first (VIII, 124): "What is the meaning of the conceptual opposition, which I introduced into aesthetics, of the Apollonian and the Dionysian, both conceived as kinds of rapture?" After such clear testimony it can no longer be a matter simply of unraveling Nietzsche's doctrine of art from the opposition of the Apollonian and the Dionysian, an opposition quite common ever since the time of its first publication, but not very commonly grasped, an opposition which nevertheless still retains its significance.

Before we pursue the opposition within the framework of our own presentation, let us ask what it is that according to Nietzsche's final explanation pervades that opposition. With this intention, let us proceed with a double question. First, what is the general essence of rapture? Second, in what sense is rapture "indispensable if there is to be art"; in what sense is rapture *the* basic aesthetic state?

To the question of the general essence of rapture Nietzsche provides a succinct answer (*Twilight of the Idols;* VIII, 123): "What is essential in rapture is the feeling of enhancement of force and plenitude." (Cf. "Toward the Physiology of Art," above: "The *feeling* of force and plenitude in rapture.") Earlier he called rapture the "physiological precondition" of art; what is now essential about the precondition is feeling. According to what we clarified above, feeling means the way we find ourselves to be with ourselves, and thereby at the same time with things, with beings that we ourselves are not. Rapture is always rapturous feeling. Where is the physiological, or what pertains to bodily states, in this? Ultimately we dare not split up the matter in such a way, as though there were a bodily state housed in the basement with feelings dwelling upstairs. Feeling, as feeling oneself to be, is precisely the way we are corporeally. Bodily being does not mean that the soul is burdened by a hulk we call the body. In feeling oneself to be, the body is already contained in advance in that self, in such a way that the body in its bodily states permeates the self. We do not "have" a body in the way we carry a knife in a sheath. Neither is the body a natural body that merely accompanies us and which we can establish, expressly or not, as being also at hand. We do not "have" a body; rather, we "are" bodily. Feeling, as feeling oneself to be, belongs to the essence of such Being. Feeling achieves from the outset the inherent internalizing tendency of the body in our Dasein. But because feeling, as feeling oneself to be, always just as essentially has a feeling for beings as a whole, every bodily state involves some way in which the things around us and the people with us lay a claim on us or do not do so. When our stomachs are "out of sorts" they can cast a pall over all things. What would otherwise seem indifferent to us suddenly becomes irritating and disturbing; what we usually take in stride now impedes us. True, the will can appeal to ways and means for suppressing the bad mood, but it cannot directly awaken or create a countermood: for moods are overcome and transformed always only by moods. Here it is essential to observe that feeling is not something that runs its course in our "inner lives." It is rather that basic mode of our Dasein by force of which and in accordance with which we are always already lifted beyond ourselves into being as a whole, which in this or that way matters to us or does not matter to us. Mood is never merely a way of being determined in our inner being for ourselves. It is above all a way of being attuned, and letting ourselves be attuned, in this or that way in mood. Mood is precisely the basic way in which we are *outside* ourselves. But that is the way we are essentially and constantly.

In all of this the bodily state swings into action. It lifts a man out beyond himself or it allows him to be enmeshed in himself and to grow listless. We are not first of all "alive," only then getting an apparatus to sustain our living which we call "the body," but we are some body who is alive.* Our being embodied is essentially other than merely being encumbered with an organism. Most of what we know from the

---

*Wir leben, indem wir leiben, "we live in that we are embodied." Heidegger plays with the German expression *wie man leibt und lebt,* "the way somebody actually is," and I have tried to catch the sense by playing on the intriguing English word "some-body." Heidegger makes this play more than once: see NI, 565 (to be published in the third volume of this series); see also *Early Greek Thinking,* p. 65.

natural sciences about the body and the way it embodies are specifications based on the established misinterpretation of the body as a mere natural body. Through such means we do find out lots of things, but the essential and determinative aspects always elude our vision and grasp. We mistake the state of affairs even further when we subsequently search for the "psychical" which pertains to the body that has already been misinterpreted as a natural body.

Every feeling is an embodiment attuned in this or that way, a mood that embodies in this or that way. Rapture is a feeling, and it is all the more genuinely a feeling the more essentially a unity of embodying attunement prevails. Of someone who is intoxicated we can only say that he "has" something like rapture. But he *is* not enraptured. The rapture of intoxication is not a state in which a man rises by himself beyond himself. What we are here calling rapture is merely—to use the colloquialism—being "soused," something that deprives us of every possible state of being.

At the outset Nietzsche emphasizes two things about rapture: first, the feeling of enhancement of force; second, the feeling of plenitude. According to what we explained earlier, such enhancement of force must be understood as the capacity to extend beyond oneself, as a relation to beings in which beings themselves are experienced as being more fully in being, richer, more perspicuous, more essential. Enhancement does not mean that an increase, an increment of force, "objectively" comes about. Enhancement is to be understood in terms of mood: to be caught up in elation—and to be borne along by our buoyancy as such. In the same way, the feeling of plenitude does not suggest an inexhaustible stockpile of inner events. It means above all an attunement which is so disposed that nothing is foreign to it, nothing too much for it, which is open to everything and ready to tackle anything— the greatest enthusiasm and the supreme risk hard by one another.

With that we come up against a third aspect of the feeling of rapture: the reciprocal penetration of all enhancements of every ability to do and see, apprehend and address, communicate and achieve release. "—In this way states are ultimately interlaced which perhaps would have reason to remain foreign to one another. For example, the feeling of religious rapture and sexual arousal (—two profound feelings coordinated quite precisely to an all but astonishing degree)" (WM, 800).

What Nietzsche means by the feeling of rapture as the basic aesthetic state may be gauged by the contrary phenomenon, the inartistic states of the sober, weary, exhausted, dry as dust, wretched, timorous, pallid creatures "under whose regard life suffers" (WM, 801, 812). Rapture is a feeling. But from the contrast of the artistic and inartistic states it becomes especially clear that by the word *Rausch* Nietzsche does not mean a fugitive state that rushes over us and then goes up in smoke. Rapture may therefore hardly be taken as an affect, not even if we give the term "affect" the more precise definition gained earlier. Here as in the earlier case it remains difficult, if not impossible, to apply uncritically terms like affect, passion, and feeling as essential definitions. We can employ such concepts of psychology, by which one divides the faculties of the psyche into classes, only as secondary references—presupposing that we are inquiring, from the beginning and throughout, on the basis of the phenomena themselves in each instance. Then perhaps the artistic state of "rapture," if it is more than a fugitive affect, may be grasped as a passion. But then the question immediately arises: to what extent? In *The Will to Power* there is a passage that can give us a pointer. Nietzsche says (WM, 814), "Artists are *not* men of *great* passion, whatever they like to tell us—and themselves as well." Nietzsche adduces two reasons why artists cannot be men of great passion. First, simply because they are artists, i.e., creators, artists must examine themselves; they lack shame before themselves, and above all they lack shame before great passion; as artists they have to exploit passion, hiding in ambush and pouncing on it, transforming it in the artistic process. Artists are too curious merely to *be* magnificent in great passion; for what passion would have confronting it is not curiosity but a sense of shame. Second, artists are also always the victims of the talent they possess, and that denies them the sheer extravagance of great passion. "One does not *get over* a passion by portraying it; rather, the passion *is over when* one portrays it" (WM,

814). The artistic state itself is never *great* passion, but still it is passion. Thus it possesses a steady and extensive reach into beings as a whole, indeed in such a way that this reach can take itself up into its own grasp, keep it in view, and compel it to take form.

From everything that has been said to clarify the general essence of rapture it ought to have become apparent that we cannot succeed in our efforts to understand it by means of a pure "physiology," that Nietzsche's use of the term "physiology of art" rather has an essentially covert meaning.

What Nietzsche designates with the word *Rausch,* which in his final publications he grasps in a unified way as the basic aesthetic state, is bifurcated early in his work into two different states. The natural forms of the artistic state are those of dream and enchantment, as we may say, adopting an earlier usage of Nietzsche's in order to avoid here the word *Rausch* which he otherwise employs. For the state he calls rapture is one in which dream and ecstatic transport first attain their art-producing essence and become the artistic states to which Nietzsche gives the names "Apollonian" and "Dionysian." The Apollonian and the Dionysian are for Nietzsche two "forces of nature and art" (WM, 1050); in their reciprocity all "further development" of art consists. The convergence of the two in the unity of one configuration is the birth of the supreme work of Greek art, tragedy. But if Nietzsche both at the beginning and at the end of his path of thought thinks the essence of art, which is to say, the essence of the metaphysical activity of life, in the selfsame opposition of the Apollonian and the Dionysian, still we must learn to know and to see that his interpretation in the two cases differs. For at the time of *The Birth of Tragedy* the opposition is still thought in the sense of Schopenhauerian metaphysics, although—rather, because—it is part of a confrontation with such metaphyics; by way of contrast, at the time of *The Will to Power* the opposition is thought on the basis of the fundamental position designated in that title. So long as we do not discern the transformation with adequate clarity and so long as we do not grasp the essence of will to power, it would be good for us to put aside for a while this opposition, which all too often becomes a vacuous catchword. The formula of Apollonian and Dionysian opposites has long been the refuge of all confused and confusing talk and writing about art and about Nietzsche. For Nietzsche the opposition remained a constant source of boundless obscurities and novel *questions.*

Nietzsche may well lay claim to the first public presentation and development of the discovery of that opposition in Greek existence to which he gives the names "Apollonian" and "Dionysian." We can surmise from various clues, however, that Jacob Burckhardt in his Basel lectures on Greek culture, part of which Nietzsche heard, was already on the trail of the opposition; otherwise Nietzsche himself would not expressly refer to Burckhardt as he does in *Twilight of the Idols* (VIII, 170–71) when he says, ". . . the most profound expert on their [the Greeks'] culture living today, such as Jacob Burckhardt in Basel." Of course, what Nietzsche could not have realized, even though since his youth he knew more clearly than his contemporaries who Hölderlin was, was the fact that Hölderlin had seen and conceived of the opposition in an even more profound and lofty manner.

Hölderlin's tremendous insight is contained in a letter to his friend Böhlendorff. He wrote it on December 4, 1801, shortly before his departure for France (*Works,* ed. Hellingrath, V, 318 ff.*). Here

---

*Hölderlin's letter to Casimir Ulrich Böhlendorff (1775–1825), a member of Hölderlin's circle of poet-friends in Homburg, contains the following lines (*Hölderlin Werke und Briefe,* Frankfurt/Main: Insel, 1969, II, 940–41):

"My friend! You have attained much by way of precision and skillful articulation and sacrificed nothing by way of warmth; on the contrary, the elasticity of your spirit, like that of a fine steel blade, has but proven mightier as a result of the schooling to which it has been subjected. . . . Nothing is more difficult for us to learn than the free employment of our national gift. And I believe that clarity of presentation is originally as natural to us as the fire of heaven was to the Greeks. On that account the Greeks are to be *surpassed* more in magnificent passion . . . than in the commanding intellect and representational skill which are typical of Homer.

"It sounds paradoxical. But I assert it once again and submit it for your examination and possible employment: what is properly national will come to have less and less priority as one's education progresses. For that reason the Greeks are not really masters of holy pathos, since it is innate in them, while from Homer on they excel in representa-

Hölderlin contrasts "the holy pathos" and "the Occidental *Junonian sobriety* of representational skill" in the essence of the Greeks. The opposition is not to be understood as an indifferent historical finding. Rather, it becomes manifest to direct meditation on the destiny and determination of the German people. Here we must be satisfied with a mere reference, since Hölderlin's way of knowing could receive adequate definition only by means of an interpretation of his work. It is enough if we gather from the reference that the variously named conflict of the Dionysian and the Apollonian, of holy passion and sober representation, is a hidden stylistic law of the historical determination of the German people, and that one day we must find ourselves ready and able to give it shape. The opposition is not a formula with the help of which we should be content to describe "culture." By recognizing this antagonism Hölderlin and Nietzsche early on placed a question mark after the task of the German people to find their essence historically. Will we understand this cipher? One thing is certain: history will wreak vengeance on us if we do not.

We are trying first of all to sketch the outline of Nietzsche's "aesthetics" as a "physiology of art" by limiting ourselves to the general phenomenon of rapture as the basic artistic state. In that regard we

---

tional skill. For that extraordinary man was so profoundly sensitive that he could capture the *Junonian sobriety* of the Western world for his Apollonian realm and adapt himself faithfully to the foreign element. . . .

"But what is one's own must be learned as thoroughly as what is foreign. For that reason the Greeks are indispensable to us. But precisely in what is our own, in what is our national gift, we will not be able to keep apace with them, since, as I said, the *free* employment of *what is one's own* is most difficult."

Hölderlin's letter has occasioned much critical debate. Heidegger discusses it in his contribution to the *Tübinger Gedenkschrift,* "Andenken," reprinted in *Erläuterungen zu Hölderlins Dichtung,* fourth, expanded ed. (Frankfurt/Main: V. Klostermann, 1971), esp. pp. 82 and 87 ff. A critical review of the literature may be found in Peter Szondi, "Hölderlins Brief an Böhlendorff vom 4. Dezember 1801," *Euphorion: Zeitschrift für Literaturgeschichte,* vol. 58 (1964), 260–75. Szondi's article hardly does justice to Heidegger's reading of the letter and in general is too polemical to be very enlightening; but it does indicate the dimensions and sources of the critical discussion in, for example, Wilhelm Michel, Friedrich Beissner, Beda Allemann, Walter Bröcker, and others.

were to answer a second question: in what sense is rapture "indispensable if there is to be art," if art is to be at all possible, if it is to be realized? What, and how, "is" art? Is art in the creation by the artist, or in the enjoyment of the work, or in the actuality of the work itself, or in all three together? How then is the conglomeration of these different things something actual? How, and where, is art? Is there "art-as-such" at all, or is the word merely a collective noun to which nothing actual corresponds?

But by now, as we inquire into the matter more incisively, everything becomes obscure and ambiguous. And if we want to know how "rapture" is indispensable if there is to be art, things become altogether opaque. Is rapture merely a condition of the commencement of art? If so, in what sense? Does rapture merely issue and liberate the aesthetic state? Or is rapture its constant source and support, and if the latter, how does such a state support "art," of which we know neither how nor what it "is"? When we say it is a configuration of will to power, then, given the current state of the question, we are not really saying anything. For what we want to grasp in the first place is what that determination means. Besides, it is questionable whether the essence of art is thereby defined in terms of art, or whether it isn't rather defined as a mode of the Being of beings. So there is only one way open to us by which we can penetrate and advance, and that is to ask further about the general essence of the aesthetic state, which we provisionally characterized as rapture. But how? Obviously, in the direction of a survey of the realm of aesthetics.

Rapture is feeling, an embodying attunement, an embodied being that is contained in attunement, attunement woven into embodiment. But attunement lays open Dasein as an enhancing, conducts it into the plenitude of its capacities, which mutually arouse one another and foster enhancement. But while clarifying rapture as a state of feeling we emphasized more than once that we may not take such a state as something at hand "in" the body and "in" the psyche. Rather, we must take it as a mode of the embodying, attuned stance toward beings as a whole, a stance which for its part determines the pitch of the attunement. Hence, if we want to characterize more broadly and fully the essential structure of the basic aesthetic mode, it behooves us to ask: what is determinative in and for this basic mode, such that it may be spoken of as aesthetic?

15. Kant's Doctrine of the Beautiful. Its Misinterpretation by Schopenhauer and Nietzsche

At the outset, we know in a rough sort of way that just as "the true" determines our behavior in thinking and knowing, and just as "the good" determines the ethical attitude, so does "the beautiful" determine the aesthetic state.

What does Nietzsche say about the beautiful and about beauty? For the answer to this question also Nietzsche provides us with only isolated statements—proclamations, as it were—and references. Nowhere do we find a structured and grounded presentation. A comprehensive, solid understanding of Nietzsche's statements about beauty might result from study of Schopenhauer's aesthetic views; for in his definition of the beautiful Nietzsche thinks and judges by way of opposition and therefore of reversal. But such a procedure is always fatal if the chosen opponent does not stand on solid ground but stumbles about aimlessly. Such is the case with Schopenhauer's views on aesthetics, delineated in the third book of his major work, *The World as Will and Representation.* It cannot be called an aesthetics that would be even remotely comparable to that of Hegel. In terms of content, Schopenhauer thrives on the authors he excoriates, namely, Schelling and Hegel. The one he does not excoriate is Kant. Instead, he thoroughly misunderstands him. Schopenhauer plays the leading role in the preparation and genesis of that misunderstanding of Kantian aesthetics to which Nietzsche too fell prey and which is still quite common today. One may say that Kant's *Critique of Judgment,* the work in which he presents his aesthetics, has been influential up to now only on the basis of misunderstandings, a happenstance of no little significance for the history of philosophy. Schiller alone grasped some essentials in relation to Kant's doctrine of the beautiful; but his insight too was buried in the debris of nineteenth-century aesthetic doctrines.

The misunderstanding of Kant's aesthetics involves an assertion by Kant concerning the beautiful. Kant's definition is developed in sections 2–5 of *The Critique of Judgment*. What is "beautiful" is what purely and simply pleases. The beautiful is the object of "sheer" delight. Such delight, in which the beautiful opens itself up to us as beautiful, is in Kant's words "devoid of all interest." He says, "*Taste* is the capacity to judge an object or mode of representation by means of delight or revulsion, *devoid of all interest. The object of such delight is called *beautiful*."*

Aesthetic behavior, i.e., our comportment toward the beautiful, is "delight devoid of all interest." According to the common notion, disinterestedness is indifference toward a thing or person: we invest nothing of our will in relation to that thing or person. If the relation to the beautiful, delight, is defined as "disinterested," then, according to Schopenhauer, the aesthetic state is one in which the will is put out of commission and all striving brought to a standstill; it is pure repose, simply wanting nothing more, sheer apathetic drift.

And Nietzsche? He says that the aesthetic state is rapture. That is manifestly the opposite of all "disinterested delight" and is therefore at the same time the keenest opposition to Kant's definition of our comportment toward the beautiful. With that in mind we understand the following observation by Nietzsche (XIV, 132): "Since Kant, all talk of art, beauty, knowledge, and wisdom has been smudged and besmirched by the concept 'devoid of interest.'" Since Kant? If this is thought to mean "through" Kant, then we have to say "No!" But if it is thought to mean since the Schopenhauerian misinterpretation of Kant, then by all means "Yes!" And for that reason Nietzsche's own effort too is misconceived.

---

*Immanuel Kant, *Kritik der Urteilskraft*, Akademieausgabe, B 16.

But then what does Kant mean by the definition of the beautiful as the object of "disinterested" delight? What does "devoid of all interest" mean? "Interest" comes from the Latin *mihi interest,* something is of importance to me. To take an interest in something suggests wanting to have it for oneself as a possession, to have disposition and control over it. When we take an interest in something we put it in the context of what we intend to do with it and what we want of it. Whatever we take an interest in is always already taken, i.e., represented, with a view to something else.

Kant poses the question of the essence of the beautiful in the following way. He asks by what means our behavior, in the situation where we find something we encounter to be beautiful, must let itself be determined in such a way that we encounter the beautiful *as* beautiful. What is the determining ground for our finding something beautiful?

Before Kant says constructively what the determining ground is, and therefore what the beautiful itself is, he first says by way of refutation what never can and never may propose itself as such a ground, namely, an interest. Whatever exacts of us the judgment "This is beautiful" can never be an interest. That is to say, in order to find something beautiful, we must let what encounters us, purely as it is in itself, come before us in its own stature and worth. We may not take it into account in advance with a view to something else, our goals and intentions, our possible enjoyment and advantage. Comportment toward the beautiful as such, says Kant, is *unconstrained favoring.* We must freely grant to what encounters us as such its way to be; we must allow and bestow upon it what belongs to it and what it brings to us.

But now we ask, is this free bestowal, this letting the beautiful be what it is, a kind of indifference; does it put the will out of commission? Or is not such unconstrained favoring rather the supreme effort of our essential nature, the liberation of our selves for the release of what has proper worth in itself, only in order that we may have it purely? Is the Kantian "devoid of interest" a "smudging" and even a "besmirching" of aesthetic behavior? Or is it not the magnificent discovery and approbation of it?

The misinterpretation of the Kantian doctrine of "disinterested delight" consists in a double error. First, the definition "devoid of all interest," which Kant offers only in a preparatory and path-breaking way, and which in its very linguistic structure displays its negative character plainly enough, is given out as the single assertion (also held to be a positive assertion) by Kant on the beautiful. To the present day it is proffered as *the* Kantian interpretation of the beautiful. Second, the definition, misinterpreted in what it methodologically tries to achieve, at the same time is not thought in terms of the content that *remains* in aesthetic behavior when interest in the object falls away. The misinterpretation of "interest" leads to the erroneous opinion that with the exclusion of interest every essential relation to the object is suppressed. The opposite is the case. Precisely by means of the "devoid of interest" the essential relation to the object itself comes into play. The misinterpretation fails to see that now for the first time the object comes to the fore as pure object and that such coming forward into appearance is the beautiful. The word "beautiful" means appearing in the radiance of such coming to the fore.*

What emerges as decisive about the double error is the neglect of actual inquiry into what Kant erected upon a firm foundation with respect to the essence of the beautiful and of art. We will bring one example forward which shows how stubbornly the ostensibly self-evident misinterpretation of Kant during the nineteenth century still obtains today. Wilhelm Dilthey, who labored at the history of aesthetics with a passion unequaled by any of his contemporaries, remarked in 1887 (*Gesammelte Schriften* VI, 119) that Kant's statement con-

---

Das Wort "schön" meint das Erscheinen im Schein solchen Vorscheins. Although the words *schön* and *Schein* vary even in their oldest forms (see Hermann Paul, *Deutsches Wörterbuch*, 6th ed. [Tübingen, M. Niemeyer, 1966], pp. 537b f. and 569b f.), their meanings converge early on in the sense of the English words "shine" and "shining," related to the words "show," "showy." Perhaps the similar relationship between the words "radiate" and "radiant" comes closest to the German *Schein* and *schön.* But it is not simply a matter of alliterative wordplay: the nexus of *schön* and *Schein* is, according to Heidegger, what Plato means by *ekphanestaton* (discussed in section 21, below); and if Nietzsche's task is to overturn Platonism, this issue must be near the very heart of the Heidegger-Nietzsche confrontation. On the relation of *Schein* and *schön* see also Martin Heidegger, "Hegel und die Griechen," in *Wegmarken*, pp. 262, 267, and elsewhere.

cerning disinterested delight "is presented by Schopenhauer with special brilliance." The passage should read, "was fatally misinterpreted by Schopenhauer."

Had Nietzsche inquired of Kant himself, instead of trusting in Schopenhauer's guidance, then he would have had to recognize that Kant alone grasped the essence of what Nietzsche in his own way wanted to comprehend concerning the decisive aspects of the beautiful. Nietzsche could never have continued, in the place cited (XIV, 132), after the impossible remark about Kant, "In *my* view what is beautiful (observed historically) is what is visible in the most honored men of an era, as an expression of what is *most worthy* of honor." For just this—purely to honor what is of worth in its appearance—is for Kant the essence of the beautiful, although unlike Nietzsche he does not expand the meaning directly to all historical significance and greatness.

And when Nietzsche says (WM, 804), "*The* beautiful exists just as little as *the* good, *the* true," that too corresponds to the opinion of Kant.

But the purpose of our reference to Kant, in the context of an account of Nietzsche's conception of beauty, is not to eradicate the firmly rooted misinterpretation of the Kantian doctrine. It is to provide a possibility of grasping what Nietzsche himself says about beauty on the basis of its own original, historical context. That Nietzsche himself did not see the context draws a boundary line that he shares with his era and its relation to Kant and to German Idealism. It would be inexcusable for us to allow the prevailing misinterpretation of Kantian aesthetics to continue; but it would also be wrongheaded to try to trace Nietzsche's conception of beauty and the beautiful back to the Kantian. Rather, what we must now do is to allow Nietzsche's definition of the beautiful to sprout and flourish in its own soil—and in that way to see to what discordance it is transplanted.

Nietzsche too defines the beautiful as what pleases. But everything depends on the operative concept of pleasure and of what pleases as such. What pleases we take to be what corresponds to us, what speaks to us. What pleases someone, what speaks to him, depends on who that someone is to whom it speaks and corresponds. Who such a person is, is defined by what he demands of himself. Hence we call "beautiful" whatever corresponds to what we demand of ourselves. Furthermore, such demanding is measured by what we take ourselves to be, what we trust we are capable of, and what we dare as perhaps the extreme challenge, one we may just barely withstand.

In that way we are to understand Nietzsche's assertion about the beautiful and about the judgment by which we find something to be beautiful (WM, 852): "To pick up the scent of what would nearly finish us off if it were to confront us in the flesh, as danger, problem, temptation—this determines even our aesthetic 'yes.' ('That is beautiful' is an *affirmation.*)" So also with *The Will to Power,* number 819: "The firm, mighty, solid, the life that rests squarely and sovereignly and conceals its strength—that is what '*pleases,*' i.e., that corresponds to what one takes oneself to be."

The beautiful is what we find honorable and worthy, as the image of our essential nature. It is that upon which we bestow "unconstrained favor," as Kant says, and we do so from the very foundations of our essential nature and for its sake. In another place Nietzsche says (XIV, 134), "Such 'getting rid of interest and the ego' is nonsense and imprecise observation: on the contrary, it is the thrill that comes of being in *our* world now, of getting rid of our anxiety in the face of things foreign!" Certainly such "getting rid of interest" in the sense of Schopenhauer's interpretation is nonsense. But what Nietzsche describes as the thrill that comes of being in our world is what Kant means by the "pleasure of reflection." Here also, as with the concept of "interest," the basic Kantian concepts of "pleasure" and "reflection" are to be discussed in terms of the Kantian philosophical effort and its transcendental procedure, not flattened out with the help of everyday notions. Kant analyzes the essence of the "pleasure of reflection," as the basic comportment toward the beautiful, in *The Critique of Judgment,* sections 37 and 39.*

---

*Neske prints §§57 and 59, but this is obviously an error: *die Lust am Schönen,* as *Lust der blossen Reflexion,* is not mentioned in §57 or §59, but *is* discussed indirectly in §37 and explicitly in §39. See especially B 155.

According to the quite "imprecise observation" on the basis of which Nietzsche conceives of the essence of interest, he would have to designate what Kant calls "unconstrained favoring" as an interest of the highest sort. Thus what Nietzsche demands of comportment toward the beautiful would be fulfilled from Kant's side. However, to the extent that Kant grasps more keenly the essence of interest and therefore excludes it from aesthetic behavior, he does not make such behavior indifferent; rather, he makes it possible for such comportment toward the beautiful object to be all the purer and more intimate. Kant's interpretation of aesthetic behavior as "pleasure of reflection" propels us toward a basic state of human being in which man for the first time arrives at the well-grounded fullness of his essence. It is the state that Schiller conceives of as the condition of the possibility of man's existence as historical, as grounding history.

According to the explanations by Nietzsche which we have cited, the beautiful is what determines us, our behavior and our capability, to the extent that we are claimed supremely in our essence, which is to say, to the extent that we ascend beyond ourselves. Such ascent beyond ourselves, to the full of our essential capability, occurs according to Nietzsche in rapture. Thus the beautiful is disclosed in rapture. The beautiful itself is what transports us into the feeling of rapture. From this elucidation of the essence of the beautiful the characterization of rapture, of the basic aesthetic state, acquires enhanced clarity. If the beautiful is what sets the standard for what we trust we are essentially capable of, then the feeling of rapture, as our relation to the beautiful, can be no mere turbulence and ebullition. The mood of rapture is rather an attunement in the sense of the supreme and most measured determinateness. However much Nietzsche's manner of speech and presentation sounds like Wagner's turmoil of feelings and sheer submergence in mere "experiences," it is certain that in this regard he wants to achieve the exact opposite. What is strange and almost incomprehensible is the fact that he tries to make his conception of the aesthetic state accessible to his contemporaries, and tries to convince them of it, by speaking the language of physiology and biology.

In terms of its concept, the beautiful is what is estimable and worthy as such. In connection with that, number 852 of *The Will to Power* says, "It is a question of *strength* (of an individual or a nation), *whether* and *where* the judgment 'beautiful' is made." But such strength is not sheer muscle power, a reservoir of "brachial brutality." What Nietzsche here calls "strength" is the capacity of historical existence to come to grips with and perfect its highest essential determination. Of course, the essence of "strength" does not come to light purely and decisively. Beauty is taken to be a "biological value":

> For consideration: the extent to which our value "beautiful" is completely anthropocentric: based on biological presuppositions concerning growth and progress—. ("Toward the Physiology of Art," no. 4 [cf. p. 94, above].)

> The fundament of all aesthetics [is given in] the general principle that aesthetic values rest on biological values, that aesthetic delights are biological delights (XIV, 165).

That Nietzsche conceives of the beautiful "biologically" is indisputable. Yet the question remains what "biological," *bios,* "life," mean here. In spite of appearances created by the words, they do *not* mean what *biology* understands them to be.

16. Rapture as Form-engendering Force

Now that the aesthetic state too has been clarified by way of an elucidation of the beautiful, we can try to survey more precisely the realm of that state. We can do this by studying the basic modes of behavior that are operative in the aesthetic state: aesthetic doing and aesthetic observing—or creation by the artist and reception by those who examine works of art.

If we ask what the essence of creation is, then on the basis of what has gone before we can answer that it is the rapturous bringing-forth of the beautiful in the work. Only in and through creation is the work realized. But because that is so, the essence of creation for its part remains dependent upon the essence of the work; therefore it can be grasped only from the Being of the work. Creation creates the work. But the essence of the work is the origin of the essence of creation.

If we ask how Nietzsche defines the work, we receive no answer. For Nietzsche's meditation on art—and precisely this meditation, as aesthetics in the extreme—does not inquire into the work as such, at least not in the first place. For that reason we hear little, and nothing essential, about the essence of creation as bringing-forth. On the contrary, only creation as a life-process is discussed, a life-process conditioned by rapture. The creative state is accordingly "an *explosive* state" (WM, 811). That is a chemical description, not a philosophical interpretation. If in the same place Nietzsche refers to vascular changes, alterations in skin tone, temperature, and secretion, his findings involve nothing more than changes in the body grasped in an extrinsic manner, even if he draws into consideration "the automatism of the entire muscular system." Such findings may be correct, but they hold also for other, pathological, bodily states. Nietzsche says it is not possible to be an artist and not be ill. And when he says that making music, making art of any kind, is also a kind of making children, it merely corresponds to that designation of rapture according to which "sexual rapture is its oldest and most original form."

But if we were to restrict ourselves to these references by Nietzsche we would heed only one side of the creative process. The other side, if it makes sense to speak here of sides at all, we must present by recalling the essence of rapture and of beauty, namely ascent beyond oneself. By such ascent we come face to face with that which corresponds to what we take ourselves to be. With that we touch upon the character of decision in creation, and what has to do with standards and with hierarchy. Nietzsche enters that sphere when he says (WM, 800), "Artists should see nothing as it is, but more fully, simply, strongly: for that, a kind of youth and spring, a kind of habitual rapture, must be proper to their lives."

Nietzsche also calls the fuller, simpler, stronger vision in creation an "idealizing." To the essential definition of rapture as a feeling of enhancement of power and plenitude (*Twilight of the Idols,* VIII, 123) Nietzsche appends: "From this feeling, one bestows upon things, one *compels* them to take from us, one violates them—this process is called *idealization.*" But to idealize is not, as one might think, merely to omit, strike, or otherwise discount what is insignificant and ancillary. Idealization is not a defensive action. Its essence consists in a *"sweeping emphasis* upon the main features." What is decisive therefore is anticipatory discernment of these traits, reaching out toward what we believe we can but barely overcome, barely survive. It is that attempt to grasp the beautiful which Rilke's "First Elegy" describes wholly in Nietzsche's sense:

> ... For the beautiful is nothing
> but the beginning of the terrible, a beginning we but barely endure;
> and it amazes us so, since calmly it disdains
> to destroy us.*

---

*Rainer Maria Rilke, *Werke in drei Bänden* (Frankfurt/Main: Insel, 1966) I, 441, from lines 4–7 of the first Duino Elegy:

Creation is an emphasizing of major features, a seeing more simply and strongly. It is bare survival before the court of last resort. It commends itself to the highest law and therefore celebrates to the full its survival in the face of such danger.

> For the artist "beauty" is something outside all hierarchical order, since in it opposites are joined—the supreme sign of power, power over things in opposition; furthermore, without tension: —that there is no further need of force, that everything so easily *follows, obeys,* and brings to its obedience the most amiable demeanor—this fascinates the will to power of the artist (WM, 803).

Nietzsche understands the aesthetic state of the observer and recipient on the basis of the state of the creator. Thus the effect of the artwork is nothing else than a reawakening of the creator's state in the one who enjoys the artwork. Observation of art follows in the wake of creation. Nietzsche says (WM, 821), "—the effect of artworks is *arousal of the art-creating state,* rapture." Nietzsche shares this conception with the widely prevalent opinion of aesthetics. On that basis we understand why he demands, logically, that aesthetics conform to the creator, the artist. Observation of works is only a derivative form and offshoot of creation. Therefore what was said of creation corresponds precisely, though derivatively, to observation of art. Enjoyment of the work consists in participation in the creative state of the artist (XIV, 136). But because Nietzsche does not unfold the essence of creation from what is to be created, namely, the work; because he develops it from the state of aesthetic behavior; the bringing-forth of the work does not receive an adequately delineated interpretation which would distinguish it from the bringing-forth of utensils by way of handicraft. Not only that. The behavior of observation is not set in relief against creation, and so it remains undefined. The view that the observation of works somehow follows in the wake of creation is so little true that

---

... Denn das Schöne ist nichts
als des Schrecklichen Anfang, den wir noch grade ertragen,
und wir bewundern es so, weil es gelassen verschmäht,
uns zu zerstören.

not even the relation of the *artist* to the work as something created is one that would be appropriate to the creator. But that could be demonstrated only by way of an inquiry into art that would begin altogether differently, proceeding from the work itself; through the presentation of Nietzsche's aesthetics offered here it ought to have become clear by now how little he treats the work of art.*

And yet, just as a keener conception of the essence of rapture led us to the inner relation to beauty, so here examination of creation and observation enables us to encounter more than mere corporeal-psychical processes. The relation to "major features" emphasized in "idealization," to the simpler and stronger aspects which the artist anticipates in what he meets, once again becomes manifest in the aesthetic state. Aesthetic feeling is neither blind and boundless emotion nor a pleasant contentment, a comfortable drifting that permeates our state of being. Rapture in itself is drawn to major features, that is, to a series of traits, to an articulation. So we must once more turn away from the apparently one-sided consideration of mere states and turn toward *what* this mood defines in our attunement. In connection with the usual conceptual language of aesthetics, which Nietzsche too speaks, we call it "form."

The artist—out of whom, back to whom, and within whom Nietzsche always casts his glance, even when he speaks of form and of the work—has his fundamental character in this: he "ascribes to no thing a value unless it knows how to become form" (WM, 817). Nietzsche explains such becoming-form here in an aside as "giving itself up," "making itself public." Although at first blush these words seem quite strange, they define the essence of form. Without Nietzsche's making explicit mention of it here or elsewhere, the definition corresponds to the original concept of form as it develops with the Greeks. We cannot discuss that origin here in greater detail.

But by way of a commentary on Nietzsche's definition let us say only

---

*The reference to an inquiry that would begin "altogether differently" is to that series of lectures Heidegger was reworking during the winter semester of 1936–37 (which is to say, during the period of these Nietzsche lectures), later published as "The Origin of the Work of Art."

this: form, *forma,* corresponds to the Greek *morphē.* It is the enclosing limit and boundary, what brings and stations a being into that which it is, so that it stands in itself: its configuration. Whatever stands in this way is what the particular being shows itself to be, its outward appearance, *eidos,* through which and in which it emerges, stations itself there as publicly present, scintillates, and achieves pure radiance.

The artist—we may now understand that name as a designation of the aesthetic state—does not comport himself to form as though it were expressive of something else. The artistic relation to form is love of form for its own sake, for what it is. Nietzsche says as much on one occasion (WM, 828), putting it in a negative way with a view to contemporary painters:

> *Not one* of them is simply a painter: they are all archeologists, psychologists, people who devise a scenario for any given recollection or theory. They take their pleasure from our erudition, our philosophy. . . . They do not love a form for what it is; they love it for what it *expresses.* They are the sons of a learned, tormented and reflective generation—a thousand miles removed from the old masters who did not read and whose only thought was to give their eyes a feast.

Form, as what allows that which we encounter to radiate in appearance, first brings the behavior that it determines into the immediacy of a relation to beings. Form displays the relation itself as the state of original comportment toward beings, the festive state in which the being itself in its essence is celebrated and thus for the first time placed in the open. Form defines and demarcates for the first time the realm in which the state of waxing force and plenitude of being comes to fulfillment. Form founds the realm in which rapture as such becomes possible. Wherever form holds sway, as the supreme simplicity of the most resourceful lawfulness, there is rapture.

Rapture does not mean mere chaos that churns and foams, the drunken bravado of sheer riotousness and tumult. When Nietzsche says "rapture" the word has a sound and sense utterly opposed to Wagner's. For Nietzsche rapture means the most glorious victory of form. With respect to the question of form in art, and with a view to

Wagner, Nietzsche says at one point (WM, 835): "An error—that what Wagner has created is a *form:* —it is formlessness. The possibility of *dramatic* structure remains to be discovered.... Whorish instrumentation."

Of course, Nietzsche does not conduct a meditation devoted expressly to the origin and essence of form in relation to art. For that his point of departure would have to have been the work of art. Yet with a bit of extra effort we can still discern, at least approximately, what Nietzsche means by form.

By "form" Nietzsche never understands the merely "formal," that is to say, what stands in need of content, what is only the external border of such content, circumscribing it but not influencing it. Such a border does not give bounds; it is itself the result of sheer cessation. It is only a fringe, not a component, not what lends consistency and pith by pervading the content and fixing it in such a way that its character as "contained" evanesces. Genuine form is the only true content.

> What it takes to be an artist is that one experience what all nonartists call "form" as *content,* as "the matter itself." With that, of course, one is relegated to an *inverted world.* For from now on one takes content to be something merely formal—including one's own life (WM, 818).

When Nietzsche tries to characterize lawfulness of form, however, he does not do so with a view to the essence of the work and the work's form. He cites only that lawfulness of form which is most common and familiar to us, the "logical," "arithmetical," and "geometrical." But logic and mathematics are for him not merely representative names designating the purest sort of lawfulness; rather, Nietzsche suggests that lawfulness of form must be traced back to logical definition, in a way that corresponds to his explanation of thinking and Being. By such tracing back of formal lawfulness, however, Nietzsche does not mean that art is nothing but logic and mathematics.

"Estimates of aesthetic value"—which is to say, our finding something to be beautiful—have as their "ground floor" those feelings that relate to logical, arithmetical, and geometrical lawfulness (XIV, 133).

The basic logical feelings are those of delight "in the ordered, the surveyable, the bounded, and in repetition." The expression "logical feelings" is deceptive. It does not mean that the feelings themselves are logical, that they proceed according to the laws of thought. The expression "logical feelings" means having a feeling for, letting one's mood be determined by, order, boundary, the overview.

Because estimates of aesthetic value are grounded on the logical feelings, they are also "more fundamental than moral estimates." Nietzsche's decisive valuations have as their standard enhancement and securement of "life." But in his view the basic logical feelings, delight in the ordered and bounded, are nothing else than "the pleasurable feelings among all organic creatures in relation to the danger of their situation or to the difficulty of finding nourishment; the familiar does one good, the sight of something that one trusts he can easily *overpower* does one good, etc." (XIV, 133).

The result, to put it quite roughly, is the following articulated structure of pleasurable feelings: underlying all, the biological feelings of pleasure that arise when life asserts itself and survives; above these, but at the same time in service to them, the logical, mathematical feelings; these in turn serve as the basis for aesthetic feelings. Hence we can trace the aesthetic pleasure derived from form back to certain conditions of the life-process as such. Our view, originally turned toward lawfulness of form, is deflected once more and is directed toward sheer states of life.

Our way through Nietzsche's aesthetics has up to now been determined by Nietzsche's basic position toward art: taking rapture, the basic aesthetic state, as our point of departure, we proceeded to consider beauty; from it we went back to the states of creation and reception; from these we advanced to what they are related to, to what determines them, i.e., form; from form we advanced to the pleasure derived from what is ordered, as a fundamental condition of embodying life; with that, we are back where we started, for life is life-enhancement, and ascendant life is rapture. The realm in which the whole process forward and backward itself takes place, the whole within which and as which rapture and beauty, creation and form, form and life have their reciprocal relation, at first remains *undefined*. So does the kind of context for and relationship between rapture and beauty, creation and form. All are proper to art. But then art would only be a collective noun and not the name of an actuality grounded and delineated in itself.

For Nietzsche, however, art is more than a collective noun. *Art is a configuration of will to power.* The indeterminateness we have indicated can be eliminated only through consideration of will to power. The essence of art is grounded in itself, clarified, and articulated in its structure only to the extent that the same is done for will to power. Will to power must originally ground the manner in which all things that are proper to art cohere.

Of course, one might be tempted to dispose of the indeterminateness in a simple way. We have only to call whatever is related to rapture "subjective," and whatever is related to beauty "objective," and in the same fashion understand creation as subjective behavior and form as objective law. The unknown variable would be the relation of the subjective to the objective: the subject-object relation. What could be more familiar than that? And yet what is more questionable than the subject-object relation as the starting point for man as subject and as the definition of the nonsubjective as object? The commonness of the distinction is not yet proof of its clarity; neither is it proof that the distinction is truly grounded.

The illusory clarity and concealed groundlessness of this schema do not help us much. The schema simply casts aside what is worthy of question in Nietzsche's aesthetics, what is worthwhile in the confrontation and therefore to be emphasized. The less we do violence to Nietzsche's "aesthetics" by building it up as an edifice of apparently obvious doctrines; the more we allow his quest and questioning to go its own way; the more surely do we come across those perspectives and basic notions in which the whole for Nietzsche possesses a unity that is fully mature, albeit obscure and amorphous. If we want to grasp the basic metaphysical position of Nietzsche's thought, we ought to clarify these notions. Therefore we must now try to simplify Nietzsche's presentations concerning art to what is essential; yet we may not relinquish the multiplicity of perspectives there, nor impose on his thoughts some dubious schema from the outside.

For our summary, which is to simplify our previous characterization of Nietzsche's conception of art, we can limit ourselves to the two predominant basic determinations, rapture and beauty. They are reciprocally related. Rapture is the basic mood; beauty does the attuning. But just how little the distinction between the subjective and the objective can contribute to our present commentary we can see easily in what follows. Rapture, which does constitute the state of the subject, can every bit as well be conceived as objective, as an actuality for which beauty is merely subjective, since there is no beauty in itself. It is certain that Nietzsche never achieved conceptual clarity here and was never able to ground these matters successfully. Even Kant, who because of his transcendental method possessed a larger number of more highly refined possibilities for interpreting aesthetics, remained trapped within the limits of the modern concept of the subject. In spite of everything, we must try to make more explicit what is essential in Nietzsche as well, going beyond him.

Rapture as a state of feeling explodes the very subjectivity of the subject. By having a feeling for beauty the subject has already come out of himself; he is no longer subjective, no longer a subject. On the other side, beauty is not something at hand like an object of sheer representation. As an attuning, it thoroughly determines the state of man. Beauty breaks through the confinement of the "object" placed at a distance, standing on its own, and brings it into essential and original correlation to the "subject." Beauty is no longer objective, no longer an object. The aesthetic state is neither subjective nor objective. Both basic words of Nietzsche's aesthetics, rapture and beauty, designate with an identical breadth the entire aesthetic state, what is opened up in it and what pervades it.

17. The Grand Style

Nietzsche has in view the whole of artistic actuality whenever he speaks of that in which art comes to its essence. He calls it *the grand style*. Here too we seek in vain when we look for an essential definition and fundamental explanation of the meaning of "style." As is typical for the realm of art, everything named in the word "style" belongs to what is most obscure. Yet the way Nietzsche ever and again invokes the "grand style," even if only in brief references, casts light on everything we have mentioned heretofore about Nietzsche's aesthetics.

> The "masses" have never had a sense for three good things in art, for elegance, logic, and beauty—*pulchrum est paucorum hominum*—; to say nothing of an even better thing, the *grand style*. Farthest removed from the grand style is Wagner: the dissipatory character and heroic swagger of his artistic means are altogether *opposed* to the grand style (XIV, 154).

Three good things are proper to art: elegance, logic, beauty; along with something even better: the grand style. When Nietzsche says that these remain foreign to the "masses," he does not mean the class concept of the "lower strata" of the population. He means "educated" people, in the sense of mediocre cultural Philistines, the kind of people who promoted and sustained the Wagner cult. The farmer and the worker who is really caught up in his machine world remain entirely unmoved by swaggering heroics. These are craved only by the frenetic petit bourgeois. His world—rather, his void—is the genuine obstacle that prevents the expansion and growth of what Nietzsche calls the grand style.

Now, in what does the grand style consist? "The grand style consists in contempt for trivial and brief beauty; it is a sense for what is rare and what lasts long" (XIV, 145).

We recall that the essence of creation is emphasis of major traits. In the grand style occurs

> . . . a triumph over the plenitude of living things; *measure* becomes master, that *tranquillity* which lies at the base of the strong soul, a soul that is slow to be moved and that resists what is all too animated. The general case, the rule, is *revered* and *emphasized;* the exception is on the contrary thrust aside, the nuance obliterated (WM, 819).

We think of beauty as being most worthy of reverence. But what is most worthy of reverence lights up only where the magnificent strength to revere is alive. To revere is not a thing for the petty and lowly, the incapacitated and underdeveloped. It is a matter of tremendous *passion;* only what flows from such passion is in the grand style (cf. WM, 1024).*

What Nietzsche calls the grand style is most closely approximated by the rigorous style, the classical style: "The classical style represents essentially such tranquillity, simplification, abbreviation, concentration —in the classical type the *supreme feeling of power* is concentrated. Slow to react: a tremendous consciousness: no feeling of struggle" (WM, 799). The grand style is the highest feeling of power. From that it is clear that if art is a configuration of will to power, then "art" here is grasped always in its highest essential stature. The word "art" does not designate the concept of a mere eventuality; it is a concept of rank. Art is not just one among a number of items, activities one engages in and enjoys now and then; art places the whole of Dasein in decision and keeps it there. For that reason art itself is subject to altogether singular conditions. In Nietzsche's view the task therefore arises: "To think to the end, without prejudice and faintness of heart, in what soil a classical

---

*Number 1024 of *The Will to Power* reads: "A period in which the old masquerade and the moralistic laundering of the affects arouses revulsion; *naked nature;* where *quanta of power* are simply admitted as being *decisive* (as *determining rank*); where the *grand style* emerges once again as a consequence of *grand passion.*"

taste may grow. To make man hard, natural, strong, more wicked: all these belong together" (WM, 849).

But not only do the grand style and wickedness belong together, emblematic of the unification of flagrant contradictions in Dasein. Two other things belong together which at first seemed incompatible to us: art as countermovement to nihilism and art as object of a physiological aesthetics.

Physiology of art apparently takes its object to be a process of nature that bubbles to the surface in the manner of an eruptive state of rapture. Such a state would evanesce without deciding anything, since nature knows no realm of decision.

But art as countermovement to nihilism is to lay the groundwork for establishment of new standards and values; it is therefore to be rank, distinction, and decision. If art has its proper essence in the grand style, this now means that measure and law are confirmed only in the subjugation and containment of chaos and the rapturous. Such is demanded of the grand style as the condition of its own possibility. Accordingly, the physiological is the basic condition for art's being able to be a creative countermovement. Decision presupposes divergence between opposites; its height increases in proportion to the depths of the conflict.

Art in the grand style is the simple tranquillity resulting from the protective mastery of the supreme plenitude of life. To it belongs the original liberation of life, but one which is restrained; to it belongs the most terrific opposition, but in the unity of the simple; to it belongs fullness of growth, but with the long endurance of rare things. Where art is to be grasped in its supreme form, in terms of the grand style, we must reach back into the most original states of embodying life, into physiology. Art as countermovement to nihilism and art as state of rapture, as object of physiology ("physics" in the broadest sense) and as object of metaphysics—these aspects of art include rather than exclude one another. The unity of such antitheses, grasped in its entire essential fullness, provides an insight into what Nietzsche himself knew —and that means willed—concerning art, its essence and essential determination.

However often and however fatally Nietzsche both in language and in thought was diverted into purely physiological, naturalistic assertions about art, it is an equally fatal misunderstanding on our part when we isolate such physiological thoughts and bandy them about as a "biologistic" aesthetics. It is even worse to confuse them with Wagner. We turn everything inside out when we make a philosophy of orgiastics out of it, as Klages does, thoroughly falsifying matters by proclaiming it Nietzsche's authentic teaching and genuine accomplishment.

In order to draw near to the essential will of Nietzsche's thinking, and remain close to it, our thinking must acquire enormous range, plus the ability to see beyond everything that is fatally contemporary in Nietzsche. His knowledge of art and his struggle on behalf of the possibility of great art are dominated by one thought, which he at one point expresses briefly in the following way: "What alone can regenerate us? Envisionment of what is perfect" (XIV, 171).

But Nietzsche was also aware of the immense difficulty of such a task. For who is to determine what the perfect is? It could only be those who are themselves perfect and who therefore know what it means. Here yawns the abyss of that circularity in which the whole of human Dasein moves. What health is, only the healthy can say. Yet healthfulness is measured according to the essential starting point of health. What truth is, only one who is truthful can discern; but the one who is truthful is determined according to the essential starting point of truth.

When Nietzsche associates art in the grand style with classical taste, he does not fall prey to some sort of classicism. Nietzsche is the first—if we discount for the moment Hölderlin—to release the "classical" from the misinterpretations of classicism and humanism. His position vis-à-vis the age of Winckelmann and Goethe is expressed clearly enough (WM, 849):

> It is an amusing comedy, which we are only now learning to laugh at, which we are now for the first time *seeing,* that the contemporaries of Herder, Winckelmann, Goethe, and Hegel claimed *to have rediscovered the classical ideal* ... and Shakespeare at the same time! And this same generation had in a rather nasty way declared itself independent of the French classical

school, as if the essential matters could not have been learned there as well as here! But they wanted "nature," "naturalness": oh, stupidity! They believed that the classic was a form of naturalness!

If Nietzsche emphasizes constantly and with conscious exaggeration the physiological aspects of the aesthetic state, it is in reaction to the poverty and lack of antithesis within classicism; he wants to put in relief the original conflict of life and thereby the roots of the necessity for a victory. The "natural" to which Nietzsche's aesthetics refers is not that of classicism: it is not something accessible to and calculable for a human reason which is apparently unruffled and quite sure of itself; it is not something without hazard, comprehensible to itself. On the contrary, Nietzsche means what is bound to nature, which the Greeks of the Golden Age call *deinon* and *deinotaton,* the frightful.*

In contrast to classicism, the classical is nothing that can be immediately divined from a particular past period of art. It is instead a basic structure of Dasein, which itself first creates the conditions for any such period and must first open itself and devote itself to those conditions. But the fundamental condition is an equally original freedom with regard to the extreme opposites, chaos and law; not the mere subjection of chaos to a form, but that mastery which enables the primal wilderness of chaos and the primordiality of law to advance under the same yoke, invariably bound to one another with equal necessity. Such mastery is unconstrained disposition over that yoke, which is as equally removed from the paralysis of form in what is dogmatic and formalistic as from sheer rapturous tumult. Wherever unconstrained disposition over that yoke is an event's self-imposed law, there is the grand style; wherever the grand style prevails, there art in the purity of its essential plenitude is actual. Art may be adjudged only in accordance with what its essential actuality is; only in accordance

---

*During the summer semester of 1935 Heidegger had elaborated the meaning of *deinon, deinotaton* in a course entitled "Introduction to Metaphysics." There he translated the word also as *das Unheimliche,* the uncanny, and *das Gewaltige,* the powerful, in his interpretation of a choral song (verses 332–75) from Sophocles' *Antigone.* See Martin Heidegger, *Einführung in die Metaphysik,* pp. 112 ff.; in the English translation pp. 123 ff.

with its essential actuality should it be conceived as a configuration of beings, that is to say, as will to power.

Whenever Nietzsche deals with art in the essential and definitive sense, he always refers to art in the grand style. Against this backdrop, his innermost antipathy to Wagner comes to light most sharply, above all because his conception of the grand style includes at the same time a fundamental decision, not only about Wagner's music, but about the essence of music as such. [Cf. these remarks from the period of *The Dawn*, 1880–81: "Music has no resonance for the transports of the spirit" (XI, 336); "The poet allows the drive for knowledge *to play;* the musician lets it take a rest" (XI, 337). Especially illuminating is a longer sketch from the year 1888 with the title " '*Music'—and the Grand Style*" (WM, 842).]*

Nietzsche's meditation on art is "aesthetics" because it examines the state of creation and enjoyment. It is the "extreme" aesthetics inasmuch as that state is pursued to the farthest perimeter of the bodily state as such, to what is farthest removed from the spirit, from the spirituality of what is created, and from its formalistic lawfulness. However, precisely in that far remove of physiological aesthetics a sudden reversal occurs. For this "physiology" is not something to which everything essential in art can be traced back and on the basis of which it can be explained. While the bodily state as such continues to participate as a condition of the creative process, it is at the same time what in the created thing is to be restrained, overcome, and surpassed. The aesthetic state is the one which places itself under the law of the grand style which is taking root in it. The aesthetic state itself is truly what it is only as the grand style. Hence such aesthetics, within

---

*The brackets appear in Heidegger's text, presumably because the reference is a kind of "footnote"; it is not likely that these remarks were added to the manuscript at the time of publication. The opening lines of *The Will to Power* number 842 are perhaps most relevant here: "The greatness of an artist is not measured by the 'beautiful feelings' he arouses: that is what the little ladies like to believe. Rather, it is measured by gradients of approximation to the grand style, by the extent to which the artist is capable of the grand style. That style has in common with great passion that it disdains to please; that it forgets about persuading; that it commands; that it *wills*.... To become master of the chaos that one is; to compel one's chaos to become form: logical, simple, unequivocal; to become mathematics, *law*—that is the grand ambition here.—"

itself, is led beyond itself. The artistic states are those which place themselves under the supreme command of measure and law, taking themselves beyond themselves in their will to advance. Such states are what they essentially are when, willing out beyond themselves, they are more than they are, and when they assert themselves in such mastery.

The artistic states are—and that means art is—nothing else than *will to power*. Now we understand Nietzsche's principal declaration concerning art as the great "stimulant of life." "Stimulant" means what conducts one into the sphere of command of the grand style.

But now we also see more clearly in what sense Nietzsche's statement about art as the great stimulant of life represents a reversal of Schopenhauer's statement which defines art as a "sedative of life." The reversal does not consist merely in the fact that "sedative" is replaced by "stimulant," that the calming agent is exchanged for an excitant. The reversal is a transformation of the essential definition of art. Such thinking about art is philosophical thought, setting the standards through which historical confrontation comes to be, prefiguring what is to come. This is something to consider, if we wish to decide in what sense Nietzsche's question concerning art can still be aesthetics, and to what extent it in any case must be such. What Nietzsche says at first with respect to music and in regard to Wagner applies to art as a whole: ". . . we no longer know how to *ground* the concepts 'model,' 'mastery,' 'perfection'—in the realm of values we grope blindly with the instincts of old love and admiration; we nearly believe that 'what is good is what pleases *us*' " (WM, 838).

In opposition to the "complete dissolution of style" in Wagner, rules and standards, and above all the grounding of such, are here demanded clearly and unequivocally; they are identified as what comes first and is essential, beyond all sheer technique and mere invention and enhancement of "means of expression." "What does all expansion of the means of expression matter when that which expresses, namely art itself, has lost the law that governs it!" Art is not only subject to rules, must not only obey laws, but is in itself legislation. Only as legislation is it truly art. What is inexhaustible, what is to be created, is the law. Art that dissolves style in sheer ebullition of feelings misses the mark, in that its discovery of law is essentially disturbed; such discovery can become actual in art only when the law drapes itself in freedom of form, in order in that way to come openly into play.

Nietzsche's aesthetic inquiry explodes its own position when it advances to its own most far-flung border. But aesthetics is by no means overcome. Such overcoming requires a still more original metamorphosis of our Dasein and our knowledge, which is something that Nietzsche only *indirectly* prepares by means of the whole of his metaphysical thought. *Our sole concern is to know the basic position of Nietzsche's thought.* At first glance, Nietzsche's thinking concerning art is aesthetic; according to its innermost will, it is metaphysical, which means it is a definition of the Being of beings. The historical fact that every true aesthetics—for example, the Kantian—explodes itself is an unmistakable sign that, although the aesthetic inquiry into art does not come about by accident, it is not what is essential.

For Nietzsche art is the essential way in which beings are made to be beings. Because what matters is the creative, legislative, form-grounding aspect of art, we can aim at the essential definition of art by asking what the creative aspect of art at any given time is. The question is not intended as a way of determining the psychological motivations that propel artistic creativity in any given case; it is meant to decide whether, when, and in what way the basic conditions of art in the grand style are there; and whether, when, and in what way they are not. Neither is this question in Nietzsche's view one for art history in the usual sense: it is for art history in the essential sense, as a question that participates in the formation of the future history of Dasein.

The question as to what has become creative in art, and what wants to become creative in it, leads directly to a number of other questions. What is it in the stimulant that properly stimulates? What possibilities are present here? How on the basis of such possibilities is the configuration of art determined? How is art the awakening of beings as beings? To what extent is it will to power?

How and where does Nietzsche think about the question concerning what is properly creative in art? He does it in those reflections that try to grasp in a more original way the distinction and opposition between the classical and romantic, in numbers 843 to 850 of *The Will to Power*. Here we cannot go into the history of the distinction and its role in art criticism, where it both clarifies and confuses. We can only pursue the matters of how Nietzsche by way of an original definition of the distinction delineates more sharply the essence of art in the grand style, and how he provides enhanced clarity for his statement that art is the stimulant of life. Of course, it is precisely these fragments that show how very much all this remains a project for the future. Here also, when clarifying the distinction between the classical and the romantic, Nietzsche has in view as his example, not the period of art around 1800, but the art of Wagner and of Greek tragedy. He thinks always on the basis of the question of the "collective artwork." That is the question of the hierarchy of the arts, the question of the form of the essential art. The terms "romantic" and "classic" are always only foreground and by way of allusion.

"A romantic is an artist whose great dissatisfaction with himself makes him creative—one who averts his glance from himself and his fellows, and looks back" (WM, 844). Here what is properly creative is discontent, the search for something altogether different; it is desire and hunger. With that, its opposite is already foreshadowed. The contrary possibility is that the creative is not a lack but plenitude, not a search but full possession, not a craving but a dispensing, not hunger but superabundance. Creation out of discontent takes "action" only in revulsion toward and withdrawal from something else. It is not active but always reactive, utterly distinct from what flows purely out of itself and its own fullness. With a preliminary glance cast toward these two basic possibilities of what is and has become creative in art, Nietzsche poses the question of "whether or not behind the antithesis of the *classical* and *romantic* that of the active and reactive lies concealed" (WM, 847). Insight into this further and more originally conceived opposition implies, however, that the classical cannot be equated with the active. For the distinction of active and reactive intersects with another, which distinguishes whether "the cause of creativity is longing after immobility, eternity, *'Being,'* or longing after destruction, change, *Becoming*" (WM, 846). The latter distinction thinks the difference between Being and Becoming, a juxtaposition that has remained dominant from the early period of Occidental thought, through its entire history, up to and including Nietzsche.

But such differentiation of longing after Being and longing after Becoming in the creative principle is still ambiguous. The ambiguity can be transformed into a clear distinction by an examination of the distinction between the active and the reactive. The latter "schema" is to be given preference over the former one and must be posited as the basic schema for the determination of the possibilities of the creative principle in art. In *The Will to Power,* number 846, Nietzsche exhibits the twofold significance of longing after Being and longing after Becoming with the help of the schema of the active and the reactive. If we use the term "schema" here, it is not to suggest an extrinsically applied framework for a mere descriptive classification and division of types. "Schema" means the guideline derived from the essence of the matter, previewing the way the decision will take.

Longing after Becoming, alteration, and therefore destruction too, can be—but need not necessarily be—"an expression of superabundant strength, pregnant with the future." Such is Dionysian art. But longing after change and Becoming can also spring from the dissatisfaction of those who hate everything that exists simply because it exists and stands. Operative here is the counterwill typical of the superfluous, the underprivileged, the disadvantaged, for whom every existent superiority constitutes in its very superiority an objection to its right to exist.

Correspondingly, the longing after Being, the will to eternalize, may derive from the possession of plenitude, from thankfulness for what is; or the perduring and binding may be erected as law and compulsion by the tyranny of a willing that wants to be rid of its inmost suffering. It therefore imposes these qualities on all things, in that way taking its revenge on them. Of such kind is the art of Richard Wagner, the art of "romantic pessimism." On the contrary, wherever the untamed and overflowing are ushered into the order of self-created law, there is classical art. But the latter cannot without further ado be conceived as the active: the purely Dionysian is also active. Just as little is the classical merely longing for Being and duration. Of such kind is romantic pessimism also. The classical is a longing for Being that flows from the fullness of gift-giving and yes-saying. With that, once more, an indication of the grand style is given.

Indeed it first seems as though the "classical style" and the "grand style" simply coincide with one another. Nevertheless, we would be thinking too cursorily were we to explain the state of affairs in this customary way. True, the immediate sense of Nietzsche's statements seems to speak for such an equation. By proceeding in that way, however, we do not heed the decisive thought. Precisely because the grand style is a bountiful and affirmative willing toward Being, its essence reveals itself only when a decision is made, indeed by means of the grand style itself, about the meaning of the Being of beings. Only on that basis is the yoke defined by which the antitheses are teamed and harnessed. But the essence of the grand style is initially given in the foreground description of the classical. Nietzsche never expresses himself about it in another way. For every great thinker always *thinks* one jump more originally than he directly *speaks*. Our interpretation must therefore try to say what is unsaid by him.

Therefore, we can demarcate the essence of the grand style only with explicit reservations. We may formulate it in the following way: the grand style prevails wherever abundance restrains itself in simplicity. But in a certain sense that is also true of the rigorous style. And even if we clarify the greatness of the grand style by saying it is that superiority which compels everything strong to be teamed with its strongest antithesis under one yoke, that too applies also to the classical type. Nietzsche himself says so (WM, 848): "In order to be the *classical* type, one must possess *all* strong, apparently contradictory gifts and desires: but in such a way that they go together under one yoke." And again (WM, 845): "Idealization of the *magnificent blasphemer* (the sense for his *greatness*) is Greek; the humiliation, defamation, vilification of the sinner is Judeo-Christian."

But whatever keeps its antithesis merely beneath it or even outside of it, as something to be battled and negated, cannot be great in the sense of the grand style, because it remains dependent upon, and lets itself be led by, what it repudiates. It remains reactive. On the contrary, in the grand style nascent law grows out of original action, which is itself the yoke. (Incidentally, we should note that the image of the "yoke" stems from the Greek mode of thought and speech.) The grand style is the active will to Being, which takes up Becoming into itself.*

But whatever is said about the classical type is said with the intention of making the grand style visible by means of what is most akin to it. Hence only what assimilates its sharpest antithesis, and not what merely holds that antithesis down and suppresses it, is truly great; such transformation does not cause the antithesis to disappear, however, but to come to its essential unfolding. We recall what Nietzsche says about the "grandiose initiative" of German Idealism, which tries to think of evil as proper to the essence of the Absolute. Nevertheless, Nietzsche would not consider Hegel's philosophy to be a philosophy in the grand style. It marks the end of the classical style.

But quite beyond the effort to establish a "definition" of the grand style, we must investigate the more essential matter of the way in which Nietzsche tries to determine what is creative in art. This we can do with the aid of a classification of artistic styles within the framework of the distinctions active-reactive and Being-Becoming. In that regard some basic determinations of Being manifest themselves: the active and reactive are conjoined in the essence of motion (*kinēsis, metabolē*). With a view to these determinations, the Greek definitions of *dynamis* and *energeia* take shape as determinations of Being in the sense of presencing. If the essence of the grand style is determined by these ultimate and primal metaphysical contexts, then they must rise to meet us wherever Nietzsche tries to interpret and grasp the Being of beings.

Nietzsche interprets the Being of beings as will to power. Art he considers the supreme configuration of will to power. The proper

---

Der grosse Stil ist der aktive Wille zum Sein, so zwar, dass dieser das Werden in sich aufhebt. The Hegelian formulation *das Werden in sich aufheben* at first seems to mean that the will to Being cancels and transcends Becoming. But the will to Being would have to be a kind of surpassing that *preserves* Becoming—else it would be, in Hegel's words, the lifeless transcendence of an empty universal, in Nietzsche's, the subterfuge of clever but weary men who must avenge themselves on Time. In the fourth and final section of his *Introduction to Metaphysics* Heidegger suggests how *Sein* and *Werden* may be, must be, thought together as *physis.*

essence of art is exemplified in the grand style. But the latter, because of its own essential unity, points to an original, concrescive unity of the active and reactive, of Being and Becoming. At the same time we must consider what the precedence of the distinction active-reactive, which is expressly emphasized over the distinction of Being and Becoming, suggests about Nietzsche's metaphysics. For formally one could subsume the distinction active-reactive under one member of the subordinate distinction of Being and Becoming—i.e., under Becoming. The articulation of the active, and of Being and Becoming, into an original unity proper to the grand style must therefore be carried out in will to power, if will to power is thought metaphysically. But will to power *is* as eternal recurrence. In the latter Nietzsche wants his thinking to fuse Being and Becoming, action and reaction, in an original unity. With that we are granted a vista onto the metaphysical horizon upon which we are to think what Nietzsche calls the grand style and art in general.

However, we would like to clear the path to the metaphysical realm first of all by passing through the essence of art. It may now become clearer why our inquiry into Nietzsche's basic metaphysical position takes art as its point of departure, and that our starting point is by no means arbitrary. The grand style is the highest feeling of power. Romantic art, springing from dissatisfaction and deficiency, is a wanting-to-be-away-from-oneself. But according to its proper essence, willing is to-want-oneself. Of course, "oneself" is never meant as what is at hand, existing just as it is; "oneself" means what first of all wants to become what it is. Willing proper does not go away from itself, but goes way beyond itself; in such surpassing itself the will captures the one who wills, absorbing and transforming him into and along with itself. Wanting-to-be-away-from-oneself is therefore basically a not-willing. In contrast, wherever superabundance and plenitude, that is, the revelation of essence which unfolds of itself, bring themselves under the law of the simple, willing wills itself in its essence, and *is* will. Such will is will to power. For power is not compulsion or violence. Genuine power does not yet prevail where it must simply hold its position in response to the threat of something that has not yet been neutralized. Power prevails only where the simplicity of calm dominates, by which the antithetical is preserved, i.e., transfigured, in the unity of a yoke that sustains the tension of a bow.

Will to power is properly there where power no longer needs the accoutrements of battle, in the sense of being merely reactive; its superiority binds all things, in that the will releases all things to their essence and their own bounds. When we are able to survey what Nietzsche thinks and demands with regard to the grand style, only then have we arrived at the peak of his "aesthetics," which at that point is no longer aesthetics at all. Now for the first time we can glance back over our own way and try to grasp what up to now has eluded us. Our path toward an understanding of Nietzsche's thought on art advanced as follows.

In order to attain that field of vision in which Nietzsche's inquiry moves, five statements (in addition to his principal statement) on art were listed and discussed along general lines, but not properly grounded. For the grounding can unfold only by way of a return back to the essence of art. But the essence of art is elaborated and determined in Nietzsche's "aesthetics." We tried to portray that aesthetics by bringing together traditional views into a new unity. The unifying center was provided by what Nietzsche calls the grand style. So long as we do not make an effort to establish internal order in Nietzsche's doctrine of art, in spite of the matter's fragmentary character, his utterances remain a tangle of accidental insights into and arbitrary observations about art and the beautiful. For that reason the path must always be held clearly in view.

It advances from rapture, as the basic aesthetic mood, to beauty, as attuning; from beauty, as the standard-giver, back to what takes its measure from beauty, to creation and reception; from these, in turn, over to that in which and as which the attuning is portrayed, to form. Finally, we tried to grasp the unity of the reciprocal relation of rapture and beauty, of creation, reception, and form, as the grand style. In the grand style the essence of art becomes actual.

18. Grounding the Five Statements on Art

How, and to what extent, can we now ground the five statements on art listed earlier?

The *first* statement says: art is for us the most familiar and perspicuous configuration of will to power. To be sure, we may view the statement as grounded only when we are familiar with other forms and stages of will to power, that is to say, only when we have possibilities for comparison. But even now elucidation of the statement is possible, merely on the basis of the clarified essence of art. Art is the configuration most familiar to us, since art is grasped aesthetically as a state; the state in which it comes to presence and from which it springs is a state proper to man, and hence to ourselves. Art belongs to a realm where we find ourselves—we are the very realm. Art does not belong to regions which we ourselves are not, and which therefore remain foreign to us, regions such as nature. But art, as a human production, does not belong simply in a general way to what is well known to us; art is *the most* familiar. The grounds for that lie in Nietzsche's conception of the kind of givenness of that in which, from the aesthetic point of view, art is actual. It is actual in the rapture of embodying life. What does Nietzsche say about the givenness of life? "Belief in the body is more fundamental than belief in the *soul*" (WM, 491). And: "Essential: to proceed from the *body* and use it as the guideline. It is the much richer phenomenon, which admits of more precise observation. Belief in the body is better established than belief in the spirit" (WM, 532).

According to these remarks the body and the physiological are also more familiar; being proper to man, they are what is most familiar to him. But inasmuch as art is grounded in the aesthetic state, which must be grasped physiologically, art is the most familiar configuration of will to power, and at the same time the most perspicuous. The aesthetic state is a doing and perceiving which we ourselves execute. We do not dwell alongside the event as spectators; we ourselves remain within the state. Our Dasein receives from it a luminous relation to beings, the sight in which beings are visible to us. The aesthetic state is the envisionment through which we constantly see, so that everything here is discernible to us. Art is the most visionary configuration of will to power.*

The *second* statement says: art must be grasped in terms of the artist. It has been shown that Nietzsche conceives of art in terms of the creative behavior of the artist; why such a conception should be necessary has not been shown. The grounding of the demand expressed in the statement is so odd that it does not seem to be a serious grounding at all. At the outset, art is posited as a configuration of will to power. But will to power, as self-assertion, is a constant creating. So art is interrogated as to that in it which is creative, superabundance or privation. But creation within art actually occurs in the productive activity of the artist. Thus, initiating the inquiry with the activity of the artist most likely guarantees access to creation in general and thereby to will to power. The statement follows from the basic premise concerning art as a configuration of will to power.

The listing and the grounding of this statement do not mean to suggest that Nietzsche holds up prior aesthetics in front of him, sees that it is inadequate, and notices too that it usually, though not exclusively, takes the man who enjoys works of art as its point of departure. With these facts staring him in the face it occurs to him to try another way for once, the way of the creators. Rather, the first and leading basic experience of art itself remains the experience that it has a significance

---

*"Visionary" is to translate *durchsichtig,* otherwise rendered as "lucid" or "perspicuous." The entire paragraph expands upon Nietzsche's statement concerning art as the most perspicuous form of will to power by interpreting the vision, *die Sicht,* and envisionment, *das Sichtige,* that art opens up for beings.

for the grounding of history, and that its essence consists in such significance. Thus the creator, the artist, must be fixed in view. Nietzsche expresses the historical essence of art early on in the following words: "Culture can proceed only on the basis of the centralizing significance of an art or an artwork" (X, 188).

The *third* statement says: art is the basic occurrence within beings as a whole. On the basis of what has gone before, this statement is the least transparent and least grounded of all, that is, within and on the basis of Nietzsche's metaphysics. Whether, and to what extent, beings are most in being in art can be decided only when we have answered two questions. First, in what does the beingness of beings consist? What is the being itself in truth? Second, to what extent can art, among beings, be more in being than the others?

The second question is not altogether foreign to us, since in the fifth statement something is asserted of art which ascribes to it a peculiar precedence. The fifth statement says: art is worth more than truth. "Truth" here means the true, in the sense of true beings; more precisely, beings that may be considered true being, being-in-itself. Since Plato, being-in-itself has been taken to be the supersensuous, which is removed and rescued from the transiency of the sensuous. In Nietzsche's view the value of a thing is measured by what it contributes to the enhancement of the actuality of beings. That art is of more value than truth means that art, as "sensuous," is more in being than the supersensuous. Granted that supersensuous being served heretofore as what is highest, if art is more in being, then it proves to be the being most in being, the basic occurrence within beings as a whole.

Yet what does "Being" mean, if the sensuous can be said to be more in being? What does "sensuous" mean here? What does it have to do with "truth"? How can it be even higher in value than truth? What does "truth" mean here? How does Nietzsche define its essence? At present all this is obscure. We do not see any way in which the *fifth* statement might be sufficiently grounded; we do not see how the statement *can* be grounded.

Such questionableness radiates over all the other statements, above all, the third, which obviously can be decided and grounded only when the fifth statement has been grounded. But the fifth statement must be presupposed if we are to understand the *fourth* as well, according to which art is the countermovement to nihilism. For nihilism, i.e., Platonism, posits the supersensuous as true being, on the basis of which all remaining beings are demoted to the level of proper nonbeing, demoted, denigrated, and declared nugatory. Thus everything hangs on the explanation and grounding of the *fifth* statement: art is worth more than truth. What is truth? In what does its essence consist?

That question is always already included in the guiding question and the grounding question of philosophy. It runs ahead of them and yet is most intrinsic to these very questions. It is the preliminary question of philosophy.

19. The Raging Discordance between Truth and Art

That the question concerning art leads us directly to the one that is preliminary to all questions already suggests that in a distinctive sense it conceals in itself essential relations to the grounding and guiding questions of philosophy. Hence our previous clarification of the essence of art will also be brought to a fitting conclusion only in terms of the question of truth.

In order to discern the connection between art and truth right from the outset, the question concerning the essence of truth and the way in which Nietzsche poses and answers the question should be prepared. Such preparation is to occur through a discussion of what it is in the essence of art that calls forth the question concerning truth. To that end we should remember once more Nietzsche's words on the connection between art and truth. He jotted them down in the year 1888 on the occasion of a meditation on his first book: "Very early in my life I took the question of the relation of *art* to *truth* seriously: and even now I stand in holy dread in the face of this discordance" (XIV, 368).

The relation between art and truth is a discordance that arouses dread.* To what extent? How, and in what respects, does art come into relation to truth? In what sense is the relation for Nietzsche a discordance? In order to see to what extent art as such comes into

---

*Ein Entsetzen erregender Zwiespalt. In the title of this section, *Der erregende Zwiespalt zwischen Wahrheit und Kunst,* the phrase *erregende Zwiespalt* is actually a condensation of the statement made here. That is to say, discordance between art and truth "rages" insofar as it *arouses dread.*

relation to truth, we must say more clearly than we have before what Nietzsche understands by "truth." In our previous discussions we gave some hints in this direction. But we have not yet advanced as far as a conceptual definition of Nietzsche's notion of truth. For that we require a preparatory reflection.

A meditation on fundamentals concerning the realm in which we are moving becomes necessary whenever we speak the word "truth" in a way that is not altogether vacuous. For without insight into these contexts we lack all the prerequisites for understanding the point where all the bypaths of Nietzsche's metaphysical thought clearly converge. It is one thing if Nietzsche himself, under the burdens that oppressed him, did not achieve sufficient perspicuity here; it is another if we who follow him renounce the task of penetrating meditation.

Every time we try to achieve clarity with regard to such basic words as truth, beauty, Being, art, knowledge, history, and freedom, we must heed two things.

First, that a clarification is necessary here has its grounds in the concealment of the essence of what is named in such words. Such clarification becomes indispensable from the moment we experience the fact that human Dasein, insofar as it is—insofar as it is itself—is steered directly toward whatever is named in such basic words and is inextricably caught up in relations with them. That becomes manifest whenever human Dasein becomes historical, and that means whenever it comes to confront beings as such, in order to adopt a stance in their midst and to ground the site of that stance definitively. Depending on what knowledge retains essential proximity to what is named in such basic words, or lapses into distance from it, the content of the name, the realm of the word, and the compelling force of the naming power vary.

When we consider this state of affairs in relation to the word "truth" in an extrinsic and desultory manner, we are accustomed to saying that the word has sundry meanings which are not sharply distinguished from one another, meanings that belong together on the basis of a common ground which we are vaguely aware of but which we do not clearly perceive. The most extrinsic form in which we encounter the ambiguity of the word is the "lexical." In the dictionary the meanings are enumerated and exhibited for selection. The life of actual language consists in multiplicity of meaning. To relegate the animated, vigorous word to the immobility of a univocal, mechanically programmed sequence of signs would mean the death of language and the petrifaction and devastation of Dasein.

Why speak of such commonplaces here? Because the "lexical" representation of the multiplicity of meanings for such a basic word easily causes us to overlook the fact that here all the meanings and the differences among them are historical and therefore necessary. Accordingly, it can never be left to caprice, and can never be inconsequential, which of the word meanings we choose in our attempt to grasp the essence named—and thus already illuminated—in the basic word and to classify it as a key word for a given discipline and area of inquiry. Every attempt of this kind is a historical decision. The leading meaning of such a basic word, which speaks to us more or less clearly, is nothing evident, although our being accustomed to it seems to suggest that. *Basic words are historical.* That does not mean simply that they have various meanings for various ages which, because they are past, we can survey historically; it means that they ground history now and in the times to come in accordance with the interpretation of them that comes to prevail. The historicity of the basic words, understood in this fashion, is one of the things that must be heeded in thinking through those basic words.

Second, we must pay attention to the way such basic words vary in meaning. Here there are principal orbits or routes; but within them meanings may oscillate. Such oscillation is not mere laxity in linguistic usage. It is the breath of history. When Goethe or Hegel says the word "education," and when an educated man of the 1890s says it, not only is the formal content of the utterance different, but the kind of world encapsulated in the saying is different, though not unrelated. When Goethe says "nature," and when Hölderlin speaks the same word, different worlds reign. Were language no more than a sequence of communicative signs, then it would remain something just as arbitrary and indifferent as the mere choice and application of such signs.

But because in the very foundations of our being language as resonant signification roots us to our earth and transports and ties us to our world, meditation on language and its historical dominion is always the action that gives shape to Dasein itself. The will to originality, rigor, and measure in words is therefore no mere aesthetic pleasantry; it is the work that goes on in the essential nucleus of our Dasein, which is historical existence.

But in what sense are there what we have called principal orbits or routes for the historical expansion of meanings among the basic words? Our example will be the word "truth." Without insight into these connections, the peculiarity, difficulty, and genuine excitement apropos of the question of truth remain closed to us; so does the possibility of understanding Nietzsche's deepest need with respect to the question of the relation of art and truth.

The assertion "Among Goethe's accomplishments in the field of science the theory of colors also belongs" is true. With the statement we have at our disposal something that is true. We are, as we say, in possession of "a truth." The assertion $2 \times 2 = 4$ is true. With this statement we have another "truth." Thus there are many truths of many kinds: things we determine in our everyday existence, truths of natural science, truths of the historical sciences. To what extent are these truths what their name says they are? To the extent that they satisfy generally and in advance whatever is proper to a "truth." Such is what makes a *true assertion* true. Just as we call the essence of the just "justice," the essence of the cowardly "cowardice," and the essence of the beautiful "beauty," so must we call the essence of the true "truth." But truth, conceived as the essence of the true, is solely one. For the essence of something is that in which everything of that kind—in our case, everything true—dovetails. If truth suggests the essence of the true, then truth is but one: it becomes impossible to talk about "truths."

Thus we already have two meanings for the word "truth," basically different but related to one another. If the word "truth" is meant in the sense which admits of no multiplicity, it names the essence of the true. On the contrary, if we take the word in the sense where a plurality is meant, then the word "truth" means not the essence of the true but any given truth as such. The essence of a matter can be conceived principally or exclusively as what may be attributed to anything that satisfies the essence of the matter. If one restricts himself to this plausible conception of essence, which, however, is neither the sole nor the original conception, as the one which is valid for many, the following may be readily deduced concerning the essential word "truth." Because being true may be asserted of every true statement as such, an abbreviated form of thought and speech can also call what is true itself a "truth." But what is meant here is "something true." Something true now is called simply "truth." The name "truth" is in an essential sense ambiguous. Truth means the one essence and also the many which satisfy the essence. Language itself has a peculiar predilection for that sort of ambiguity. We therefore encounter it early on and constantly. The inner grounds for the ambiguity are these: inasmuch as we speak, and that means comport ourselves to beings through speech, speaking on the basis of beings and with reference back to them, we mean for the most part beings themselves. The being in question is always this or that individual and specific being. At the same time it is a being as such, that is, it is of such a genus and species, such an essence. This house as such is of the essence and species "house."

When we mean something true, we of course understand the essence of truth along with it. We must understand the latter if, whenever we intend something true, we are to know what we have in front of us. Although the essence itself is not expressly and especially named, but always only previewed and implied, the word "truth," which names the essence, is nevertheless used for true things themselves. The name for the essence glides unobtrusively into our naming such things that participate in that essence. Such slippage is aided and abetted by the fact that for the most part we let ourselves be determined by beings themselves and not by their essence as such.

The manner in which we examine the basic words therefore moves along two principal routes: the route of the essence, and that which veers away from the essence and yet is related back to it. But an interpretation which is as old as our traditional Western logic and grammar makes this apparently simple state of affairs even simpler and therefore more ordinary. It is said that the essence—here the essence of the true, which makes everything true be what it is—because it is valid for many true things, is the generally and universally valid. The truth of the essence consists in nothing else than such universal validity. Thus truth, as the essence of the true, is the universal. However, the "truth" which is one of a plurality, "truths," the individual truth, true propositions, are "cases" that fall under the universal. Nothing is clearer than that. But there are various kinds of clarity and transparency, among them a kind that thrives on the fact that what seems to be lucid is really vacuous, that the least possible amount of thought goes into it, the danger of obscurity being thwarted in that way. But so it is when one designates the essence of a thing as the universal concept. That in certain realms—not all—the essence of something holds for many particular items (manifold validity) is a consequence of the essence, but it does not hit upon its essentiality.

The equating of essence with the character of the universal, even as an essential conclusion which has but conditional validity, would of itself not have been so fatal had it not for centuries barred the way to a decisive question. The essence of the true holds for the particular assertions and propositions which, as individuals, differ greatly from one another according to content and structure. The true is in each case something various, but the essence, as the universal which is valid for many, is one. But universal validity, which is valid for many things that belong together, is now made what is universally valid without qualification. "Universally valid" now means not only valid for many particular items that belong together, but also what is always and everywhere valid in itself, immutable and eternal, transcending time.

The result is the proposition of the immutability of essences, including the essence of truth. The proposition is logically correct but metaphysically untrue. Viewed in terms of the particular "cases" of the many true statements, the essence of the true is that in which the many dovetail. The essence in which the many dovetail must be one and the same thing for them. But from that it by no means follows that the essence in itself cannot be changeable. For, supposing that the essence of truth did change, that which changes could always still be a "one" which holds for "many," the transformation not disturbing that relationship. But what is preserved in the metamorphosis is what is unchangeable in the essence, which essentially unfolds in its very transformation. The essentiality of essence, its inexhaustibility, is thereby affirmed, and also its genuine selfhood and selfsameness. The latter stands in sharp contrast to the vapid selfsameness of the monotonous, which is the only way the unity of essence can be thought when it is taken merely as the universal. If one stands by the conception of the selfsameness of the essence of truth which is derived from traditional logic, he will immediately (and from that point of view quite correctly) say: "The notion of a change of essence leads to relativism; there is only one truth and it is the same for everybody; every relativism is disruptive of the general order and leads to sheer caprice and anarchy." But the right to such an objection to the essential transformation of truth stands and falls with the appropriateness of the representation of the "one" and the "same" therein presupposed, which is called the absolute, and with the right to define the essentiality of essence as manifold validity. The objection that essential transformation leads to relativism is possible only on the basis of deception concerning the essence of the absolute and the essentiality of essence.

That digression must suffice for our present effort to unfold what Nietzsche in his discussions of the relation between art and truth understands by "truth." According to what we have shown, we must first ask upon which route of meaning the word "truth" moves for Nietzsche in the context of his discussions of the relationship between art and truth. The answer is that it moves along the route which deviates from the essential route. That means that in the fundamental question which arouses dread Nietzsche nevertheless does not arrive at the proper question of truth, in the sense of a discussion of the essence of the true. That essence is presupposed as evident. For Nietzsche truth is not the essence of the true but the true itself, which satisfies the essence of truth. It is of decisive importance to know that Nietzsche does not pose the question of truth proper, the question concerning the essence of the true and the truth of essence, and with it the question of the ineluctable possibility of its essential transformation. Nor does he ever stake out the domain of the question. This we must know, not only in order to judge Nietzsche's position with regard to the question of the relation of art and truth, but above all in order to estimate and measure in a fundamental way the degree of originality of the inquiry encompassed by Nietzsche's philosophy as a whole. That the question of the essence of truth is missing in Nietzsche's thought is an oversight unlike any other; it cannot be blamed on him alone, or him first of all—if it can be blamed on anyone. The "oversight" pervades the entire history of Occidental philosophy since Plato and Aristotle.

That many thinkers have concerned themselves with the concept of truth; that Descartes interprets truth as certitude; that Kant, not independent of that tendency, distinguishes an empirical and a transcendental truth; that Hegel defines anew the important distinction between abstract and concrete truth, i.e., truth of science and truth of speculation; that Nietzsche says "truth" is error; all these are advances of thoughtful inquiry. And yet! They all leave untouched the essence of truth itself. No matter how far removed Nietzsche is from Descartes and no matter how much he emphasizes the distance between them, in what is essential he still stands close to Descartes. All the same, it would be pedantic to insist that the use of the word "truth" be kept within the strict bounds of particular routes of meaning. For as a basic word it is at the same time a universal word; thus it is entrenched in the laxity of linguistic usage.

We must ask with greater penetration what Nietzsche understands by truth. Above we said that he means the true. Yet what is the true? What is it here that satisfies the essence of truth; in what is that essence itself determined? The true is true being, what is in truth actual. What does "in truth" mean here? Answer: what is in truth known. For our knowing is what can be true or false right from the start. Truth is truth of knowledge. Knowledge is so intrinsically the residence of truth that a knowing which is untrue cannot be considered knowledge. But knowledge is a way of access to beings; the true is what is truly known, the actual. The true is established as something true in, by, and for knowledge alone. Truth is proper to the realm of knowledge. Here decisions

are made about the true and the untrue. And depending on the way
the essence of knowledge is demarcated, the essential concept of truth
is defined.

Our knowing as such is always an approximation to what is to be
known, a measuring of itself upon something. As a consequence of the
character of measurement, knowing implies a relation to some sort of
standard. The standard, and our relation to it, can be interpreted in
various ways. In order to clarify the interpretive possibilities with regard to the essence of knowing, we will describe the principal trait of
two basically different types. By way of exception, and for the sake of
brevity, we will take up two terms which are not to suggest any more
than what we will make of them here: the conceptions of knowledge
in "Platonism" and "Positivism."

20. Truth in Platonism and Positivism. Nietzsche's Attempt to Overturn Platonism on the Basis of the Fundamental Experience of Nihilism

We say "Platonism," and not Plato, because here we are dealing with the conception of knowledge that corresponds to that term, not by way of an original and detailed examination of Plato's works, but only by setting in rough relief one particular aspect of his work. Knowing is approximation to what is to be known. What is to be known? The being itself. Of what does it consist? Where is its Being determined? On the basis of the Ideas and *as* the *ideai*. They "are" what is apprehended when we look at things to see how they look, to see what they give themselves out to be, to see their what-being (*to ti estin*). What makes a table a table, table-being, can be seen; to be sure, not with the sensory eye of the body, but with the eye of the soul. Such sight is apprehension of what a matter is, its Idea. What is so seen is something nonsensuous. But because it is that in the light of which we first come to know what is sensuous—that thing there, as a table—the nonsensuous at the same time stands above the sensuous. It is the supersensuous and the proper what-being and Being of the being. Therefore, knowledge must measure itself against the supersensuous, the Idea; it must somehow bring forward what is not sensuously visible for a face-to-face encounter: it must put forward or present.* Knowledge is presentative measurement

---

*"To put forward or present" is an attempt to translate the hyphenated word *vor-stellen,* which without the hyphen is usually translated as "to represent."

of self upon the supersensuous. Pure nonsensuous presentation, which unfolds in a mediating relation that derives from what is represented, is called *theōria*. Knowledge is in essence theoretical.

The conception of knowledge as "theoretical" is undergirded by a particular interpretation of Being; such a conception has meaning and is correct only on the basis of metaphysics. To preach the "eternally immutable essence of science" is therefore either to employ an empty turn of phrase that does not take seriously what it says, or to mistake the basic facts concerning the origin of the concept of Western science. The "theoretical" is not merely something distinguished and differentiated from the "practical," but is itself grounded in a particular basic experience of Being. The same is true also of the "practical," which for its part is juxtaposed to the "theoretical." Both of these, and the difference between them, are to be grasped solely from the essence of Being which is relevant in each case, which is to say, they are to be grasped metaphysically. Neither does the practical change on the basis of the theoretical, nor does the theoretical change on the basis of the practical: both change always simultaneously on the basis of their fundamental metaphysical position.

The interpretation of knowledge in positivism differs from that in Platonism. To be sure, knowing here too is a measuring. But the standard which representation must respect, right from the start and constantly, differs: it is what lies before us from the outset, what is constantly placed before us, the *positum*. The latter is what is given in sensation, the sensuous. Here too measurement is an immediate presenting or putting forward ("sensing"), which is defined by a mediating interrelation of what is given by way of sensation, a judging. The essence of judgment in turn can itself be interpreted in various ways—a matter we will not pursue any further here.

Without deciding prematurely that Nietzsche's conception of knowledge takes one of these two basic directions—Platonism or positivism—or is a hybrid of both, we can say that the word "truth" for him means as much as the true, and the true what is known in truth. Knowing is a theoretical-scientific grasp of the actual in the broadest sense.

That suggests in a general way that Nietzsche's conception of the essence of truth keeps to the realm of the long tradition of Western thought, no matter how much Nietzsche's particular interpretations of that conception deviate from earlier ones. But also in relation to our particular question concerning the relation of art and truth, we have just now taken a decisive step. According to our clarification of the guiding conception of truth, what are here brought into relation are, putting it more strictly, on the one hand, art, and on the other, theoretical-scientific knowledge. Art, grasped in Nietzsche's sense in terms of the artist, is creation; creation is related to beauty. Correspondingly, truth is the object related to knowledge. Thus the relation of art and truth that is here in question, the one which arouses dread, must be conceived as the relation of art and scientific knowledge, and correlatively the relation of beauty and truth.

But to what extent is the relation for Nietzsche a discordance? To what extent do art and knowledge, beauty and truth at all enter into noteworthy relation? Surely not on the basis of the wholly extrinsic grounds, definitive for the usual philosophies and sciences of culture, that art exists and that science is right there beside it; the fact that both belong to a culture; and the fact that if one wants to erect a system of culture, one must also provide information about the interrelations of these cultural phenomena. Were Nietzsche's point of inquiry merely that of the philosophy of culture, intending to erect a tidy system of cultural phenomena and cultural values, then the relation of art and truth could surely never become for it a discordance, much less one that arouses dread.

In order to see how for Nietzsche art and truth can and must in some way come into noteworthy relation, let us proceed with a renewed clarification of his concept of truth, since we have already treated sufficiently the other member of the relation, art. In order to characterize more precisely Nietzsche's concept of truth, we must ask in what way he conceives of knowledge and what standard he applies to it. How does Nietzsche's conception of knowledge stand in relation to the two basic tendencies of epistemological interpretation described above, Platonism and positivism? Nietzsche once says, in a brief observation found among the early sketches (1870–71) for his first treatise, "My philosophy an *inverted Platonism:* the farther removed from true being, the purer, the finer, the better it is. Living in semblance as goal" (IX, 190). That is an astonishing preview in the thinker of his entire later philosophical position. For during the last years of his creative life he labors at nothing else than the overturning of Platonism. Of course, we may not overlook the fact that the "inverted Platonism" of his early period is enormously different from the position finally attained in *Twilight of the Idols.* Nevertheless, on the basis of Nietzsche's own words we can now define with greater trenchancy his conception of truth, which is to say, his conception of the true.

For Platonism, the Idea, the supersensuous, is the true, true being. In contrast, the sensuous is *mē on.* The latter suggests, not nonbeing pure and simple, *ouk on,* but *mē*—what may not be addressed as being even though it is not simply nothing. Insofar as, and to the extent that, it may be called being, the sensuous must be measured upon the supersensuous; nonbeing possesses the shadow and the residues of Being which fall from true being.

To overturn Platonism thus means to reverse the standard relation: what languishes below in Platonism, as it were, and would be measured against the supersensuous, must now be put on top; by way of reversal, the supersensuous must now be placed in its service. When the inversion is fully executed, the sensuous becomes being proper, i.e., the true, i.e., truth. The true is the sensuous. That is what "positivism" teaches. Nevertheless, it would be premature to interpret Nietzsche's conception of knowledge and of the kind of truth pertaining to it as "positivistic," although that is what usually happens. It is indisputable that prior to the time of his work on the planned magnum opus, *The Will to Power,* Nietzsche went through a period of extreme positivism; these were the years 1879–81, the years of his decisive development toward maturity. Such positivism, though of course transformed, became a part of his later fundamental position also. But what matters is precisely the transformation, especially in relation to the overturning of Platonism as a whole. In that inversion Nietzsche's philosophical thought proper comes to completion. For Nietzsche the compelling task from early on was to think through the philosophy of Plato, indeed from two different sides. His original profession as a classical philologist brought him to Plato, partly through his teaching duties, but above all through a philosophical inclination to Plato. During the Basel years he held lectures on Plato several times: "Introduction to the Study of the Platonic Dialogues" in 1871–72 and 1873–74, and "Plato's Life and Teachings" in 1876 (see XIX, 235 ff.).

But here again one discerns clearly the philosophical influence of Schopenhauer. Schopenhauer himself grounds his entire philosophy, indeed consciously and expressly, on Plato and Kant. Thus in the Preface to his major work, *The World as Will and Representation* (1818), he writes:

> Hence *Kant's* is the sole philosophy a basic familiarity with which is all but presupposed by what will be presented here. —If, however, the reader has in addition lingered awhile in the school of the divine Plato, he will be all the more receptive and all the better prepared to hear me.

As a third inspiration Schopenhauer then names the Indian Vedas. We know how much Schopenhauer misinterprets and vulgarizes the Kantian philosophy. The same happens with regard to Plato's philosophy. In the face of Schopenhauer's coarsening of the Platonic philosophy, Nietzsche, as a classical philologist and a considerable expert in that area, is not so defenseless as he is with respect to Schopenhauer's Kant-interpretation. Even in his early years (through the Basel lectures) Nietzsche achieves a remarkable autonomy and thereby a higher truth in his Plato interpretation than Schopenhauer does in his. Above all he rejects Schopenhauer's interpretation of the apprehension of the Ideas as simple "intuition." He emphasizes that apprehension of the Ideas is "dialectical." Schopenhauer's opinion concerning such apprehension, that it is intuition, stems from a misunderstanding of Schelling's teaching concerning "intellectual intuition" as the basic act of metaphysical knowledge.

However, the interpretation of Plato and of Platonism which tends to follow the direction of philology and the history of philosophy, although it is an aid, is not the decisive path for Nietzsche's philosophical advance toward the Platonic doctrine and confrontation with it. It is not the decisive path of his experiencing an insight into the necessity of overturning Platonism. Nietzsche's fundamental experience is his growing insight into the basic development of our history. In his view it is nihilism. Nietzsche expresses incessantly and passionately the fundamental experience of his existence as a thinker. To the blind, to those who cannot see and above all do not want to see, his words easily sound overwrought, as though he were raving. And yet when we plumb the depths of his insight and consider how very closely the basic historical development of nihilism crowds and oppresses him, then we may be inclined to call his manner of speech almost placid. One of the essential formulations that designate the event of nihilism says, "God is dead." (Cf. now *Holzwege*, 1950, pp. 193–247.)* The phrase "God is dead" is not an atheistic proclamation: it is a formula for the fundamental experience of an event in Occidental history.

Only in the light of that basic experience does Nietzsche's utterance, "My philosophy is inverted Platonism," receive its proper range and intensity. In the same broad scope of significance, therefore, Nietzsche's interpretation and conception of the essence of truth must be conceived. For that reason we ought to remember what Nietzsche understands by nihilism and in what sense alone that word may be used as a term for the history of philosophy.

By nihilism Nietzsche means the historical development, i.e., event, that the uppermost values devalue themselves, that all goals are an-

---

*See the English translation, "The Word of Nietzsche: 'God is Dead,' " in Martin Heidegger, *The Question Concerning Technology and Other Essays,* translated by William Lovitt (New York: Harper & Row, 1978). Heidegger's reference, placed in parentheses, apparently was added in 1961. Note that the "event" of nihilism, cited four times in this and the following paragraphs, occasions perhaps the earliest "terminological" use of the word *Ereignis* in Heidegger's published writings. (Cf. the use of the word *Geschehnis* in the *Holzwege* article, p. 195, and in *Einführung in die Metaphysik,* p. 4.) The word's appearance in the context of Nietzsche's account of nihilism assumes even more importance when we recall a parenthetical remark in the "Protocol" to the Todtnauberg Seminar on "Zeit und Sein" (*Zur Sache des Denkens* [Tübingen: M. Niemeyer, 1969], p. 46): "The relationships and contexts which constitute the essential structure of *Ereignis* were worked out between 1936 and 1938," which is to say, precisely at the time of the first two Nietzsche lecture courses.

nihilated, and that all estimates of value collide against one another.
Such collision Nietzsche describes at one point in the following way:

> . . . we call good someone who does his heart's bidding, but also the one who
> only tends to his duty;
> we call good the meek and the reconciled, but also the courageous, un-
> bending, severe;
> we call good somone who employs no force against himself, but also the
> heroes of self-overcoming;
> we call good the utterly loyal friend of the true, but also the man of piety,
> one who transfigures things;
> we call good those who are obedient to themselves, but also the pious;
> we call good those who are noble and exalted, but also those who do not
> despise and condescend;
> we call good those of joyful spirit, the peaceable, but also those desirous
> of battle and victory;
> we call good those who always want to be first, but also those who do not
> want to take precedence over anyone in any respect.
> (From unpublished material composed during the period of *The Gay
> Science,* 1881–82; see XII, 81.)

There is no longer any goal in and through which all the forces of
the historical existence of peoples can cohere and in the direction of
which they can develop; no goal of such a kind, which means at the
same time and above all else no goal of such power, that it can by virtue
of its power conduct Dasein to its realm in a unified way and bring it
to creative evolution. By establishment of the goal Nietzsche understands the metaphysical task of ordering beings as a whole, not merely
the announcement of a provisional whither and wherefore. But a genuine establishment of the goal must at the same time ground its goal.
Such grounding cannot be exhaustive if, in its "theoretical" exhibition
of the reasons which justify the goal to be established, it asseverates that
such a move is "logically" necessary. To ground the goal means to
awaken and liberate those powers which lend the newly established goal
its surpassing and pervasive energy to inspire commitment. Only in
that way can historical Dasein take root and flourish in the realm
opened and identified by the goal. Here, finally, and that means primor-

dially, belongs the growth of forces which sustain and propel preparation of the new realm, the advance into it, and the cultivation of what
unfolds within it, forces which induce it to undertake bold deeds.

Nietzsche has all this in view when he speaks of nihilism, goals, and
establishment of goals. But he also sees the necessary range of such
establishment, a range determined by the incipient dissolution of all
kinds of order all over the earth. It cannot apply to individual groups,
classes, and sects, nor even to individual states and nations. It must be
European at least. That does not mean to say that it should be "interna-
tional." For implied in the essence of a creative establishment of goals
and the preparation for such establishment is that it comes to exist and
swings into action, as historical, only in the unity of the fully historical
Dasein of men in the form of particular nations. That means neither
isolation from other nations nor hegemony over them. Establishment
of goals is in itself confrontation, the initiation of struggle. *But the
genuine struggle is the one in which those who struggle excel, first the
one then the other, and in which the power for such excelling unfolds
within them.*

Meditation of such kind on the historical event of nihilism and on
the condition for overcoming it utterly—meditation on the basic metaphysical position needed to that end, thinking through the ways and
means of awakening and outfitting such conditions—Nietzsche some-
times calls "grand politics."* That sounds like the "grand style." If we
think both as belonging originally together, we secure ourselves against
misinterpretations of their essential sense. Neither does the "grand
style" want an "aesthetic culture," nor does the "grand politics" want
the exploitative power politics of imperialism. The grand style can be
created only by means of the grand politics, and the latter has the most

---

*Nietzsche uses the phrase *die grosse Politik* during the period of the preparation of
Beyond Good and Evil; cf. WM, 463 and 978, both notes from the year 1885. The source
for Heidegger's entire discussion of *Zielsetzung* seems to be section 208 of *Beyond Good
and Evil.* Cf. also the entire eighth part of that work, "Nations and Fatherlands." We
should also note that *die grosse Politik* occupied the very center of interest in Nietzsche
in Germany after World War I: not only the Stefan George circle and Alfred Baeumler,
but even Karl Jaspers (see his *Nietzsche,* Bk. II, chap. 4), emphasized it.

intrinsic law of its will in the grand style. What does Nietzsche say of the grand style? "What makes the *grand style:* to become master of one's *happiness,* as of one's *unhappiness:* —" (from plans and ideas for an independent sequel to *Zarathustra,* during the year 1885; see XII, 415). To be master over one's happiness! That is the hardest thing. To be master over unhappiness: that can be done, if it has to be. But to be master of one's happiness. . . .

In the decade between 1880 and 1890 Nietzsche thinks and questions by means of the standards of the "grand style" and in the field of vision of "grand politics." We must keep these standards and the scope of the inquiry in view if we are to understand what is taken up into Book One and Book Two of *The Will to Power,* which present the insight that the basic force of Dasein, the self-assuredness and power of such force to establish a goal, is lacking. Why is the basic force that is needed in order to attain a creative stance in the midst of beings missing? Answer: because it has been in a state of advanced atrophy for a long time, and because it has been perverted into its opposite. The major debility of the basic force of Dasein consists in the calumniation and denegration of the fundamental orienting force of "life" itself. Such defamation of creative life, however, has its grounds in the fact that things are posited *above* life which make negation of it desirable. The desirable, the ideal, is the supersensuous, interpreted as genuine being. This interpretation of being is accomplished in the Platonic philosophy. The theory of Ideas founds the ideal, and that means the definitive preeminence of the supersensuous, in determining and dominating the sensuous.

Here a new interpretation of Platonism emerges. It flows from a fundamental experience of the development of nihilism. It sees in Platonism the primordial and determining grounds of the possibility of nihilism's upsurgence and of the rise of life-negation. Christianity is in Nietzsche's eyes nothing other than "Platonism for the people." As Platonism, however, it is nihilism. But with the reference to Nietzsche's opposition to the nihilistic tendency of Christianity, his position as a whole with respect to the historical phenomenon of Christianity is not delineated exhaustively. Nietzsche is far too perspicacious and too sovereignly intelligent not to know and acknowledge that an essential presupposition for his own behavior, the probity and discipline of his inquiry, is a consequence of the *Christian* education that has prevailed for centuries. To present two pieces of evidence from among the many available:

> *Probity* as a *consequence* of long moral training: the *self-critique of morality* is at the same time a *moral* phenomenon, an event of morality (XIII, 121).

> We are no longer Christians: we have grown out of Christianity, not because we dwelled too far from it, but because we dwelled too near it, even more, because we have grown *from* it—it is our more rigorous and fastidious piety itself that *forbids* us today to be Christians (XIII, 318).

Within the field of vision maintained by meditation on nihilism, "inversion" of Platonism takes on another meaning. It is not the simple, almost mechanical exchange of one epistemological standpoint for another, that of positivism. Overturning Platonism means, first, shattering the preeminence of the supersensuous as the ideal. Beings, being what they are, may not be despised on the basis of what should and ought to be. But at the same time, in opposition to the philosophy of the ideal and to the installation of what ought to be and of the "should," the inversion sanctions the investigation and determination of that which is—it summons the question "What is being itself?" If the "should" is the supersensuous, then being itself, that which is, conceived as liberated from the "should," can only be the sensuous. But with that the essence of the sensuous is not given; its definition is given up. In contrast, the realm of true being, of the true, and thereby the essence of truth, is demarcated; as before, however, already in Platonism, the true is to be attained on the path of knowledge.

In such inversion of Platonism, invoked and guided by the will to overcome nihilism, the conviction shared with Platonism and held to be evident is that truth, i.e., true being, must be secured on the path of knowledge. Since, according to the inversion, the sensuous is now the true, and since the sensuous, as being, is now to provide the basis for the new foundation of Dasein, the question concerning the sensuous and with it the determination of the true and of truth receive enhanced significance.

The interpretation of truth or true being as the sensuous is of course, considered formally, an overturning of Platonism, inasmuch as Platonism asserts that genuine being is supersensuous. Yet such inversion, and along with it the interpretation of the true as what is given in the senses, must be understood in terms of the overcoming of nihilism. But the definitive interpretation of art, if it is posited as the countermovement to nihilism, operates within the same perspective.

Against Platonism, the question "What is true being?" must be posed, and the answer to it must be, "The true is the sensuous." Against nihilism, the creative life, preeminently in art, must be set to work. But art creates out of the sensuous.

Now for the first time it becomes clear to what extent art and truth, whose relationship in Nietzsche's view is a discordance that arouses dread, can and must come into relation at all, a relation that is more than simply comparative, which is the kind of interpretation of both art and truth offered by philosophies of culture. Art and truth, creating and knowing, meet one another in the single guiding perspective of the rescue and configuration of the sensuous.

With a view to the conquest of nihilism, that is, to the foundation of the new valuation, art and truth, along with meditation on the essence of both, attain equal importance. According to their essence, intrinsically, art and truth come together in the realm of a new historical existence.

What sort of relationship do they have?

21. The Scope and Context of Plato's Meditation on the Relationship of Art and Truth

According to Nietzsche's teaching concerning the artist, and seen in terms of the one who creates, art has its actuality in the rapture of embodying life. Artistic configuration and portrayal are grounded essentially in the realm of the sensuous. Art is affirmation of the sensuous. According to the doctrine of Platonism, however, the supersensuous is affirmed as genuine being. Platonism, and Plato, would therefore logically have to condemn art, the affirmation of the sensuous, as a form of nonbeing and as what ought not to be, as a form of *mē on*. In Platonism, for which truth is supersensuous, the relationship to art apparently becomes one of exclusion, opposition, and antithesis; hence, one of discordance. If, however, Nietzsche's philosophy is reversal of Platonism, and if the true is thereby affirmation of the sensuous, then truth is the same as what art affirms, i.e., the sensuous. For inverted Platonism, the relationship of truth and art can only be one of univocity and concord. If in any case a discordance should exist in Plato (which is something we must still ask about, since not every distancing can be conceived as discordance), then it would have to disappear in the reversal of Platonism, which is to say, in the cancellation of such philosophy.

Nevertheless, Nietzsche says that the relationship is a discordance, indeed, one which arouses dread. He speaks of the discordance that arouses dread, not in the period *prior to* his own overturning of Platonism, but precisely during the period in which the inversion is decided for him. In 1888 Nietzsche writes in *Twilight of the Idols*, "On the contrary, the grounds upon which 'this' world [i.e., the sensuous] was designated as the world of appearances ground the reality of this world —*any other* kind of reality is absolutely indemonstrable" (VIII, 81). During the same period when Nietzsche says that the sole true reality, i.e., the true, is the sensuous world, he writes concerning the relationship of art and truth, ". . . and even now [i.e., in the autumn of 1888] I stand in holy dread in the face of this discordance."

Where is the path that will take us to the hidden, underlying sense of this remarkable phrase concerning the relationship of art and truth? We have to get there. For only from that vantage point will we be able to see Nietzsche's basic metaphysical position in its own light. It would be a good idea to take as our point of departure that basic philosophical position in which a discordance between art and truth at least seems to be possible, i.e., Platonism.

The question as to whether in Platonism a conflict between truth (or true being) and art (or what is portrayed in art) necessarily and therefore actually exists can be decided only on the basis of Plato's work itself. If a conflict exists here, it must come to the fore in statements which, comparing art and truth, say the opposite of what Nietzsche decides in evaluating their relationship.

Nietzsche says that art is worth more than truth. It must be that Plato decides that art is worth less than truth, that is, less than knowledge of true being as philosophy. Hence, in the Platonic philosophy, which we like to display as the very blossom of Greek thought, the result must be a depreciation of art. This among the Greeks—of all people—who affirmed and founded art as no other Occidental nation did! That is a disturbing matter of fact; nevertheless, it is indisputable. Therefore we must show at the outset, even if quite briefly, how the depreciation of art in favor of truth appears in Plato, and see to what extent it proves to be necessary.

But the intention of the following digression is by no means merely one of informing ourselves about Plato's opinion concerning art in this respect. On the basis of our consideration of Plato, for whom a sundering of art and truth comes to pass, we want to gain an indication of where and how we can find traces of discordance in Nietzsche's inversion of Platonism. At the same time, on our way we should provide a richer and better defined significance for the catchword "Platonism."

We pose two questions. First, what is the scope of those determinations which in Plato's view apply to what we call "art"? Second, in what context is the question of the relationship of art and truth discussed?

Let us turn to the first question. We customarily appeal to the word *technē* as the Greek designation of what we call "art." What *technē* means we suggested earlier (cf. p. 80). But we must be clear about the fact that the Greeks have no word at all that corresponds to what we mean by the word "art" in the narrower sense. The word "art" has for us a multiplicity of meanings, and not by accident. As masters of thought and speech, the Greeks deposited such multiple meanings in the majority of their sundry univocal words. If by "art" we mean primarily an ability in the sense of being well versed in something, of a thoroughgoing and therefore masterful *know-how,* then this for the Greeks is *technē.* Included in such know-how, although never as the essential aspect of it, is knowledge of the rules and procedures for a course of action.

In contrast, if by "art" we mean an ability in the sense of an acquired capacity to carry something out which, as it were, has become second nature and basic to Dasein, ability as behavior that accomplishes something, then the Greek says *meletē, epimeleia,* carefulness of concern (see Plato's *Republic,* 374).* Such carefulness is more than practiced diligence; it is the mastery of a composed resolute openness to beings; it is "care." We must conceive of the innermost essence of *technē* too as such care, in order to preserve it from the sheer "technical"

---

*Cf. especially *Republic* 374e 2: the task of the guardians requires the greatest amount of *technēs te kai epimeleias.* Socrates has been arguing that a man can perform only one *technē* well, be he shoemaker, weaver, or warrior. Here *technē* seems to mean "skill" or "professional task." In contrast, *meletainō* means to "take thought or care for," "to attend to, study, or pursue," "to exercise and train." *Hē meletē* is "care," "sustained attention to action." *Epimeleia* means "care bestowed upon a thing, attention paid to it." Schleiermacher translates *epimeleia* as *Sorgfalt,* meticulousness or diligence. Such is perhaps what every *technē* presupposes. *Epimeleia* would be a welcome addition to the discussion of *cura, Sorge,* in *Being and Time,* section 42.

interpretation of later times. The unity of *melete* and *techne* thus characterizes the basic posture of the forward-reaching disclosure of Dasein, which seeks to ground beings on their own terms.

Finally, if by "art" we mean *what is brought forward in a process of bringing-forth,* what is produced in production, and the producing itself, then the Greek speaks of *poiein and poiesis.* That the word *poiesis* in the emphatic sense comes to be reserved for designation of the production of something in words, that *poiesis* as "poesy" becomes the special name for the art of the word, poetic creation, testifies to the primacy of such art within Greek art as a whole. Therefore it is not accidental that when Plato brings to speech and to decision the relationship of art and truth he deals primarily and predominantly with poetic creation and the poet.

Turning to the second question, we must now consider where and in what context Plato poses the question concerning the relationship of art and truth. For the way he poses and pursues that question determines the form of the interpretation for the whole of Plato's multifaceted meditation on art. Plato poses the question in the "dialogue" which bears the title *Politeia* [*Republic*], his magnificent discussion on the "state" as the basic form of man's communal life. Consequently, it has been supposed that Plato asks about art in a "political" fashion, and that such a "political" formulation would have to be opposed to, or distinguished essentially from, the "aesthetic" and thereby in the broadest sense "theoretical" point of view. We can call Plato's inquiry into art political to the extent that it arises in connection with *politeia;* but we have to know, and then say, what "political" is supposed to mean. If we are to grasp Plato's teaching concerning art as "political," we should understand that word solely in accordance with the concept of the essence of the *polis* that emerges from the dialogue itself. That is all the more necessary as this tremendous dialogue in its entire structure and movement aims to show that the sustaining ground and determining essense of all political Being consists in nothing less than the "theoretical," that is, in essential knowledge of *dike* and *dikaiosyne.* This Greek word is translated as "justice," but that misses the proper sense, inasmuch as justice is transposed

straightaway into the moral or even the merely "legal" realm. But *dikē*
is a metaphysical concept, not originally one of morality. It names
Being with reference to the essentially appropriate articulation of all
beings.* To be sure, *dikē* slips into the twilight zone of morality
precisely on account of the Platonic philosophy. But that makes it all
the more necessary to hold onto its metaphysical sense, because
otherwise the Greek backgrounds of the dialogue on the state do not
become visible. Knowledge of *dikē,* of the articulating laws of the Being
of beings, is philosophy. Therefore the decisive insight of the entire
dialogue on the state says, *dei tous philosophous basileuein (archein)*:
it is essentially necessary that philosophers be the rulers (see *Republic,*
Bk. V, 473). The statement does not mean that philosophy professors
should conduct the affairs of state. It means that the basic modes of
behavior that sustain and define the community must be grounded in
essential knowledge, assuming of course that the community, as an
order of being, grounds itself on its own basis, and that it does not wish
to adopt standards from any other order. The unconstrained
self-grounding of historical Dasein places itself under the jurisdiction
of knowledge, and not of faith, inasmuch as the latter is understood as
the proclamation of truth sanctioned by divine revelation. All
knowledge is at bottom commitment to beings that come to light under
their own power. Being becomes visible, according to Plato, in the
"Ideas." They constitute the Being of beings, and therefore are
themselves the true beings, the true.

Hence, if one still wants to say that Plato is here inquiring politically
into art, it can only mean that he evaluates art, with reference to its
position in the state, upon the essence and sustaining grounds of the
state, upon knowledge of "truth." Such inquiry into art is "theoretical"
in the highest degree. The distinction between political and theoretical
inquiry no longer makes any sense at all.

---

*Cf. Martin Heidegger, *An Introduction to Metaphysics,* pp. 134–35 and 139–40.
(N.B.: in the Anchor Books edition, p. 139, line 11, the words *technē* and dikē are
misplaced: *dikē* is the overpowering order, *technē* the violence of knowledge). On *dikē,*
cf. also "The Anaximander Fragment" (1936) in Martin Heidegger, *Early Greek Thinking,* pp. 41–47.

That Plato's question concerning art marks the beginning of "aesthetics" does not have its grounds in the fact that it is generally theoretical, which is to say, that it springs from an interpretation of Being; it results from the fact that the "theoretical," as a grasp of the Being of beings, is based on a *particular* interpretation of Being. The *idea*, the envisioned outward appearance, characterizes Being precisely for that kind of vision which recognizes in the visible as such pure presence. "Being" stands in essential relation to, and in a certain way means as much as, self-showing and appearing, the *phainesthai* of what is *ekphanes*.* One's grasp of the Ideas, with regard to the possible accomplishment of that grasp, though not to its established goal, is grounded upon *erōs*, which in Nietzsche's aesthetics corresponds to rapture. What is most loved and longed for in *erōs*, and therefore the Idea that is brought into fundamental relation, is what at the same time appears and radiates most brilliantly. The *erasmiōtaton*, which at the same time is *ekphanestaton*, proves to be the *idea tou kalou*, the Idea of the beautiful, beauty.

Plato deals with the beautiful and with Eros primarily in the *Symposium*. The questions posed in the *Republic* and *Symposium* are conjoined and brought to an original and basic position with a view to the fundamental questions of philosophy in the dialogue *Phaedrus*. Here Plato offers his most profound and extensive inquiry into art and the beautiful in the most rigorous and circumscribed form. We refer to these other dialogues so that we do not forget, at this very early stage, that the discussions of art in the *Republic*—for the moment the sole important ones for us—do not constitute the whole of Plato's meditation in that regard.

But in the context of the dialogue's guiding question concerning the state, how does the question of art come up? Plato asks about the structure of communal life, what must guide it as a whole and in totality, and what component parts belong to it as what is to be guided. He does not describe the form of any state at hand, nor does he

---

*On the meaning of *phainesthai* see section 7A of *Being and Time;* in *Basic Writings,* pp. 74–79.

elaborate a utopian model for some future state. Rather, the inner order of communal life is projected on the basis of Being and man's fundamental relation to Being. The standards and principles of education for correct participation in communal life and for active existence are established. In the pursuit of such inquiry, the following question emerges, among others: does art too, especially the art of poetry, belong to communal life; and, if so, how? In Book Three (1–18)* that question becomes the object of the discussion. Here Plato shows in a preliminary way that what art conveys and provides is always a portrayal of beings; although it is not inactive, its producing and making, *poiein,* remain *mimēsis,* imitation, copying and transforming, poetizing in the sense of inventing. Thus art in itself is exposed to the danger of continual deception and falsehood. In accord with the essence of its activity, art has no direct, definitive relation to the true and to true being. That fact suffices to produce one irremediable result: in and for the hierarchy of modes of behavior and forms of achievement within the community, art cannot assume the highest rank. If art is admitted into the community at all, then it is only with the proviso that its role be strictly demarcated and its activities subject to certain demands and directives that derive from the guiding laws of the Being of states.

At this point we can see that a decision may be reached concerning the essence of art and its necessarily limited role in the state only in terms of an original and proper relation to the beings that set the standard, only in terms of a relationship that appreciates *dikē,* the matter of order and disorder with respect to Being. For that reason, after the preliminary conversations about art and other forms of achievement in the state, we arrive at the question concerning our basic relation to Being, advancing to the question concerning true comportment toward beings, and hence to the question of truth. On our way through these conversations, we encounter at the beginning of the seventh book the discussion of the essence of truth, based on the Allegory of the Cave. Only after traversing this long and broad path

---

*I.e., topics 1–18 in Schleiermacher's arrangement; in the traditional Stephanus numbering, 386a–412b.

to the point where philosophy is defined as masterful knowledge of the Being of beings do we turn back, in order to ground those statements which were made earlier in a merely provisional manner, among them the statements concerning art. Such a return transpires in the tenth and final book.

Here Plato shows first of all what it means to say that art is *mimēsis,* and then why, granting that characteristic, art can only occupy a subordinate position. Here a decision is made about the metaphysical relation of art and truth (but only in a certain respect). We shall now pursue briefly the chief matter of Book Ten, without going into particulars concerning the movement of the dialogue, and also without referring to the transformation and refinement of what is handled there in Plato's later dialogues.

One presupposition remains unchallenged: all art is *mimēsis.* We translate that word as "imitation." At the outset of Book Ten the question arises as to what *mimēsis* is. Quite likely we are inclined to assume that here we are encountering a "primitivistic" notion of art, or a one-sided view of it, in the sense of a particular artistic style called "naturalism," which copies things that are at hand. We should resist both preconceptions from the start. But even more misleading is the opinion that when art is grasped as *mimēsis* the result is an arbitrary presupposition. For the clarification of the essence of *mimēsis* which is carried out in Book Ten not only defines the word more precisely but also traces the matter designated in the word back to its inner possibility and to the grounds that sustain such possibility. Those grounds are nothing other than basic representations the Greeks entertained concerning beings as such, their understanding of Being. Since the question of truth is sister to that of Being, the Greek concept of truth serves as the basis of the interpretation of art as *mimēsis.* Only on that basis does *mimēsis* possess sense and significance—but also necessity. Such remarks are needed in order that we fix our eyes on the correct point of the horizon for the following discussion. What we will consider there, after two thousand years of tradition and habituation of thought and representation, consists almost entirely of commonplaces. But seen from the point of view of Plato's age, it is all first discovery and definitive utterance. In order to correspond to the mood of this dialogue, we would do well to put aside for the moment our seemingly greater sagacity and our superior air of "knowing all about it already." Of course, here we have to forgo recapitulation of the entire sequence of individual steps in the dialogue.

22. Plato's *Republic:* The Distance of Art (*Mimēsis*) from Truth (*Idea*)

Let us formulate our question once again. How does art relate to truth? Where does art stand in the relationship? Art is *mimēsis*. Its relation to truth must be ascertainable in terms of the essence of *mimēsis*. What is *mimēsis?* Socrates says to Glaucon (at 595 c): *Mimēsin holōs echois an moi eipein hoti pot' estin; oude gar toi autos pany ti synnoō ti bouletai einai.* "Imitation, viewed as a whole: can you tell me at all what that is? For I myself as well am totally unable to discern what it may be."

Thus the two of them begin their conversation, *episkopountes,* "keeping firmly in view the matter itself named in the word." This they do *ek tēs eiōthuias methodou,* "in the manner to which they are accustomed to proceeding, being in pursuit of the matter," since that is what the Greek word "method" means. That customary way of proceeding is the kind of inquiry Plato practiced concerning beings as such. He expressed himself about it continually in his dialogues. Method, the manner of inquiry, was never for him a fixed technique; rather, it developed in cadence with the advance toward Being. If therefore at our present position method is formulated in an essential statement, such a designation by Platonic thought concerning the Ideas corresponds to that stage of the Platonic philosophy which is reached when Plato composes the dialogue on the state. But that stage is by no means the ultimate one. In the context of our present inquiry this account of method is of special significance.

Socrates (i.e., Plato) says in that regard (at 596 a): *eidos gar pou ti hen hekaston eiōthamen tithesthai peri hekasta ta polla, hois tauton onoma epipheromen.* "We are accustomed to posing to ourselves (letting lie before us) one *eidos,* only one of such kind for each case, in relation to the cluster (*peri*) of those many things to which we ascribe the same name." Here *eidos* does not mean "concept" but the outward appearance of something. In its outward appearance this or that thing does not become present, come into presence, in its particularity; it becomes present as that which it is. To come into presence means Being; Being is therefore apprehended in discernment of the outward appearance. How does that proceed? In each case one outward appearance is posed. How is that meant? We may be tempted to have done with the statement, which in summary fashion is to describe the method, by saying that for a multiplicity of individual things, for example, particular houses, the Idea (house) is posited. But with this common presentation of the kind of thought Plato developed concerning the Ideas, we do not grasp the heart of the method. It is not merely a matter of positing the Idea, but of finding that approach by which what we encounter in its manifold particularity is brought together with the unity of the *eidos,* and by which the latter is joined to the former, both being established in relationship to one another. What is established, i.e., brought to the proper approach, i.e., located and presented for the inquiring glance, is not only the Idea but also the manifold of particular items that can be related to the oneness of its unified outward appearance. The procedure is therefore a mutual accommodation between the many particular things and the appropriate oneness of the "Idea," in order to get both in view and to define their reciprocal relation.

The essential directive in the procedure is granted by language, through which man comports himself toward beings in general. In the word, indeed in what is immediately uttered, both points of view intersect: on the one hand, that concerning what in each case is immediately addressed, this house, this table, this bedframe; and on the other hand, that concerning what this particular item in the word is addressed *as*—this thing *as* house, with a view to its outward appearance. Only when we read the statement on method in terms of such an interpretation do we hit upon the full Platonic sense. We have long been accustomed to looking at the many-sided individual thing simultaneously with a view to its universal. But here the many-sided individual appears as such in the scope of its outward appearance as such, and in that consists the Platonic discovery. Only when we elaborate upon that discovery does the statement cited concerning "method" provide us with the correct directive for the procedure now to be followed in pursuit of *mimēsis.*

Mimēsis means copying, that is, presenting and producing something in a manner which is typical of something else. Copying is done in the realm of production, taking it in a very broad sense. Thus the first thing that occurs is that a manifold of produced items somehow comes into view, not as the dizzying confusion of an arbitrary multiplicity, but as the many-sided individual item which we name with *one* name. Such a manifold of produced things may be found, for example, in *ta skeuē,* "utensils" or "implements" which we find commonly in use in many homes. *Pollai pou eisi klinai kai trapedzai* (596 b): ". . . many, which is to say, many according to number and also according to the immediate view, are the bedframes and tables there." What matters is not that there are many bedframes and tables at hand, instead of a few; the only thing we must see is what is co-posited already in such a determination, namely, that there are many bedframes, many tables, yet just *one* Idea "bedframe" and *one* Idea "table." In each case, the one of outward appearance is not only one according to number but above all is one and the same; it is the one that continues to exist in spite of all changes in the apparatus, the one that maintains its consistency. In the outward appearance, whatever it is that something which encounters us "is," shows itself. To Being, therefore, seen Platonically, permanence belongs. All that becomes and suffers alteration, as impermanent, has no Being. Therefore, in the view of Platonism, "Being" stands always in exclusive opposition to "Becoming" and change. We today, on the contrary, are used to addressing also what changes and occurs, and precisely that, as "real" and as genuine being. In opposition to that, whenever Nietzsche says "Being" he always means it Platonically—even after the reversal of Platonism. That is to say, he means it in antithesis to "Becoming."

Alla ideai ge pou peri tauta ta skeuē dyō, mia men klinēs, mia de trapedzēs. "But, of course, the Ideas for the clusters of these implements are two: one in which 'bedframe' becomes manifest, and one in which 'table' shows itself." Here Plato clearly refers to the fact that the permanence and selfsameness of the "Ideas" is always *peri ta polla,* "*for* the cluster of the many and *as* embracing the many." Hence it is not some arbitrary, undefined permanence. But the philosophic search does not thereby come to an end. It merely attains the vantage point from which it may ask: how is it with those many produced items, those implements, in relation to the "Idea" that is applicable in each case? We pose the question in order to come to know something about *mimēsis.* We must therefore cast about, within the realm of our vision, with greater penetration, still taking as our point of departure the many implements. They are not simply at hand, but are at our disposal for use, or are already in use. They "are" with that end in view. As produced items, they are made for the general use of those who dwell together and are with one another. Those who dwell with one another constitute the *dēmos,* the "people," in the sense of public being-with-one-another, those who are mutually known to and involved with one another. For them the implements are made. Whoever produces such implements is therefore called a *dēmiourgos,* a worker, manufacturer, and maker of something for the sake of the *dēmos.* In our language we still have a word for such a person, although, it is true, we seldom use it and its meaning is restricted to a particular realm: *der Stellmacher,* one who constructs frames, meaning wagon chassis (hence the name *Wagner*).* That implements and frames are made by a frame-maker—that is no astonishing piece of wisdom! Certainly not.

All the same, we ought to think through the simplest things in the

---

Der Stellmacher is a wheelwright, maker of wheeled vehicles; but he makes the frames (*Gestelle*) for his wagons as well. Heidegger chooses the word because of its kinship with *herstellen,* to produce. He employs the word *Ge-stell* in his essay on "The Origin of the Work of Art" (in the Reclam edition, p. 72). Much later, in the 1950s, Heidegger employs it as the name for the essence of technology; cf. *Vorträge und Aufsätze* (Pfullingen: G. Neske, 1954), p. 27 ff., and *Ursprung des Kunstwerkes,* "Zusatz" (1956), Reclam edition, pp. 97–98.

simplest clarity of their relationships. In this regard, the everyday state
of affairs by which the framemaker frames and produces frames gave
a thinker like Plato something to think about—for one thing, this: in
the production of tables the tablemaker proceeds *pros tēn idean blepōn
poiei*, making this or that table "while at the same time looking to the
Idea." He keeps an "eye" on the outward appearance of tables in
general. And the outward appearance of such a thing as a table? How
is it with that, seen from the point of view of production? Does the
tablemaker produce the outward appearance as well? No. *Ou gar pou
tēn ge idean autēn dēmiourgei oudeis tōn dēmiourgōn.* "For in no case
does the craftsman produce the Idea itself." How should he, with axe,
saw, and plane be able to manufacture an Idea? Here an end (or
boundary) becomes manifest, which for all "practice" is insurmounta-
ble, indeed an end or boundary *precisely with respect to what "practice" itself needs* in order to be "practical." For it is an essential matter
of fact that the tablemaker cannot manufacture the Idea with his tools;
and it is every bit as essential that he look to the Idea in order to be
who he is, the producer of tables. In that way the realm of a workshop
extends far beyond the four walls that contain the craftsman's tools and
produced items. The workshop possesses a vantage point from which
we can see the outward appearance or Idea of what is immediately on
hand and in use. The framemaker is a maker who in his making must
be on the lookout for something he himself cannot make. The Idea is
prescribed to him and he must *subscribe* to it. Thus, as a maker, he
is already somehow one who copies or imitates. Hence there is nothing
at all like a *pure* "practitioner," since the practitioner himself necessarily and from the outset is always already *more* than that. Such is the
basic insight that Plato strives to attain.

But there is something else we have to emphasize in the fact that
craftsmen manufacture implements. For the Greeks themselves it was
clearly granted, but for us it has become rather hazy, precisely because
of its obviousness. And that is the fact that what is manufactured or
produced, which formerly was not in being, now "is." It "is." We
understand this "is." We do not think very much about it. For the
Greeks the "Being" of manufactured things was defined, but different-

ly than it is for us. Something produced "is" because the Idea lets it
be seen as such, lets it come to presence in its outward appearance, lets
it "be." Only to that extent can what is itself produced be said "to be."
Making and manufacturing therefore mean to bring the outward appearance to show itself in something else, namely, in what is manufactured, to "pro-duce" the outward appearance, not in the sense of
manufacturing it but of letting it radiantly appear. What is manufactured "is" only to the extent that in it the outward appearance, Being,
radiates. To say that something manufactured "is" means that in it the
presence of its outward appearance shows itself. A worker is one who
fetches the outward appearance of something into the presence of
sensuous visibility. That seems to delineate sufficiently what, and how,
it is that the craftsman properly makes, and what he cannot make.
Every one of these pro-ducers of serviceable and useful implements and
items keeps to the realm of the one "Idea" that guides him: the
tablemaker looks to the Idea of table, the shoemaker to that of shoe.
Each is proficient to the extent that he limits himself purely to his own
field. Else he botches the job.

But how would it be if there were a man, *hos panta poiei, hosaper
heis hekastos tōn cheirotechnōn* (596 c), "who pro-duced everything
that every single other craftsman" is able to make? That would be a
man of enormous powers, uncanny and astonishing. In fact there is
such a man: *hapanta ergadzetai,* "he produces anything and everything." He can produce not only implements, *alla kai ta ek tēs gēs
phuomena hapanta poiei kai zōia panta ergadzetai,* "but also what
comes forth from the earth, producing plants and animals and everything else"; *kai heauton,* "indeed, himself too," and besides that, earth
and sky, *kai theous,* "even the gods," and everything in the heavens and
in the underworld. But such a producer, standing above all beings and
even above the gods, would be a sheer wonderworker! Yet there is such
a *dēmiourgos,* and he is nothing unusual; each of us is capable of
achieving such production. It is all a matter of observing *tini tropōi
poiei,* "in what way he produces."

While meditating on what is produced, and on production, we must
pay heed to the *tropos.* We are accustomed to translating that Greek

word, correctly but inadequately, as "way" and "manner." *Tropos* means how one is turned, in what direction he turns, in what he maintains himself, to what he applies himself, where he turns to and remains tied, and with what intention he does so. What does that suggest for the realm of pro-duction? One may say that the way the shoemaker proceeds is different from that in which the tablemaker goes to work. Certainly, but the difference here is defined by what in each case is to be produced, by the requisite materials, and by the kind of refinements or operations such materials demand. Nevertheless, the same *tropos* prevails in all these ways of producing. How so? This query is to be answered by that part of the discussion we shall now follow.

Kai tis ho tropos houtos; "And what *tropos* is that," which makes possible a production that is capable of producing *hapanta,* "anything and everything," to the extent designated, which is in no way limited? Such a *tropos* presents no difficulties: by means of it one can go ahead and produce things everywhere and without delay. *Tachista de pou, ei 'theleis labōn katoptron peripherein pantachēi* (596 d), "but you can do it quickest if you just take a mirror and point it around in all directions."

Tachy men hēlion poiēseis kai ta en tōi ouranōi, tachy de gēn, tachy de sauton te kai talla zōia kai skeuē kai phyta kai panta hosa nyndē elegeto. "That way you will quickly produce the sun and what is in the heavens; quickly too the earth; and quickly also you yourself and all other living creatures and implements and plants and everything else we mentioned just now."

With this turn of the conversation we see how essential it is to think of *poiein*—"making"—as *pro-ducing* in the Greek sense. A mirror accomplishes such production of outward appearance; it allows all beings to become present just as they outwardly appear.

But at the same time, this is the very place to elaborate an important distinction in the *tropos* of production. It will enable us for the first time to attain a clearer concept of the *dēmiourgos* and thereby also of *mimēsis,* "copying." Were we to understand *poiein*—"making"—in some indefinite sense of manufacturing, then the example of the mirror would have no effect, since the mirror does not manufacture the sun.

But if we understand pro-duction in a Greek manner, in the sense of bringing forth the Idea (bringing the outward appearance of something into something else, no matter in what way), then the mirror *does* in this particular sense *pro-duce* the sun.

With regard to "pointing the mirror in all directions," and to its mirroring, Glaucon must therefore agree immediately: *Nai,* "Certainly," that is a producing of "beings"; but he adds, *phainomena, ou mentoi onta ge pou tēi alētheiai.* But what shows itself in the mirror "only looks like, but all the same is not, something present in unconcealment," which is to say, undistorted by the "merely outwardly appearing as," i.e., undistorted by semblance. Socrates supports him: *kalōs, . . . kai eis deon erchēi tōi logōi.* "Fine, and by saying that you go to the heart of what is proper (to the matter)." Mirroring does produce beings, indeed as self-showing, but not as beings in un-concealment or nondistortion. Juxtaposed to one another here are *on phainomenon* and *on tēi alētheiai,* being as self-showing and being as undistorted; by no means *phainomenon* as "semblance" and "the merely apparent," on the one hand, and *on tēi alētheiai* as "Being," on the other; in each case it is a matter of *on*—"what is present"—but in different ways of presencing. But is that not the same, the self-showing and the undistorted? Yes and no. Same with respect to *what* becomes present (house), same to the extent that in each case it is a presencing; but in each case the *tropos* differs. In one case the "house" becomes present by showing itself and appearing in, and by means of, the glittering surface of the mirror; in the other the "house" is present by showing itself in stone and wood. The more firmly we hold on to the selfsameness, the more significant the distinction must become. Plato here is wrestling with the conception of the varying *tropos,* that is, at the same time and above all, with the determination of that "way" in which *on* itself shows itself most purely, so that it does not portray itself by means of something else but presents itself in such a way that its outward appearance, *eidos,* constitutes its Being. Such self-showing is the *eidos* as *idea.*

Two kinds of presence result: the house (i.e., the *idea*) shows itself in the mirror or in the "house" itself at hand. Consequently, two kinds of production and producers must be differentiated and clarified. If we call every pro-ducer a *dēmiourgos,* then one who mirrors is a particular type of *dēmiourgos.* Therefore Socrates continues: *tōn toioutōn gar oimai dēmiourgōn kai ho zōgraphos estin.* "For I believe that the painter too belongs to that kind of pro-ducing," which is to say the mirroring kind. The artist lets beings become present, but as *phainomena,* "showing themselves by appearing through something else." *Ouk alēthē . . . poiein ha poiei,* "he does not bring forward what he produces as unconcealed." He does not produce the *eidos. Kaitoi tropōi ge tini kai ho zōgraphos klinēn poiei.* "All the same, the painter too produces [a] bedframe"—*tropōi tini,* "in a certain way." *Tropos* here means the kind of presence of the *on* (the *idea*); hence it means that in which and through which *on* as *idea* produces itself and brings itself into presence. The *tropos* is in one case the mirror, in another the painted surface, in another the wood, in all of which the table comes to presence.

We are quick on the uptake, so we say that some of them produce "apparent" things, others "real" things. But the question is: what does "real" in this case mean? And is the table manufactured by the carpenter the "real" table according to the Greeks; is it in being? To ask it another way: when the carpenter manufactures this or that table, any given table, does he thereby produce the table that is in being; or is manufacturing a kind of bringing forward that will never be able to produce the table "itself"? But we have already heard that there is also something which he does *not* pro-duce, something which he, as framemaker, with the means available to him, cannot pro-duce: *ou to eidos* (*tēn idean*) *poiei,* "but he does not produce the pure outward appearance (of something like a bedframe) in itself." He presupposes it as already granted to him and thereby brought forth unto and produced for him.

Now, what is the *eidos* itself? What is it in relation to the individual bedframe that the framemaker produces? *To eidos . . . ho dē phamen einai ho esti klinē,* "the outward appearance, of which we say that it is what the bedframe is," and thereby *what* it is *as such:* the *ho esti, quid est, quidditas,* whatness. It is obviously that which is essential in

beings, by means of which they "first and last are," *teleōs on* (597 a).
But if the craftsman does not pro-duce precisely this *eidos* in itself, but
in each case merely looks to it as something already brought to him;
and if *eidos* is what is properly in being among beings; then the
craftsman does not produce the Being of beings either. Rather, he
always produces this or that being—*ouk ... ho esti klinē, alla klinēn
tina,* "not the what-being of the bedframe, but some bedframe or
other."

So it is that the craftsman, who grapples with a reality you can hold
in your hands, is not in touch with beings themselves, *on tēi alētheiai.*
Therefore, Socrates says, *mēden ara thaumadzōmen ei kai touto (to
ergon tou dēmiourgou) amydron ti tynchanei on pros alētheian.* "In
no way would it astonish us, therefore, if even this (what is manufactured by the craftsman) proves to be something obscure and hazy in
relation to unconcealment." The wood of the bedframe, the amassed
stone of the house, in each case bring the *idea* forth into appearance;
yet such pro-duction dulls and darkens the original luster of the *idea.*
Hence the house which we call "real" is in a certain way reduced to
the level of an image of the house in a mirror or painting. The Greek
word *amydron* is difficult to translate: for one thing it means the
darkening and distorting of what comes to presence. But then such
darkening, over against what is undistorted, is something lusterless and
feeble; it does not command the inner power of the presencing of
beings themselves.

Only now do the speakers attain the position from which Socrates
may demand that they try to illuminate the essence of *mimēsis* on the
basis of what they have so far discussed. To that end he summarizes
and describes in a more pointed way what they have already ascertained.

The approach to their considerations established that there are, for
example, many individual bedframes set up in houses. Such a "many"
is easy to see, even when we look around us in a lackadaisical sort of
way. Therefore, Socrates (Plato) says at the beginning of the discussion,
with a very profound, ironic reference to what is to follow and which
we are now on the verge of reaching (596 a), *polla toi oxyteron blepon-
tōn amblyteron horōntes proteroi eidon.* "A variety and multiplicity is

what those who look with dull eyes see, rather than those who examine things more keenly." Those who examine things more keenly see fewer things, but for that reason they see what is essential and simple. They do not lose themselves in a sheer variety that has no essence. Dull eyes see an incalculable multiplicity of sundry particular bedframes. Keen eyes see something else, even—and especially—when they linger upon one single bedframe at hand. For dull eyes the many always amounts to "a whole bunch," understood as "quite a lot," hence as abundance. In contrast, for keen eyes the simple is simplified. In such simplification, essential plurality originates. That means: the first (one), produced by the god, (the pure) one-and-the-same outward appearance, the Idea; the second, what is manufactured by the carpenter; the third, what the painter conjures in images. What is simple is named in the word *klinē*. But *trittai tines klinai hautai gignontai* (597 b). We must translate: "In a certain way, a first, a second, and a third bedframe have resulted here." *Mia men hē en tēi physei ousa*, "for what is being in nature is *one*." We notice that the translation does not succeed. What is *physis*, "nature," supposed to mean here? No bedframes appear in nature; they do not grow as trees and bushes do. Surely *physis* still means emergence for Plato, as it does primarily for the first beginnings of Greek philosophy, emergence in the way a rose emerges, unfolding itself and showing itself out of itself. But what we call "nature," the countryside, nature out-of-doors, is only a specially delineated sector of nature or *physis* in the essential sense: that which of itself unfolds itself in presencing. *Physis* is the primordial Greek grounding word for Being itself, in the sense of the presence that emerges of itself and so holds sway.

Hē en tēi physei ousa, the bedframe "which is in nature," means that what is essential in pure Being, as present of itself, in other words, what emerges by itself, stands in opposition to what is pro-duced only by something else. *Hē physei klinē:* what pro-duces itself as such, without mediation, by itself, in its pure outward appearance. What presences in this way is the purely, straightforwardly envisioned *eidos,* which is not seen by virtue of any medium, hence the *idea*. That such a thing lights up, emerges, *phyei,* no man can bring about. Man cannot produce the *idea;* he can only be stationed before it. For that reason, of the *physei klinē* Socrates says: *hēn phaimen an, hōs egōimai, theon ergasasthai,* "of which we may well say, as I believe, that a god produced it and brought it forth."

Mia de ge hēn ho tektōn. "But it is a different bedframe which the craftsman manufactures." *Mia de hēn ho zōgraphos.* "And again another which the painter brings about."

The threefold character of the one bedframe, and so naturally of every particular being that is at hand, is captured in the following statement (597 b): *Zōgraphos dē, klinopoios, theos, treis houtoi epistatai trisin eidesi klinōn.* "Thus the painter, the framemaker, the god—these three are *epistatai,* those who dedicate themselves to, or preside over, three types of outward appearance of the bedframe." Each presides over a distinct type of self-showing, which each sees to in his own way; he is the overseer for that type, watching over and mastering the self-showing. If we translate *eidos* here simply as "type," three types of bedframes, we obfuscate what is decisive. For Plato's thought is here moving in the direction of visualizing how the selfsame shows itself in various ways: three ways of self-showing; hence, of presence; hence, three metamorphoses of Being itself. What matters is the unity of the basic character that prevails throughout self-showing in spite of all difference: appearing in this or that fashion and becoming present in outward appearance.

Let us also observe something else that accompanied us everywhere in our previous considerations: whenever we mentioned genuine being we also spoke of *on tēi alētheiai,* being "in truth." Grasped in a Greek manner, however, "truth" means nondistortion, openness, namely for the self-showing itself.

The interpretation of Being as eidos, *presencing in outward appearance, presupposes the interpretation of truth as* alētheia, *nondistortion.* We must heed that if we wish to grasp the relation of art (*mimēsis*) and truth in Plato's conception correctly, which is to say, in a Greek manner. Only in such a realm do Plato's questions unfold. From it they derive the possibility of receiving answers. Here at the peak of the Platonic interpretation of the Being of beings as *idea,* the question arises as to why the god allowed only one *idea* to go forth for each realm of individual things, for example, bedframes. *Eite ouk ebouleto, eite tis anankē epēn mē pleon ē mian en tēi physei apergasasthai auton klinēn* (597 c). "Either he desired, or a certain necessity compelled him, not to permit more than one bedframe to emerge in outward appearance." *Dyo de toiautai ē pleious oute ephuteuthēsan hypo tou theou oute mē phyōsin.* "Two or more such Ideas neither were brought forward by the god, nor will they ever come forth." What is the reason for that? Why is there always only one Idea for one thing?

Let us illustrate briefly Plato's answer, with a glance back to the essence of the true, which we discussed earlier, the true in its singularity and immutability.

What would happen if the god were to allow several Ideas to emerge for one thing and its manifold nature—"house" and houses, "tree" and trees, "animal" and animals? The answer: *ei dyo monas poiēseien, palin an mia anaphaneiē hēs ekeinai an au amphoterai to eidos echoien, kai eiē an ho estin klinē ekeinē all' oukh hai dyo.* "If instead of the single 'Idea' house he were to allow more to emerge, even if only two, then one of them would have to appear with an outward appearance that both would have to have as their own; and the what-being of the bedframe or the house would be that one, whereas both could not be." Hence unity and singularity are proper to the essence of the *idea.* Now, according to Plato, where does the ground for the singularity of each of the Ideas (essences) lie? It does not rest in the fact that when two Ideas are posited the one allows the other to proceed to a higher level; it rests in the fact that the god, who knew of the ascent of representation from a manifold to a unity, *boulomenos einai ontōs klinēs poiētēs ontōs ousēs, alla mē klinēs tinos mēde klinopoios tis, mian physei autēn ephysen* (597 d), "wanted to be the essential producer of the essential thing, not of any given particular thing, and not like some sort of framemaker." Because the god wanted to be such a god, he allowed such things—for example, bedframes—"to come forth in the unity and singularity of their essence." In what, then, is the essence of the Idea, and thereby of Being, ultimately grounded for Plato? In the initiating action of a creator whose essentiality appears to be saved only when what he creates is in each case something singular, a one; and also there where allowance is made in the representation of a manifold for an ascent to the representation of its one.

The grounding of this interpretation of Being goes back to the initiating action of a creator and to the presupposition of a one which in each case unifies a manifold. For us a question lies concealed here. How does Being, as presencing and letting come to presence, cohere with the one, as unifying? Does the reversion to a creator contain an answer to the question, or does the question remain unasked, since Being as presencing is not thought through, and the unifying of the one not defined with reference to Being as presencing?

Every single being, which we today take to be the particular item which is "properly real," manifests itself in three modes of outward appearance. Accordingly, it can be traced back to three ways of self-showing or being pro-duced. Hence there are three kinds of producers.

First, the god who lets the essence emerge—*physin phyei*. He is therefore called *phytourgos,* the one who takes care of and holds in readiness the emergence of pure outward appearance, so that man can discern it.*

Second, the craftsman who is the *dēmiourgos klinēs*. He produces a bed according to its essence, but lets it appear in wood, that is, in the kind of thing where the bedframe stands as this particular item at our disposal for everyday use.

Third, the painter who brings the bedframe to show itself in his picture. May he therefore be called a *dēmiourgos?* Does he work for the *dēmos,* participating in the public uses of things and in communal life? No! For neither does he have disposition over the pure essence, as the god does (he rather darkens it in the stuff of colors and surfaces), nor does he have disposition over and use of what he brings about with respect to what it is. The painter is not *dēmiourgos* but *mimētēs hou ekeinoi dēmiourgoi,* "a copier of the things of which those others are

---

*Schleiermacher translates *phytourgos* (*Republic,* 597 d 5) as *Wesensbildner,* "shaper of essences"; the word literally means gardener, "worker with plants." Aeschylus' suppliant maidens use the word as an epithet of Zeus the Father (*Supp.* 592).

the producers for the public." What, consequently, is the *mimētēs?* The copier is *ho tou tritou gennēmatos apo tēs physeōs* (597 e); he is *epistatēs;* "he presides and rules over" one way in which Being, the *idea,* is brought to outward appearance, *eidos.* What he manufactures —the painting—is *to triton gennēma,* "the third kind of bringing-forth," third *apo tēs physeōs,* "reckoned in terms of the pure emergence of the *idea,* which is first." In the pictured table, "table" is somehow manifest in general, showing its *idea* in some way; and the table in the picture also manifests a particular wooden frame, and thus is somehow what the craftsman properly makes: but the pictured table shows both of them in something else, in shades of color, in some third thing. Neither can a usable table come forward in such a medium, nor can the outward appearance show itself purely as such. The way the painter pro-duces a "table" into visibility is even farther removed from the Idea, the Being of the being, than the way the carpenter produces it.

The distance from Being and its pure visibility is definitive for the definition of the essence of the *mimētēs.* What is decisive for the Greek-Platonic concept of *mimēsis* or imitation is not reproduction or portraiture, not the fact that the painter provides us with the same thing once again; what is decisive is that this is precisely what he cannot do, that he is even less capable than the craftsman of duplicating the same thing. It is therefore wrongheaded to apply to *mimēsis* notions of "naturalistic" or "primitivistic" copying and reproducing. Imitation is subordinate pro-duction. The *mimētēs* is defined in essence by his position of distance; such distance results from the hierarchy established with regard to ways of production and in the light of pure outward appearance, Being.

But the subordinate position of the *mimētēs* and of *mimēsis* has not yet been sufficiently delineated. We need to clarify in what way the painter is subordinate to the carpenter as well. A particular "real" table offers different aspects when viewed from different sides. But when the table is in use such aspects are indifferent; what matters is the particular table, which is one and the same. *Mē ti diapherei autē heautēs* (598 a), "it is distinguished (in spite of its various aspects) in no way from itself." Such a single, particular, and selfsame thing the carpenter can manufacture. In contrast, the painter can bring the table into view only from one particular angle. What he pro-duces is consequently but *one* aspect, *one* way in which the table appears. If he depicts the table from the front, he cannot paint the rear of it. He produces the table always in only one view or *phantasma* (598 b). What defines the character of the painter as *mimētēs* is not only that he cannot at all produce any particular usable table, but also that he cannot even bring that one particular table fully to the fore.

But *mimēsis* is the essence of all art. Hence a position of distance with respect to Being, to immediate and undistorted outward appearance, to the *idea,* is proper to art. In regard to the opening up of Being, that is, to the display of Being in the unconcealed, *alētheia,* art is subordinate.

Where, then, according to Plato, does art stand in relation to truth (*alētheia*)? The answer (598 b): *Porrō ara pou tou alēthous hē mimētikē estin.* "So, then, art stands far removed from truth." What art pro-duces is not the *eidos* as *idea* (*physis,*) but *touto eidōlon,* which is but the semblance of pure outward appearance. *Eidōlon* means a little *eidos,* but not just in the sense of stature. In the way it shows and appears, the *eidōlon* is something slight. It is a mere residue of the genuine self-showing of beings, and even then in an alien domain, for example, color or some other material of portraiture. Such diminution of the way of pro-ducing is a darkening and distorting. *Tout' ara estai kai ho tragōidopoios, eiper mimētēs esti, tritos tis apo basileōs kai tēs alētheias pephykōs, kai pantes hoi alloi mimētai* (597 e). "Now, the tragedian will also be of such kind, if he is an 'artist,' removed three times, as it were, from the master who rules over the emergence of pure Being; according to his essence he will be reduced to third place with regard to truth (and to the grasp of it in pure discernment); and of such kind are the other 'artists' as well."

A statement by Erasmus which has been handed down to us is supposed to characterize the art of the painter Albrecht Dürer. The statement expresses a thought that obviously grew out of a personal conversation which that learned man had with the artist. The statement runs: *ex situ rei minus, non unam speciem sese oculis offerentem exprimit:* by showing a particular thing from any given angle, he, Dürer the painter, brings to the fore not only one single isolated view which offers itself to the eye. Rather—we may complete the thought in the following way—by showing any given individual thing as this particular thing, in its singularity, he makes Being itself visible: in a particular hare, the Being of the hare; in a particular animal, the animality. It is clear that Erasmus here is speaking against Plato. We may presume that the humanist Erasmus knew the dialogue we have been discussing and its passages on art. That Erasmus and Dürer could speak in such a fashion presupposes that a transformation of the understanding of Being was taking place.*

In the sequence of sundry ways taken by the presence of beings, hence by the Being of beings, art stands far below truth in Plato's metaphysics. We encounter here a distance. Yet distance is not discordance, especially not if art—as Plato would have it—is placed under the guidance of philosophy as knowledge of the essence of beings. To pursue Plato's thoughts in that direction, and so to examine the further contents of Book Ten, is not germane to our present effort.

---

*Compare to the above Heidegger's reference to Albrecht Dürer in *Der Ursprung des Kunstwerkes,* Reclam edition, p. 80; "The Origin of the Work of Art," in *Poetry, Language, Thought,* p. 70.

23. Plato's *Phaedrus*: Beauty and Truth in Felicitous Discordance

Our point of departure was the question as to the nature of the discordance between art and truth in Nietzsche's view. The discordance must loom before him on the basis of the way he grasps art and truth philosophically. According to his own words, Nietzsche's philosophy is inverted Platonism. If we grant that there is in Platonism a discordance between art and truth, it follows that such discordance would in Nietzsche's view have to vanish as a result of the cancellation which overturns Platonism. But we have just seen that there is no discordance in Platonism, merely a distance. Of course, the distance is not simply a quantitative one, but a distance of order and rank. The result is the following proposition, which would apply to Plato, although couched in Nietzsche's manner of speech: truth is worth more than art. Nietzsche says, on the contrary: art is worth more than truth. Obviously, the discordance lies hidden in these propositions. But if in distinction to Plato the relation of art and truth is reversed within the hierarchy; and if for Nietzsche that relation is a discordance, then it only follows that for Plato too the relation is a discordance, but of a reverse sort. Even though Nietzsche's philosophy may be understood as the reversal of Platonism, that does not mean that through such reversal the discordance between art and truth must vanish. We can only say that if there is a discordance between art and truth in Plato's teaching, and if Nietzsche's philosophy represents a reversal of Platonism, then such discordance must come to the fore in Nietzsche's philosophy in the reverse form. Hence Platonism can be for us a directive for the discov-

ery and location of the discordance in Nietzsche's thought, a directive
that would indicate by way of reversal. In that way Nietzsche's knowledge of art and truth would finally be brought to its sustaining ground.

What does discordance mean? Discordance is the opening of a gap
between two things that are severed. Of course, a mere gap does not
yet constitute a discordance. We do speak of a "split" in relation to the
gap that separates two soaring cliffs; yet the cliffs are not in discordance
and never could be; to be so would require that they, of themselves,
relate to each other. Only two things that are related to one another
can be opposed to each other. But such opposition is not yet discordance. For it is surely the case that their being opposed to one another
presupposes a being drawn toward and related to each other, which is
to say, their converging upon and agreeing with one another in one
respect. Genuine political opposition—not mere dispute—can arise
only where the selfsame political order is willed; only here can ways and
goals and basic principles diverge. In every opposition, agreement prevails in one respect, whereas in other respects there is variance. But
whatever diverges in the same respect in which it agrees slips into
discordance. Here the opposition springs from the divergence of what
once converged, indeed in such a way that precisely by being apart they
enter into the supreme way of belonging together. But from that we
also conclude that severance is something different from opposition,
that it does not need to be discordance, but may be a concordance.
Concordance too requires the twofold character implied in severance.

Thus "discordance" is ambiguous. It may mean, first, a severance
which at bottom can be a concordance; second, one which must be a
discordance (abscission). For the present we purposely allow the word
"discordance" to remain in such ambiguity. For if a discordance prevails in Nietzsche's inverted Platonism, and if that is possible only to
the extent that there is discordance already in Platonism; and if the
discordance is in Nietzsche's view a dreadful one; then for Plato it must
be the reverse, that is to say, it must be a severance which nevertheless
is concordant. In any case, any two things that are supposed to be able
to enter into discordance must be balanced against one another, be of
the same immediate origin, of the same necessity and rank. There can

be an "above" and "below" in cases of mere distance and opposition, but never in the case of discordance, for the former do not share an equivalent standard of measure. The "above" and "below" are fundamentally different; in the essential respect they do not agree.

Therefore, so long as art in the *Republic* remains in third position when measured in terms of truth, a distance and a subordination obtain between art and truth—but a discordance is not possible. If such discordance between art and truth is to become possible, art must first of all be elevated to equal rank. But is there as a matter of fact a "discordance" between art and truth? Indeed Plato speaks—in the *Republic,* no less (607 b)—in a shadowy and suggestive way of the *palaia men tis diaphora philosophiai te kai poiētikēi,* "of a certain ancient quarrel between philosophy and poetry," which is to say, between knowledge and art, truth and beauty. Yet even if *diaphora* here is to suggest more than a quarrel—and it is—in this dialogue it is not and cannot be a matter of "discordance." For if art must become equal in rank with truth, so as to become "discordant" with it, then it becomes necessary to consider art in yet another respect.

That other respect in which art must be viewed can only be the same one in which Plato discusses truth. Only that one and the same respect grants the presupposition for a severance. We must therefore investigate in what other regard—in contrast to the conversation carried on in the *Republic*—Plato treats the question of art.

If we scrutinize the traditional configuration of Plato's philosophy as a whole we notice that it consists of particular conversations and areas of discussion. Nowhere do we find a "system" in the sense of a unified structure planned and executed with equal compartments for all essential questions and issues. The same is true of Aristotle's philosophy and of Greek philosophy in general. Various questions are posed from various points of approach and on various levels, developed and answered to varying extents. Nevertheless, a certain basic way of proceeding prevails in Plato's thought. Everything is gathered into the guiding question of philosophy—the question as to what beings are.

Although the congelation of philosophical inquiry in the doctrines and handbooks of the Schools is prepared in and by the philosophy of

Plato, we must be chary of thinking about his questions on the guidelines of particular dogmatic phrases and formulations found in the later philosophical disciplines. Whatever Plato says about truth and knowledge, or beauty and art, we may not conceive of it and pigeonhole it according to later epistemology, logic, and aesthetics. Of course that does not preclude our posing the question, in relation to Plato's meditation on art, of whether and where the issue of beauty is also treated in his philosophy. Granted that we must allow the whole matter to remain open, we may ask about the nature of the relation between art and beauty—a relation that long ago was accepted as a matter of course.

In his discussions Plato often speaks of "the beautiful" without taking up the question of art. To one of his dialogues the tradition has appended the express subtitle *peri tou kalou,* "On the Beautiful." It is that conversation which Plato called *Phaedrus,* after the youth who serves as the interlocutor in it. But the dialogue has received other subtitles over the centuries: *peri psychēs,* "On the Soul," and *peri tou erōtos,* "On Love." That alone is enough to produce uncertainty concerning the contents of the dialogue. All those things—the beautiful, the soul, and love—are discussed, and not merely incidentally. But the dialogue speaks also of *technē,* art, in great detail; also of *logos,* speech and language, with great penetration; of *alētheia,* truth, in a quite essential way, of *mania*—madness, rapture, ecstasy—in a most compelling manner; and finally, as always, of the *ideai* and of Being.

Every one of these words could with as much (or as little) right serve as the subtitle. Nevertheless, the content of the dialogue is by no means a jumbled potpourri. Its rich content is shaped so remarkably well that this dialogue must be accounted the most accomplished one in all essential respects. It therefore may not be taken to be the earliest work of Plato, as Schleiermacher believed; just as little does it belong to the final period; it rather belongs to those years which comprise the *akmē* of Plato's creative life.

Because of the inner greatness of this work of Plato's, we cannot hope to make the whole of it visible at once and in brief; that is even less possible here than it was in the case of the *Republic.* Our remarks concerning the title suffice to show that the *Phaedrus* discusses art, truth, speech, rapture, and the beautiful. Now we will pursue only what is said concerning the beautiful in relation to the true. We do this in order to estimate whether, to what extent, and in what way, we can speak of a severance of the two.

Decisive for correct understanding of what is said here about the beautiful is knowledge of the context and the scope in which the beautiful comes to language. To begin with a negative determination: the beautiful is discussed neither in the context of the question of art nor in explicit connection with the question of truth. Rather, the beautiful is discussed with the range of the original question of man's relation to beings as such. But precisely because Plato reflects upon the beautiful within the realm of that question, its connection with truth and art comes to the fore. We can demonstrate that on the basis of the latter half of the dialogue.

We will first of all select several guiding statements, in order to make visible the scope in which the beautiful is discussed. Second, we will comment upon what is said there about the beautiful, while remaining within the limits of our task. Third, and finally, we will ask about the kind of relation between beauty and truth which confronts us there.

Turning to the first matter, we note that the beautiful is discussed with the scope characteristic of man's relation to beings as such. In that regard we must consider the following statement (249 e): *pasa men anthrōpou psychē physei tetheatai ta onta, ē ouk an ēlthen eis tode to zōion.* "Every human soul, rising of itself, has already viewed beings in their Being; otherwise it would never have entered into this form of life." In order for man to be this particular embodying/living man, he must already have viewed Being. Why? What is man, after all? That is not stated in so many words; it remains tacit and presupposed. Man is the essence that comports itself to beings as such. But he could not be such an essence, that is to say, beings could not show themselves to him as beings, if he did not always ahead of time have Being in view by means of "theory." Man's "soul" must have viewed Being, since Being cannot be grasped by the senses. The soul "nourishes itself," *trephetai,* upon Being. Being, the discerning relation to Being, guarantees man his relation to beings.

If we did not know what variation and equality were, we could never encounter various things; we could never encounter things at all. If we did not know what sameness and contrariety were, we could never comport ourselves toward ourselves as selfsame in each case; we would never be with ourselves, would never be our selves at all. Nor could we ever experience something that stands over against us, something other than ourselves. If we did not know what order and law, or symmetry and harmonious arrangement were, we could not arrange and construct anything, could not establish and maintain anything in existence. The form of life called man would simply be impossible if the view upon Being did not prevail in it in a fundamental and paramount way.

But now we must catch a glimpse of man's other essential determination. Because the view upon Being is exiled in the body, Being can never be beheld purely in its unclouded brilliance; it can be seen only under the circumstance of our encountering this or that particular being. Therefore the following is generally true of the view upon Being which is proper to man's soul: *mogis kathorōsa ta onta* (248 a), "it just barely views being [as such], and only with effort." For that reason most people find knowledge of Being quite laborious, and consequently *ateleis tēs tou ontos theas aperchontai* (248 b), "the *thea*, the view upon Being, remains *atelēs* to them, so that it does not achieve its end, does not encompass everything that is proper to Being." Hence their view of things is but half of what it should be: it is as though they looked cockeyed at things. Most people, the cockeyed ones, give it up. They divert themselves from the effort to gain a pure view upon Being, *kai apelthousai trophēi doxastēi chrōntai*, "and in turning away are no longer nourished by Being." Instead, they make use of the *trophē doxastē*, the nourishment that falls to them thanks to *doxa*, i.e., what offers itself in anything they may encounter, some fleeting appearance which things just happen to have.

But the more the majority of men in the everyday world fall prey to mere appearance and to prevailing opinions concerning beings, and the more comfortable they become with them, feeling themselves confirmed in them, the more Being "conceals itself" (*lanthanei*) from man. The consequence for man of the concealment of Being is that he is overcome by *lēthē,* that concealment of Being which gives rise to the illusion that there is no such thing as Being. We translate the Greek word *lēthē* as "forgetting," although in such a way that "to forget" is thought in a metaphysical, not a psychological, manner. The majority of men sink into oblivion of Being, although—or precisely because—they constantly have to do solely with the things that are in their vicinity. For such things are not beings; they are only such things *ha nyn einai phamen* (249 c), "of which we now say that they are." Whatever matters to us and makes a claim on us here and now, in this or that way, as this or that thing, is—to the extent that it is at all—only a *homoiōma,* an approximation to Being. It is but a fleeting appearance of Being. But those who lapse into oblivion of Being do not even know of the appearance as an appearance. For otherwise they would at the same time have to know of Being, which comes to the fore even in fleeting appearances, although "just barely." They would then emerge from oblivion of Being. Instead of being slaves to oblivion, they would preserve *mnēmē* in recollective thought on Being. *Oligai dē leipontai hais to tēs mnēmēs hikanōs parestin* (250 a 5): "Only a few remain who have at their disposal the capacity to remember Being." But even these few are not able without further ado to see the appearance of what they encounter in such a way that the Being in it comes to the fore for them. Particular conditions must be fulfilled. Depending on how Being gives itself, the power of self-showing in the *idea* becomes proper to it, and therewith the attracting and binding force.

As soon as man lets himself be bound by Being in his view upon it, he is cast beyond himself, so that he is stretched, as it were, between himself and Being and is outside himself. Such elevation beyond oneself and such being drawn toward Being itself is *erōs.* Only to the extent that Being is able to elicit "erotic" power in its relation to man is man capable of thinking about Being and overcoming oblivion of Being.

The proposition with which we began—that the view upon Being is proper to the essence of man, so that he can be as man—can be understood only if we realize that the view upon Being does not enter on the scene as a mere appurtenance of man. It belongs to him as his most intrinsic possession, one which can be quite easily disturbed and deformed, and which therefore must always be recovered anew. Hence the need for whatever makes possible such recovery, perpetual renewal, and preservation of the view upon Being. That can only be something which in the immediate, fleeting appearances of things encountered also brings Being, which is utterly remote, to the fore most readily. But that, according to Plato, is the beautiful. When we defined the range and scope in which the beautiful comes to language we were basically already saying what the beautiful is, with regard to the possibility and the preservation of the view upon Being.

We proceed now to the second stage, adducing several statements in order to make the matter clearer. These statements are to establish the essential definition of the beautiful and thereby to prepare the way for the third stage, namely, a discussion of the relation of beauty and truth in Plato. From the metaphysical founding of communal life in Plato's dialogue on the state we know that what properly sets the standard is manifested in *dikē* and *dikaiosynē*, that is, in the well-wrought jointure of the order of Being. But viewed from the standpoint of the customary oblivion of Being, the supreme and utterly pure essence of Being is what is most remote. And to the extent that the essential order of Being shows itself in "beings," that is to say, in whatever we call "beings," it is here very difficult to discern. Fleeting appearances are inconspicuous; what is essential scarcely obtrudes. In the *Phaedrus* (250 b) Plato says accordingly: *dikaiosynēs men oun kai sōphrosynēs kai hosa alla timia psychais ouk enesti phengos ouden en tois tēide homoiōmasin.* "In justice and in temperance, and in whatever men ultimately must respect above all else, there dwells no radiance whenever men encounter them as fleeting appearances." Plato continues: *alla di' amydrōn organōn mogis autōn kai oligoi epi tas eikonas iontes theōntai to tou eikasthentos genos.* "On the contrary, we grasp Being with blunt instruments, clumsily, scarcely at all; and few of those who approach the appearances in question catch a glimpse of the original source, i.e., the essential origin, of what offers itself in fleeting appearances." The train of thought continues as Plato interposes a striking antithesis: *kallos de,* "With beauty, however," it is different. *Nun de kallos monon tautēn esche moiran, hōst' ekphanestaton einai* *kai erasmiōtaton* (250 d). "But to beauty alone has the role been allotted [i.e., in the essential order of Being's illumination] to be the most radiant, but also the most enchanting." The beautiful is what advances most directly upon us and captivates us. While encountering us as a being, however, it at the same time liberates us to the view upon Being. The beautiful is an element which is disparate within itself; it grants entry into immediate sensuous appearances and yet at the same time soars toward Being; it is both captivating and liberating.* Hence it is the beautiful that snatches us from oblivion of Being and grants the view upon Being.

The beautiful is called that which is most radiant, that which shines in the realm of immediate, sensuous, fleeting appearances: *kateilēphamen auto dia tēs enargestatēs aisthēseōs tōn hemeterōn stilbon enargestata.* "The beautiful itself is given [to us men, here] by means of the most luminous mode of perception at our disposal, and we possess the beautiful as what most brightly glistens." *Opsis gar hēmin oxytate tōn dia tou sōmatos erchetai aisthēseōn.* "For vision, viewing, is the keenest way we can apprehend things through the body." But we know that *thea,* "viewing," is also the supreme apprehending, the grasping of Being. The look reaches as far as the highest and farthest remoteness of Being; simultaneously, it penetrates the nearest and brightest proximity of fleeting appearances. The more radiantly and brightly fleeting appearances are apprehended as such, the more brightly does that of which they are the appearances come to the fore—Being. According to its most proper essence, the beautiful is what is most radiant and

---

*Heidegger translates *erasmiōtaton* as *das Entrückendste,* modifying it now as *das Berückend-Entrückende.* Although both German words could be rendered by the English words "to entrance, charm, enchant," their literal sense is quite different. *Rücken* suggests sudden change of place; the prefixes (*be-, ent-*) both make the verb transitive. But *berücken* suggests causing to move toward, *entrücken* causing to move away. Heidegger thus tries to express the disparate, i.e., genuinely erotic character of the beautiful, which both captivates and liberates us, by choosing two German words that manifest a kind of felicitous discordance. The same formulation appears in *"Wie wenn am Feiertage . . ."* (1939–40) in Martin Heidegger, *Erläuterungen zu Hölderlins Dichtung,* pp. 53–54.

sparkling in the sensuous realm, in a way that, as such brilliance, it lets Being scintillate at the same time. Being is that to which man from the outset remains essentially bound; it is in the direction of Being that man is liberated.

Since the beautiful allows Being to scintillate, and since the beautiful itself is what is most attractive, it draws man through and beyond itself to Being as such. We can scarcely coin an expression that would render what Plato says in such a lucid way about radiance through those two essential words, *ekphanestaton kai erasmiōtaton.*

Even the Latin translation from Renaissance times obscures everything here when it says, *At vero pulchritudo sola habuit sortem, ut maxime omnium et perspicua sit et amabilis* ["But true beauty alone has been destined to be the most transparent of things and the loveliest of all"]. Plato does not mean that the beautiful itself, as an object, is "perspicuous and lovely." It is rather what is most luminous and what thereby most draws us on and liberates us.

From what we have presented, the essence of the beautiful has become clear. It is what makes possible the recovery and preservation of the view upon Being, which devolves from the most immediate fleeting appearances and which can easily vanish in oblivion. Our capacity to understand, *phronēsis,* although it remains related to what is essential, of itself has no corresponding *eidōlon,* no realm of appearances which brings what it has to grant us into immediate proximity and yet at the same time elevates us toward what is properly to be understood.

The third question, inquiring about the relationship between beauty and truth, now answers itself. To be sure, up to now truth has not been treated explicitly. Nevertheless, in order to achieve clarity concerning the relation of beauty and truth, it suffices if we think back to the major introductory statement and read it in the way Plato himself first introduces it. The major statement says that the view upon Being is proper to the essence of man, that by force of it man can comport himself to beings and to what he encounters as merely apparent things. At the place where that thought is first introduced (249 b), Plato says, not that the basic condition for the form of man is that he *tetheatai ta onta,* that he "has beings as such in view ahead of time," but *ou gar hē ge mēpote idousa tēn alētheian eis tode hēxei to schēma,* that "the soul would never have assumed this form if it had not earlier viewed the unconcealment of beings, i.e., beings in their unconcealment."

The view upon Being opens up what is concealed, making it unconcealed; it is the basic relation to the true. That which truth essentially brings about, the unveiling of Being, that and nothing else is what beauty brings about. It does so, scintillating in fleeting appearances, by liberating us to the Being that radiates in such appearances, which is to say, to the openedness of Being, to truth. Truth and beauty are in essence related to the selfsame, to Being; they belong together in one, the one thing that is decisive: to open Being and to keep it open.

Yet in that very medium where they belong together, they must diverge for man, they must separate from one another. For the openedness of Being, truth, can only be nonsensuous illumination, since for Plato Being is nonsensuous. Because Being opens itself only to the view upon Being, and because the latter must always be snatched from oblivion of Being, and because for that reason it needs the most direct radiance of fleeting appearances, the opening up of Being must occur at that site where, estimated in terms of truth, the *mē on (eidōlon),* i.e., nonbeing, occurs. But that is the site of beauty.

When we consider very carefully that art, by bringing forth the beautiful, resides in the sensuous, and that it is therefore far removed from truth, it then becomes clear why truth and beauty, their belonging together in one notwithstanding, still must be two, must separate from one another. But the severance, discordance in the broad sense, is not in Plato's view one which arouses dread; it is a felicitous one. The beautiful elevates us beyond the sensuous and bears us back into the true. Accord prevails in the severance, because the beautiful, as radiant and sensuous, has in advance sheltered its essence in the truth of Being as supersensuous.

Viewed more discerningly, a discordance in the strict sense lies here as well. But it belongs to the essence of Platonism that it efface that discordance by positing Being in such a way that it can do so without the effacement becoming visible as such. But when Platonism is overturned everything that characterizes it must also be overturned; whatever it can cloak and conceal, whatever it can pronounce felicitous, on the contrary, must out, and must arouse dread.

24. Nietzsche's Overturning of Platonism

We conducted an examination of the relation of truth and beauty in Plato in order to sharpen our view of things. For we are attempting to locate the place and context in Nietzsche's conception of art and truth where the severance of the two must occur, and in such a way that it is experienced as a discordance that arouses dread.

Both beauty and truth are related to Being, indeed by way of unveiling the Being of beings. Truth is the immediate way in which Being is revealed in the thought of philosophy; it does not enter into the sensuous, but from the outset is averted from it. Juxtaposed to it is beauty, penetrating the sensuous and then moving beyond it, liberating in the direction of Being. If beauty and truth in Nietzsche's view enter into discordance, they must previously belong together in one. That one can only be Being and the relation to Being.

Nietzsche defines the basic character of beings, hence Being, as will to power. Accordingly, an original conjunction of beauty and truth must result from the essence of will to power, a conjunction which simultaneously must become a discordance. When we try to discern and grasp the discordance we cast a glance toward the unified essence of will to power. Nietzsche's philosophy, according to his own testimony, is inverted Platonism. We ask: in what sense does the relation of beauty and truth which is peculiar to Platonism become a different sort of relation through the overturning?

The question can easily be answered by a simple recalculation, if "overturning" Platonism may be equated with the procedure of standing all of Plato's statements on their heads, as it were. To be sure, Nietzsche himself often expresses the state of affairs in that way, not only in order to make clear what he means in a rough and ready fashion, but also because he himself often thinks that way, although he is aiming at something else.

Only late in his life, shortly before the cessation of his labors in thinking, does the full scope required by such an inversion of Platonism become clear to him. That clarity waxes as Nietzsche grasps the necessity of the overturning, which is demanded by the task of overcoming nihilism. For that reason, when we elucidate the overturning of Platonism we must take the structure of Platonism as our point of departure. For Plato the supersensuous is the true world. It stands over all, as what sets the standard. The sensuous lies below, as the world of appearances. What stands over all is alone and from the start what sets the standard; it is therefore what is desired. After the inversion—that is easy to calculate in a formal way—the sensuous, the world of appearances, stands above; the supersensuous, the true world, lies below. With a glance back to what we have already presented, however, we must keep a firm hold on the realization that the very talk of a "true world" and "world of appearances" no longer speaks the language of Plato.

But what does that mean—the sensuous stands above all? It means that it is the true, it is genuine being. If we take the inversion strictly in this sense, then the vacant niches of the "above and below" are preserved, suffering only a change in occupancy, as it were. But as long as the "above and below" define the formal structure of Platonism, Platonism in its essence perdures. The inversion does not achieve what it must, as an overcoming of nihilism, namely, an overcoming of Platonism in its very foundations. Such overcoming succeeds only when the "above" in general is set aside as such, when the former positing of something true and desirable no longer arises, when the true world—in the sense of the ideal—is expunged. What happens when the true world is expunged? Does the apparent world still remain? No. For the apparent world can be what it is only as a counterpart of the true. If the true world collapses, so must the world of appearances. Only then is Platonism overcome, which is to say, inverted in such a way that philosophical thinking twists free of it. But then where does such thinking wind up?

During the time the overturning of Platonism became for Nietzsche a twisting free of it, madness befell him. Heretofore no one at all has recognized this reversal as Nietzsche's final step; neither has anyone perceived that the step is clearly taken only in his final creative year (1888). Insight into these important connections is quite difficult on the basis of the book *The Will to Power* as it lies before us in its present form, since the textual fragments assembled here have been removed from a great number of manuscripts written during the years 1882 to 1888. An altogether different picture results from the examination of Nietzsche's original manuscripts. But even without reference to these, there is a section of the treatise *Twilight of the Idols,* composed in just a few days during that final year of creative work (in September of 1888, although the book did not appear until 1889), a section which is very striking, because its basic position differs from the one we are already familiar with. The section is entitled "How the 'True World' Finally Became a Fable: the History of an Error" (VIII, 82–83; cf. WM, 567 and 568, from the year 1888.*)

The section encompasses a little more than one page. (Nietzsche's handwritten manuscript, the one sent to the printer, is extant.) It belongs to those pieces the style and structure of which betray the fact that here, in a magnificent moment of vision, the entire realm of Nietzsche's thought is permeated by a new and singular brilliance. The title, "How the 'True World' Finally Became a Fable," says that here a history is to be recounted in the course of which the supersensuous, posited by Plato as true being, not only is reduced from the higher to the lower rank but also collapses into the unreal and nugatory. Nietzsche divides the history into six parts, which can be readily recognized as the most important epochs of Western thought, and which lead directly to the doorstep of Nietzsche's philosophy proper.

---

*In these two complex notes Nietzsche defines the "perspectival relation" of will to power. Whereas in an earlier note (WM, 566) he spoke of the "true world" as "always the apparent world *once again,*" he now (WM, 567) refrains from the opposition of true and apparent worlds as such: "Here there remains not a shadow of a *right* to speak of *Schein* . . .," which is to say, of a world of mere appearances.

For the sake of our own inquiry we want to trace that history in all brevity, so that we can see how Nietzsche, in spite of his will to subvert, preserved a luminous knowledge concerning what had occurred prior to him.

The more clearly and simply a decisive inquiry traces the history of Western thought back to its few essential stages, the more that history's power to reach forward, seize, and commit grows. This is especially the case where it is a matter of overcoming such history. Whoever believes that philosophical thought can dispense with its history by means of a simple proclamation will, without his knowing it, be dispensed with by history; he will be struck a blow from which he can never recover, one that will blind him utterly. He will think he is being original when he is merely rehashing what has been transmitted and mixing together traditional interpretations into something ostensibly new. The greater a revolution is to be, the more profoundly must it plunge into its history.

We must measure Nietzsche's brief portrayal of the history of Platonism and its overcoming by this standard. Why do we emphasize here things that are evident? Because the form in which Nietzsche relates the history might easily tempt us to take it all as a mere joke, whereas something very different is at stake here (cf. *Beyond Good and Evil,* no. 213, "What a philosopher is," VII, 164 ff.).

The six divisions of the history of Platonism, culminating in emergence from Platonism, are as follows.

"1. The true world, attainable for the wise, the pious, the virtuous man—he lives in it, *he is it.*"

Here the founding of the doctrine by Plato is established. To all appearances, the true world itself is not handled at all, but only how man adopts a stance toward it and to what extent it is attainable. And the essential definition of the true world consists in the fact that it is attainable here and now for man, although not for any and every man, and not without further ado. It is attainable for the virtuous; it is the supersensuous. The implication is that virtue consists in repudiation of the sensuous, since denial of the world that is closest to us, the sensuous world, is proper to the Being of beings. Here the "true world" is not yet anything "Platonic," that is, not something unattainable, merely desirable, merely "ideal." Plato himself is who he is by virtue of the fact that he unquestioningly and straightforwardly functions on the basis of the world of Ideas as the essence of Being. The supersensuous is the *idea*. What is here envisioned in the eyes of Greek thought and existence is truly seen, and experienced in such simple vision, as what makes possible every being, as that which becomes present to itself (see *Vom Wesen des Grundes,* 1929, part two). Therefore, Nietzsche adds the following commentary in parentheses: "(Oldest form of the idea, relatively sensible, simple, convincing. Circumlocution for the sentence 'I, Plato, *am* the truth.')" The thought of the Ideas and the interpretation of Being posited here are creative in and of themselves. Plato's work is not yet Platonism. The "true world" is not yet the object of a doctrine; it is the power of Dasein; it is what lights up in becoming present; it is pure radiance without cover.

"2. The true world, unattainable for now, but promised for the wise, the pious, the virtuous man ('for the sinner who repents')."

With the positing of the supersensuous as true being, the break with the sensuous is now expressly ordained, although here again not straightaway: the true world is unattainable only in this life, for the duration of earthly existence. In that way earthly existence is denigrated and yet receives its proper tension, since the supersensuous is promised as the "beyond." Earth becomes the "earthly." The essence and existence of man are now fractured, but that makes a certain ambiguity possible. The possibility of "yes and no," of "this world as well as that one," begins; the apparent affirmation of this world, but with a reservation; the ability to go along with what goes on in this world, but keeping that remote back door ajar. In place of the unbroken essence of the Greek, which while unbroken was not without hazard but was passionate, which grounded itself in what was attainable, which drew its definitive boundaries here, which not only bore the intractability of fate but in its affirmation struggled for victory—in place of that essence begins something insidious. In Plato's stead, Platonism now rules. Thus:

"(Progress of the idea: it becomes more subtle, insidious, ungraspable —*it becomes woman*, it becomes Christian. . . .)" The supersensuous is no longer present within the scope of human existence, present for it and for its sensuous nature. Rather, the whole of human existence becomes this-worldly to the extent that the supersensuous is interpreted as the "beyond." In that way the true world now becomes even truer, by being displaced ever farther beyond and away from this world; it grows ever stronger in being, the more it becomes what is promised and the more zealously it is embraced, i.e., believed in, as what is promised. If we compare the second part of the history with the first, we see how Nietzsche in his description of the first part consciously sets Plato apart from all Platonism, protecting him from it.

"3. The true world, unattainable, indemonstrable, unpromisable, but even as thought, a consolation, an obligation, an imperative."

This division designates the form of Platonism that is achieved by the Kantian philosophy. The supersensuous is now a postulate of practical reason; even outside the scope of all experience and demonstration it is demanded as what is necessarily existent, in order to salvage adequate grounds for the lawfulness of reason. To be sure, the accessibility of the supersensuous by way of cognition is subjected to critical doubt, but only in order to make room for belief in the requisition of reason. Nothing of the substance and structure of the Christian view of the world changes by virtue of Kant; it is only that all the light of knowledge is cast on experience, that is, on the mathematical-scientific interpretation of the "world." Whatever lies outside of the knowledge possessed by the sciences of nature is not denied as to its existence but is relegated to the indeterminateness of the unknowable. Therefore: "(The old sun, basically, but seen through haze and skepticism; the idea rarified, grown pallid, Nordic, Königsbergian.)" A transformed world —in contrast to the simple clarity by which Plato dwelled in direct contact with the supersensuous, as discernible Being. Because he sees through the unmistakable Platonism of Kant, Nietzsche at the same time perceives the essential difference between Plato and Kant. In that way he distinguishes himself fundamentally from his contemporaries, who, not accidentally, equate Kant and Plato—if they don't interpret Plato as a Kantian who didn't quite make it.

"4. The true world—unattainable? In any case, unattained. And as unattained also *unknown*. Consequently, also, not consolatory, redemptive, obligating: to what could something unknown obligate us? . . ."

With the fourth division, the form to which Platonism commits itself as a consequence of the bygone Kantian philosophy is historically attained, although without an originally creative overcoming. It is the age following the dominance of German Idealism, at about the middle of the last century. With the help of its own chief principle, the theoretical unknowability of the supersensuous, the Kantian system is unmasked and exploded. If the supersensuous world is altogether unattainable for cognition, then nothing can be known about it, nothing can be decided for or against it. It becomes manifest that the supersensuous does not come on the scene as a part of the Kantian philosophy on the grounds of basic philosophical principles of knowledge but as a consequence of uneradicated Christian-theological presuppositions.* In that regard Nietzsche on one occasion observes of Leibniz, Kant, Fichte, Schelling, Hegel, and Schopenhauer, "They are all mere Schleiermachers" (XV, 112). The observation has two edges: it means not only that these men are at bottom camouflaged theologians but also that they are what that name suggests—*Schleier-macher,* makers of veils, men who veil things. In opposition to them stands the somewhat halfhearted rejection of the supersensuous as something unknown, to which, after Kant, no cognition can in principle attain. Such rejection is a kind of first glimmer of "probity" of meditation amid the

---

***Unerschütterter theologisch-christlicher Voraussetzungen.* The formulation is reminiscent of Heidegger's words in *Being and Time,* section 44 C: "The assertion of 'eternal truths' and the confusion of the phenomenally grounded 'ideality' of Dasein with an idealized absolute subject belong to those residues of Christian theology in philosophical problems which have not yet been radically extruded [*zu den längst noch nicht radikal ausgetriebenen Resten von christlicher Theologie innerhalb der philosophischen Problematik.*]"

captiousness and "counterfeiting" that came to prevail with Platonism. Therefore: "(Gray morning. First yawnings of reason. Cockcrow of positivism.)" Nietzsche descries the rise of a new day. Reason, which here means man's knowing and inquiring, awakens and comes to its senses.

"5. The 'true world'—an idea which is of use for nothing, which is no longer even obligating—an idea become useless, superfluous, *consequently,* a refuted idea: let us abolish it!"

With this division Nietzsche designates the first segment of his own way in philosophy. The "true world" he now sets in quotation marks. It is no longer his own word, the content of which he himself could still affirm. The "true world" is abolished. But notice the reason: because it has become useless, superfluous. In the shimmering twilight a new standard of measure comes to light: whatever does not in any way at any time involve man's Dasein can make no claim to be affirmed. Therefore: "(Bright day; breakfast; return of *bon sens* and of cheerfulness; Plato's embarrassed blush; pandemonium of all free spirits.)" Here Nietzsche thinks back on the years of his own metamorphosis, which is intimated clearly enough in the very titles of the books he wrote during that time: *Human, All Too Human* (1878), *The Wanderer and His Shadow* (1880), *The Dawn* (1881), and *The Gay Science* (1882). Platonism is overcome inasmuch as the supersensuous world, as the true world, is abolished; but by way of compensation the sensuous world remains, and positivism occupies it. What is now required is a confrontation with the latter. For Nietzsche does not wish to tarry in the dawn of morning; neither will he rest content with mere forenoon. In spite of the fact that the supersensuous world as the true world has been cast aside, the vacant niche of the higher world remains, and so does the blueprint of an "above and below," which is to say, so does Platonism. The inquiry must go one step farther.

"6. The true world we abolished: which world was left? the apparent one perhaps? ... But no! *along with the true world we have also abolished the apparent one!*"

That Nietzsche appends a sixth division here shows that, and how, he must advance beyond himself and beyond sheer abolition of the supersensuous. We sense it directly from the animation of the style and manner of composition—how the clarity of this step conducts him for the first time into the brilliance of full daylight, where all shadows dwindle. Therefore: "(Midday; moment of the shortest shadow; end of the longest error; highpoint of humanity; INCIPIT ZARATHUSTRA.)" Thus the onset of the final stage of his own philosophy.

The portrayal of all six divisions of the history of Platonism is so arranged that the "true world," the existence and legitimacy of which is under consideration, is in each division brought into connection with the type of man who comports himself to that world. Consequently, the overturning of Platonism and the ultimate twist out of it imply a metamorphosis of man. At the end of Platonism stands a decision concerning the transformation of man. That is how the phrase "highpoint of humanity" is to be understood, as the peak of decision, namely, decision as to whether with the end of Platonism man as he has been hitherto is to come to an end, whether he is to become that kind of man Nietzsche characterized as the "last man," or whether that type of man can be overcome and the "overman" can begin: "Incipit Zarathustra." By the word "overman" Nietzsche does not mean some miraculous, fabulous being, but the man who surpasses former man. But man as he has been hitherto is the one whose Dasein and relation to Being have been determined by Platonism in one of its forms or by a mixture of several of these. The last man is the necessary consequence of unsubdued nihilism. The great danger Nietzsche sees is that it will all culminate in the last man, that it will peter out in the spread of the increasingly insipid last man. "The opposite of the overman is the *last man:* I created him at the same time I created the former" (XIV, 262).

That suggests that the end first becomes visible as an end on the basis of the new beginning. To put it the other way round, overman's identity first becomes clear when the last man is perceived as such.

Now all we must do is bring into view the extreme counterposition to Plato and Platonism and then ascertain how Nietzsche successfully adopts a stance within it. What results when, along with the true world, the apparent world too is abolished?

The "true world," the supersensuous, and the apparent world, the sensuous, together make out what stands opposed to pure nothingness; they constitute beings as a whole. When both are abolished everything collapses into the vacuous nothing. That cannot be what Nietzsche means. For he desires to overcome nihilism in all its forms. When we recall that, and how, Nietzsche wishes to ground art upon embodying life by means of his physiological aesthetics, we note that this implies an affirmation of the sensuous world, not its abolition. However, according to the express wording of the final division of the history of Platonism, "the apparent world is abolished." Certainly. But the sensuous world is the "apparent world" only according to the interpretation of Platonism. With the abolition of Platonism the way first opens for the affirmation of the sensuous, and along with it, the nonsensuous world of the spirit as well. It suffices to recall the following statement from *The Will to Power,* no. 820:

> For myself and for all those who live—are *permitted* to live—without the anxieties of a puritanical conscience, I wish an ever greater spiritualization and augmentation of the senses. Yes, we ought to be grateful to our senses for their subtlety, fullness, and force; and we ought to offer them in return the very best of spirit we possess.

What is needed is neither abolition of the sensuous nor abolition of the nonsensuous. On the contrary, what must be cast aside is the misinterpretation, the deprecation, of the sensuous, as well as the extravagant elevation of the supersensuous. A path must be cleared for a new interpretation of the sensuous on the basis of a new hierarchy of the sensuous and nonsensuous. The new hierarchy does not simply wish to reverse matters within the old structural order, now reverencing the sensuous and scorning the nonsensuous. It does not wish to put what was at the very bottom on the very top. A new hierarchy and new valuation mean that the ordering *structure* must be changed. To that extent, overturning Platonism must become a twisting free of it. How far the latter extends with Nietzsche, how far it can go, to what extent it comes to an overcoming of Platonism and to what extent not—those are necessary critical questions. But they should be posed only when we have reflected in accordance with the thought that Nietzsche most intrinsically willed—beyond everything captious, ambiguous, and deficient which we might very easily ascribe to him here.

25. The New Interpretation of Sensuousness and the Raging Discordance between Art and Truth

We are now asking what new interpretation and ordering of the sensuous and nonsensuous results from the overturning of Platonism. To what extent is "the sensuous" the genuine "reality"? What transformation accompanies the inversion? What metamorphosis underlies it? We must ask the question in this last form, because it is not the case that things are inverted first, and then on the basis of the new position gained by the inversion the question is posed, "What is the result?" Rather, the overturning derives the force and direction of its motion from the new inquiry and its fundamental experience, in which true being, what is real, "reality," is to be defined afresh.

We are not unprepared for these questions, provided we have traversed the path of the entire lecture course, which from the outset has aimed in their direction.

We unfolded all our questions concerning art for the explicit and exclusive purpose of bringing the new reality, above all else, into sharp focus. In particular, the presentation of Nietzsche's "physiological aesthetics" was elaborated in such a way that we now only need to grasp in a more fundamental manner what was said there. We do that in order to pursue his interpretation of the sensuous in its principal direction, which means, to see how he achieves a stand for his thought after both the true and the apparent worlds of Platonism have been abolished.

Nietzsche recognizes rapture to be the basic actuality of art. In contrast to Wagner, he understands the feeling of increment of force, plenitude, and the reciprocal enhancement of all capacities, as a being beyond oneself, hence a coming to oneself in the supreme lucidity of Being—not a visionless tumult. But in Nietzsche's view that implies at the same time the emergence of the abyss of "life," of life's essential contradictions, not as moral evil or as something to be negated, but as what is to be affirmed. The "physiological," the sensuous-corporeal, in itself possesses this beyond-itself. The inner constitution of the sensuous was clarified by emphasis on the relation of rapture to beauty, and of creation and enjoyment to form. What is proper to form is the constant, order, overview, boundary, and law. The sensuous in itself is directed toward overview and order, toward what can be mastered and firmly fixed. What makes itself known here with regard to the essence of the "sensuous" we now need grasp only in its principal relations, in order to see how for Nietzsche the sensuous constitutes reality proper.

What lives is exposed to other forces, but in such a way that, striving against them, it deals with them according to their form and rhythm, in order to estimate them in relation to possible incorporation or elimination. According to this angle of vision, everything that is encountered is interpreted in terms of the living creature's capacity for life. The angle of vision, and the realm it opens to view, themselves draw the borderlines around what it is that creatures can or cannot encounter. For example, a lizard hears the slightest rustling in the grass but it does not hear a pistol shot fired quite close by. Accordingly, the creature develops a kind of interpretation of its surroundings and thereby of all occurrence, not incidentally, but as the fundamental process of life itself: "The *perspectival* [is] the basic condition of all life" (VII, 4).

With a view to the basic constitution of living things Nietzsche says (XIII, 63), "The essential aspect of organic beings is a *new* manifold, which is itself an occurrence." The living creature possesses the character of a perspectival preview which circumscribes a "line of horizon" about him, within whose scope something can come forward into appearance for him at all. Now, in the "organic" there is a multiplicity of drives and forces, each of which has its perspective. The manifold of perspectives distinguishes the organic from the inorganic. Yet even the latter has its perspective; it is just that in the inorganic, in attraction and repulsion, the "power relations" are clearly fixed (XIII, 62). The mechanistic representation of "inanimate" nature is only a hypothesis for purposes of calculation; it overlooks the fact that here too relations of forces and concatenations of perspectives hold sway. Every point of force per se is perspectival. As a result it becomes manifest "that there is no inorganic world" (XIII, 81). Everything "real" is alive, is "perspectival" in itself, and asserts itself in its perspective against others. On that basis we can understand Nietzsche's note from the years 1886–87 (XIII, 227–28):

> Fundamental question: whether the *perspectival* is proper to the *being,* and is not only a form of observation, a relation between different beings? Do the various forces stand in relation, so that the relation is tied to a perceptual optics? That would be possible if *all Being were essentially something which perceives.*

We would not have to go far to find proof to show that this conception of beings is precisely that of Leibniz, except that Nietzsche eliminates the latter's theological metaphysics, i.e., his Platonism. All being is in itself perspectival-perceptual, and that means, in the sense now delineated, "sensuous."

The sensuous is no longer the "apparent," no longer the penumbra; it alone is what is real, hence "true." And what becomes of semblance? Semblance itself is proper to the essence of the real. We can readily see that in the perspectival character of the actual. The following statement provides an opening onto the matter of semblance within the perspectivally constructed actual: "With the organic world begin *indeterminateness* and *semblance*" (XIII, 288; cf. also 229). In the unity of an organic being there is a multiplicity of drives and capacities (each of which possesses its perspective) which struggle against one another. In such a multiplicity the univocity of the particular perspective in which the actual in any given case stands is lost. The equivocal character of what shows itself in several perspectives is granted, along with the indeterminate, which now appears one way, then another, which first proffers this appearance, then that one. But such appearance becomes semblance in the sense of mere appearance only when what becomes manifest in one perspective petrifies and is taken to be the sole definitive appearance, to the disregard of the other perspectives that crowd round in turn.

In that way, palpable things, "objects," emerge for creatures in what they encounter; things that are constant, with enduring qualities, by which the creature can get its bearings. The entire range of what is fixed and constant is, according to the ancient Platonic conception, the region of "Being," the "true." Such Being, viewed perspectivally, is but the one-sided, entrenched appearance, which is taken to be solely definitive. It thus becomes mere appearance; Being, the true, is mere appearance, error.

> *Error* begins in the organic world. "Things," "substances," properties, act-"ivities" [*Tätig"keiten"*]—one should not read all that into the inorganic world! They are the specific errors by virtue of which organisms live (XIII, 69).

In the organic world, the world of embodying life, where man too resides, "error" begins. That should not be taken as meaning that creatures, in distinction to members of the inorganic realm, can go astray. It means that those beings which in the definitive perspectival horizon of a creature appear to constitute its firmly established, existent world, in their Being are but appearance, mere appearance. Man's logic serves to make what he encounters identical, constant, ascertainable. Being, the true, which logic "firmly locates" (petrifies), is but semblance; a semblance, an apparentness, that is essentially necessary to the creature as such, which is to say, a semblance that pertains to his survival, his establishment of self amidst ceaseless change. Because the real is perspectival in itself, apparentness as such is proper to reality. Truth, i.e., true being, i.e., what is constant and fixed, because it is the petrifying of any single given perspective, is always only an apparentness that has come to prevail, which is to say, it is always error. For that reason Nietzsche says (WM, 493), "*Truth is the kind of error* without which a certain kind of living being could not live. The value for *life* ultimately decides."

Truth, that is, the true as the constant, is a kind of semblance that is justified as a necessary condition of the assertion of life. But upon deeper meditation it becomes clear that all appearance and all apparentness are possible only if something comes to the fore and shows itself at all. What in advance enables such appearing is the perspectival itself. That is what genuinely radiates, bringing something to show itself. When Nietzsche uses the word semblance [*Schein*] it is usually ambiguous. He knows it, too. "There are fateful words which appear to express an insight but which in truth *hinder* it; among them belongs the word 'semblance,' 'appearance' " (XIII, 50). Nietzsche does not become master of the fate entrenched in that word, which is to say, in the matter. He says (*ibid.*), " 'Semblance' as I understand it is the actual and sole reality of things." That should be understood to mean not that reality is something apparent, but that being-real is in itself perspectival, a bringing forward into appearance, a letting radiate; that it is in itself a shining. Reality is radiance.

> Hence I do not posit "semblance" in opposition to "reality," but on the contrary take semblance to be the reality which resists transformation into an imaginative "world of truth." A particular name for that reality would be "will to power," designated of course intrinsically and not on the basis of its ungraspable, fluid, Protean nature (XIII, 50; from the year 1886, at the latest).

Reality, Being, is *Schein* in the sense of perspectival letting-shine. But proper to that reality at the same time is the multiplicity of perspectives, and thus the possibility of illusion and of its being made fast, which means the possibility of truth as a kind of *Schein* in the sense of "mere" appearance. If truth is taken to be semblance, that is, as mere appearance and error, the implication is that truth is the fixed semblance which is necessarily inherent in perspectival shining—it is illusion. Nietzsche often identifies such illusion with "the lie": "One who tells the truth ends by realizing that he always lies" (XII, 293).

Indeed Nietzsche at times defines perspectival shining as *Schein* in the sense of illusion and deception, contrasting illusion and deception to truth, which, as "Being," is also at bottom error.

We have already seen that creation, as forming and shaping, as well as the aesthetic pleasures related to such shaping, are grounded in the essence of life. Hence art too, and precisely it, must cohere most intimately with perspectival shining and letting shine. Art in the proper sense is art in the grand style, desirous of bringing waxing life itself to power. It is not an immobilizing but a liberating for expansion, a clarifying to the point of transfiguration, and this in two senses: first, stationing a thing in the clarity of Being; second, establishing such clarity as the heightening of life itself.

Life is in itself perspectival. It waxes and flourishes with the height and heightening of the world which is brought forward perspectivally to appearance, with the enhancement of the shining, that is, of what brings a thing to scintillate in such a way that life is transfigured. "Art and nothing but art!" (WM, 853, section II). Art induces reality, which is in itself a shining, to shine most profoundly and supremely in scintillating transfiguration. If "metaphysical" means nothing else than the essence of reality, and if reality consists in shining, we then understand the statement with which the section on art in *The Will to Power* closes (WM, 853): " ... 'art as the proper task of life, art as its *metaphysical* activity . . . .' " Art is the most genuine and profound will to semblance, namely, the scintillation of what transfigures, in which the supreme lawfulness of Dasein becomes visible. In contrast, truth is any given fixed apparition that allows life to rest firmly on a particular perspective and to preserve itself. As such fixation, "truth" is an immobilizing of life, and hence its inhibition and dissolution. "We have art so that we *do not perish from the truth*" (WM, 822). It is *"not possible . . . to live with the truth,"* if life is always enhancement of life; the "will to truth," i.e., to fixed apparition, is "already a symptom of degeneration" (XIV, 368). Now it becomes clear what the fifth and concluding proposition concerning art avers: *art is worth more than truth.*

Both art and truth are modes of perspectival shining. But the value of the real is measured according to how it satisfies the essence of reality, how it accomplishes the shining and enhances reality. *Art, as transfiguration, is more enhancing to life than truth, as fixation of an apparition.*

Now too we perceive to what extent the relation of art and truth must be a discordance for Nietzsche and for his philosophy, as inverted Platonism. Discordance is present only where the elements which sever the unity of their belonging-together diverge from one another by virtue of that very unity. The unity of their belonging-together is granted by the *one* reality, perspectival shining. To it belong both apparition and scintillating appearance as transfiguration. In order for the real (the living creature) to *be* real, it must on the one hand ensconce itself within a particular horizon, thus perduring in the illusion of truth. But in order for the real to *remain* real, it must on the other hand simultaneously transfigure itself by going beyond itself, surpassing itself in the scintillation of what is created in art—and that means it has to advance against the truth. While truth and art are proper to the essence of reality with equal originality, they must diverge from one another and go counter to one another.

But because in Nietzsche's view semblance, as perspectival, also possesses the character of the nonactual, of illusion and deception, he must say, "The will to *semblance,* to illusion, to deception, to Becoming and change is deeper, more 'metaphysical' [that is to say, corresponding more to the essence of Being] than the will to *truth,* to actuality, to Being" (XIV, 369). This is expressed even more decisively in *The Will to Power,* no. 853, section I, where semblance is equated with "lie": "*We need the lie* in order to achieve victory over this reality, this 'truth,' which is to say, in order to *live* . . . . That the lie is necessary for life is itself part and parcel of the frightful and questionable character of existence."

Art and truth are equally necessary for reality. As equally necessary they stand in severance. But their relationship first arouses dread when we consider that creation, i.e., the metaphysical activity of art, receives yet another essential impulse the moment we descry the most tremendous event—the death of the God of morality. In Nietzsche's view, existence can now be endured only in creation. Conducting reality to the power of its rule and of its supreme possibilities alone guarantees Being. But creation, as art, is will to semblance; it stands in severance from truth.

Art as will to semblance is the supreme configuration of will to power. But the latter, as the basic character of beings, as the essence of reality, is in itself that Being which wills itself by willing to be Becoming. In that way Nietzsche in will to power attempts to think the original unity of the ancient opposition of Being and Becoming. Being, as permanence, is to let Becoming *be* a Becoming. The origin of the thought of "eternal recurrence" is thereby indicated.

In the year 1886, in the middle of the period when he labored on the planned major work, Nietzsche's first treatise, *The Birth of Trage-dy from the Spirit of Music* (1872), appeared in a new edition. It bore the altered title *The Birth of Tragedy, or Greek Civilization and Pessi-mism; New Edition, with an Attempt at Self-criticism* (see I, 1–14). The task which that book had first ventured to undertake remained the same for Nietzsche.

He pinpoints the task in a passage that is often quoted but just as often misinterpreted. The correct interpretation devolves from the entirety of this lecture course. Rightly grasped, the passage can serve as a rubric that characterizes the course's starting point and the direc-tion of its inquiry. Nietzsche writes (I, 4):

> ... Nevertheless, I do not wish to suppress entirely how unpleasant it now seems to me, how alien it stands before me now, after sixteen years—before an eye which has grown older, a hundred times more fastidious, but by no means colder, an eye which would not be any the less prepared to undertake the very task that audacious book ventured for the first time: *to see science under the optics of the artist, but art under the optics of life*. ...

Half a century has elapsed for Europe since these words were penned. During the decades in question the passage has been misread again and again, precisely by those people who exerted themselves to resist the increasing uprooting and devastation of science. From Nietzsche's words they gathered the following: the sciences may no longer be conducted in an arid, humdrum manner, they may no longer "gather dust," far removed from "life"; they have to be shaped "artistically," so that they are attractive, pleasing, and in good taste—all that, because the artistically shaped sciences must be related to "life," remain in proximity to "life," and be readily useful for "life."

Above all, the generation that studied at the German universities between 1909 and 1914 heard the passage interpreted in this way. Even in the form of the misinterpretation it was a help to us. But there was no one about who could have provided the correct reading of it. That would have required re-asking the grounding question of Occidental philosophy, questioning in the direction of Being by way of actual inquiry.

To explain our understanding of the phrase cited, *"to see science under the optics of the artist, but art under the optics of life,"* we must refer to four points, all of which, after what we have discussed, will by now be familiar to us.

First, "science" here means knowing as such, the relation to truth.

Second, the twofold reference to the "optics" of the artist and of life indicates that the "perspectival character" of Being becomes essential.

Third, the equation of art and the artist directly expresses the fact that art is to be conceived in terms of the artist, creation, and the grand style.

Fourth, "life" here means neither mere animal and vegetable Being nor that readily comprehensible and compulsive busyness of everyday existence; rather, "life" is the term for Being in its new interpretation, according to which it is a Becoming. "Life" is neither "biologically" nor "practically" intended; it is meant metaphysically. The equation of Being and life is not some sort of unjustified expansion of the biological, although it often seems that way, but a transformed interpretation of the biological on the basis of Being, grasped in a superior way—this, of course, not fully mastered, in the timeworn schema of "Being and Becoming."

Nietzsche's phrase suggests that on the basis of the essence of Being art must be grasped as the fundamental occurrence of beings, as the properly creative. But art conceived in that way defines the arena in which we can estimate how it is with "truth," and in what relation art and truth stand. The phrase does not suggest that artistic matters be jumbled with the "conduct of science," much less that knowledge be subjected to aesthetic rehabilitation. Nor does it mean that art has to follow on the heels of life and be of service to it; for it is art, the grand style, which is to legislate the Being of beings in the first place.

The phrase demands knowledge of the event of nihilism. In Nietzsche's view such knowledge at the same time embraces the will to overcome nihilism, indeed by means of original grounding and questioning.

To see science "under the optics of the artist" means to estimate it according to its creative force, neither according to its immediate utility nor in terms of some vacuous "eternal significance."

But creation itself is to be estimated according to the originality with which it penetrates to Being, neither as the mere achievement of an individual nor for the entertainment of the many. Being able to estimate, to esteem, that is, to act in accordance with the standard of Being, is itself creation of the highest order. For it is preparation of readiness for the gods; it is the Yes to Being. "Overman" is the man who grounds Being anew—in the rigor of knowledge and in the grand style of creation.

APPENDIX, ANALYSIS, AND GLOSSARY

Appendix

A manuscript page from the lecture course *Nietzsche: Der Wille zur Macht als Kunst,* Winter Semester 1936–37

It was Heidegger's practice to write out his lectures on unlined sheets measuring approximately 21 by 34 centimeters, the width of the page exceeding the length. (These dimensions would be somewhat larger than those of a "legal pad" turned on its side.) The left half of each manuscript sheet is covered recto with a dense, minuscule script, constituting the main body of the lecture. The right half is reserved for major emendations. It is characteristic of Heidegger's manner of composition that this half is almost as densely covered as the first. Heidegger's script is the so-called *Sütterlinschrift,* devised by Ludwig Sütterlin (1865–1917), quite common in the southern German states. It is said to be a "strongly rounded" script but to the English and American penman it still seems preeminently Gothic, vertical and angular. To the exasperated Innocent Abroad it seems a partner in that general conspiracy of Continental scripts other than the "Latin" to make each letter look like every other letter.

The manuscript page reproduced following p. 223 is the one mentioned in the Editor's Preface, Archive number A 33/14. It begins with the words *der Grundirrtum Schopenhauers,* found in the Neske edition at NI, 50, line 25, and ends with the words *nichts zu tun,* found at the close of section 7, NI, 53, line 24. Hence this single page of holograph constitutes three entire pages of the printed German text. (Of course I should note that Neske's page is rather generously spaced.) The

English translation of the German text taken from this manuscript page is found on pp. 40–43 above.

The right half of the manuscript page contains five major emendations to the text and one addition to an emendation. These changes are not substitutions for something in the body of the lecture; they are expansions and elaborations of what is found there. (The addition to the emendation is a text from Nietzsche's *The Gay Science* in support of Heidegger's argument.) Precisely when these emendations were made is impossible to tell, but the handwriting suggests that they are roughly contemporaneous with the main body of the text, added in all probability before the lecture was delivered. Only in rare cases (the revised clause and the bracketed phrase discussed below) is there any evidence that changes on the holograph page may have been made substantially later—for example at the time of the publication of *Nietzsche* in 1961.

The Neske edition reproduces the lecture notes of A 33/14 word for word up to the phrase *gesetzte will* at NI, 51, line 7. At that point, the insertion of the first emendation is indicated. It is a lengthy addition, amounting to fifteen printed lines. Here the Neske edition varies in some respects from the holograph. A comparison of the two passages may be instructive:

Neske edition	*Holograph*
Der Wille bringt jeweils von sich her eine durchgängige Bestimmtheit in sein Wollen. Jemand, der nicht weiß, was er will, will gar nicht und kann überhaupt nicht wollen; ein Wollen im allgemeinen gibt es nicht; "denn der Wille ist, als Affekt des Befehls, das entscheidende Abzeichen der Selbstherrlichkeit und Kraft" ("Die fröhliche Wissenschaft," 5. Buch, 1886; V, 282). Dagegen kann das Streben unbestimmt sein, sowohl hinsichtlich dessen, was eigentlich angestrebt ist, als auch mit Bezug auf das	⁀ Der Wille bringt so seinem Wesen nach in sich selbst heraus immer eine Bestimmtheit im Ganzen; jemand der nicht weiß, was er will, will gar nicht u. <u>kann</u> übhpt. nicht wollen; ein Wollen im Allgemeinen gibt es; wohl dagegen kann das Streben [*word crossed out*] unbedingt sein—sowohl hinsichtlich dessen, <u>was</u> eigentlich angestrebt ist—als auch mit Bezug auf das <u>Strebende</u> selbst. [*At this point a mark to the left of the emendation indicates that the passage from* The Gay Science *is to be inserted—but its*

Strebende selbst. Im Streben und Drängen sind wir in ein Hinzu . . . mit hineingenommen und wissen selbst nicht, was im Spiel ist. Im bloßen Streben nach etwas sind wir nicht eigentlich vor uns selbst gebracht, und deshalb ist hier auch keine Möglichkeit, über uns hinaus zu streben, sondern wir streben bloß und gehen in solchem Streben mit Entschlossenheit zu sich—ist immer: über sich hinaus wollen.

precise location is not indicated.] Im Streben u. Drängen sind wir in ein Hin zu-etwas mit hineingenommen —u. wissen selbst nicht was [*word crossed out*] im Spiel ist. Im blossen Streben nach etwas—sind wir nicht eigentlich vor uns selbst gebracht u. deshalb ist hier auch keine Möglichkeit—über uns hinaus zu [*word crossed out*] streben—sondern wir streben bloß [-en *crossed out*] u. gehen in solchem Streben auf [?]. Entschlossenheit zu sich ist immer über sich hinaus wollen.

The changes introduced in the Neske edition are of five sorts. First, a more variegated punctuation replaces the series of semicolons and dashes. Second, the number of stressed words (italics, reproducing underlinings) is greatly reduced. Third, obvious oversights (such as the omission of the word *nicht* after the phrase *ein Wollen im allgemeinen gibt es*) are corrected, abbreviated words written out, and crossed-out words and letters deleted. Fourth, a precise location for the quotation from *The Gay Science* is found. Fifth, and most important, several phrases are entirely recast. Thus *Hin zu-etwas* (underlined) becomes Hinzu . . . (not italicized), and the entire opening clause is revised. The holograph version of the latter would read, in translation, "Thus will, according to its essence, in itself always brings out a determinateness in the totality." The Neske lines say, "In each case will itself furnishes a thoroughgoing determinateness to its willing." When this change occurred is impossible to determine; it may well have come at the time of publication. (The *Abschrift* or typewritten copy here follows the holograph.)

At the end of this long emendation the problem mentioned in the Preface arises. The last word runs up against the edge of the page and could as easily be *mit* as *auf*. (The practice of adding a diacritical mark over the non-umlauted *u*, which often makes it resemble a dotted *i*, complicates the situation here.) The meaning of the sentence depends to a great extent upon the separable prefix: it is according to the *sense* of the holograph page that I read it as *auf*. What is quite clear is that the main body of the text continues with a new sentence: *Entschlossenheit zu sich ist immer....* The words *Wille dagegen* are inserted in the *Abschrift* in order to emphasize the distinction between "will" and "striving." Although the origin, date, and status of the *Abschrift* are unknown, I have retained them in my own reading. Finally, I have added *als* in order to make the apposition of "will" and "resolute openness" clear.

The Neske edition prints the remainder of A 33/14 with only a few alterations, all but one of them minor ones. Two further major emendations from the right half of the page are incorporated into the main body of the text without any disturbing consequences (NI, 51, line 30 to NI, 52, line 2; and NI, 52, lines 22–29). The published text of NI, 52, lines 20–21 alters the holograph rendering only slightly. Then comes the second important change. Three lines in the holograph which are set off by brackets, lines which would have appeared at NI, 53, line 18, are omitted. When Heidegger added the brackets or "bracketed out" the passage is, again, not clear. The lines read:

> Man ist glücklich beim Irrationalismus—jenem Sumpf, in dem alle Denkfaulen und Denkmüden einträchtlich sich treffen, aber dabei meistens noch allzu "rational" reden und schreiben.

In translation:

> People are delighted with irrationalism—that swamp where all those who are too lazy or too weary to think convene harmoniously; but for the most part they still talk and write all too "rationally."

Heidegger often bracketed out such sardonic remarks when a lecture manuscript was on its way to becoming a book, apparently because he considered such off-the-cuff remarks more obtrusive in print than in speech. (Cf. for example the following remarks published in Walter Biemel's edition of the lecture course *Logik: Aristoteles,* volume 21 of the Heidegger *Gesamtausgabe,* Frankfurt/Main, 1976: on fraudulent logic courses, p. 12; on Heinrich Rickert's gigantomachia, p. 91; on two kinds of Hegelian confusion, pp. 260 and 267; and on the hocus-pocus of spiritualism and subjectivism, p. 292. These are remarks which we are delighted to read but which Heidegger himself, had he edited the text, might have deleted.)

Finally, on the right half of the holograph page a general reference to WM 84 and 95 appears. These two aphorisms in *The Will to Power* juxtapose the Nietzschean sense of will as mastery to the Schopenhauerian sense of will as desire. The reference's identifying mark does not appear anywhere in the text or in the other emendations, so that the reference has nowhere to go; in the Neske edition it is omitted.

By way of conclusion I may note that the Neske edition is generally closer to the holograph than is the sole extant *Abschrift*. The text we possess—notwithstanding the one major difficulty cited—seems remarkably faithful to Heidegger's handwritten lecture notes, assuming that the relation of A 33/14 to the relevant pages of the Neske edition is typical. Whether or not that is so the editor of volume 43 of the *Gesamtausgabe* will have to determine.*

---

*In the third edition of Heidegger's *Nietzsche* (without date, but available since the mid-1970s) the Neske Verlag altered the passage discussed above by adding a period to NI, 51, line 22, between the words *mit* and *Entschlossenheit*. (Cf. p. 227 of this volume, line 10 in the first column.) The passage would thus read: "For that reason it is not possible for us to strive beyond ourselves; rather, we merely strive, and go along with such striving. Resolute openness to oneself—is always: willing out beyond oneself." The addition of the period is a significant improvement in the text, but I still prefer the full reading suggested in this Appendix and employed on p. 41 of the translation.

The third edition does not correct the erroneous duplication of the word *nicht* at NI, 189, line 5 from the bottom.

I am grateful to Ursula Willaredt of Freiburg, whose painstaking checking of the page proofs uncovered this change in the third Neske edition of *Nietzsche*.

Analysis

By DAVID FARRELL KRELL

> No judgment renders an account of the world, but art can teach us to
> reiterate it, just as the world reiterates itself in the course of eternal
> returns.... To say "yes" to the world, to reiterate it, is at the same
> time to recreate the world and oneself; it is to become the great artist,
> the creator.
>
> A. CAMUS, *Man in Rebellion*, 1951

Early in 1961 Brigitte Neske designed a set of handsome book jackets
for one of the major events in her husband's publishing career. Along
the spine of the volumes two names appeared, black and white on a
salmon background, neither name capitalized: heidegger nietzsche.
Both were well known. The latter was famous for having been, as he
said, "born posthumously." And that apparently helped to give rise to
the confusion: when the volumes first appeared in Germany no one was
sure whether they were heidegger's books on nietzsche or nietzsche's
books on heidegger.

Readers of this and the other English volumes may find themselves
recalling this little joke more than once and for more than one reason.

Aus-einander-setzung, "a setting apart from one another," is the
word Heidegger chooses in his Foreword to these volumes to characterize his encounter with Nietzsche. That is also the word by which he
translates *polemos* in Heraclitus B53 and B80. Is Heidegger then at war
with Nietzsche? Are his lectures and essays on Nietzsche polemics? In
the first part of his lecture course "What Calls for Thinking?" Heidegger cautions his listeners that all polemic "fails from the outset to

assume the attitude of thinking."[1] In Heidegger's view *polemos* is a name for the lighting or clearing of Being in which beings become present to one another and so can be distinguished from one another. Heraclitus speaks of *ton polemon xynon*, a setting apart from one another that serves essentially to bring together, a contest that unites. In these volumes the English word "confrontation" tries to capture the paradoxical sense of Heidegger's *Aus-einander-setzung* with Nietzsche's philosophy. Before we say anything about Heidegger's "interpretation" of Nietzsche we should pause to consider the *koinōnia* or community of both thinkers. For at the time Heidegger planned a series of lectures on Nietzsche he identified the task of his own philosophy as the effort "to bring Nietzsche's accomplishment to a full unfolding."[2] The magnitude of that accomplishment, however, was not immediately discernible. Heidegger's first attempt to delineate Nietzsche's accomplishment and to circumscribe his confrontation with Nietzsche traces the profile of will to power as art.

I. THE STRUCTURE AND MOVEMENT OF THE LECTURE COURSE

The published text of Heidegger's 1936–37 lecture course, "Nietzsche: Will to Power as Art," consists of twenty-five unnumbered sections.[3] Although no more comprehensive parts or divisions appear, the course unfolds in three stages. Sections 1–10 introduce the theme of Nietzsche as metaphysician and examine the nature of "will," "power," and "will to power" in his thought. Sections 12–18 pursue the significance of art in Nietzsche's thinking. Sections 20–25 compare his conception of art to that in Platonism—the philosophy which Nietzsche sought to overturn—and in Plato's dialogues. But if the first

---

[1]Martin Heidegger, *Was heisst Denken?* (Tübingen: M. Niemeyer, 1954), p. 49. Cf. the English translation, *What Is Called Thinking?*, tr. Fred D. Wieck and J. Glenn Gray (New York: Harper & Row, 1968), p. 13; cf. also Martin Heidegger, *Basic Writings*, ed. D. F. Krell (New York: Harper & Row, 1977), p. 354.

[2]Martin Heidegger, *Einführung in die Metaphysik* (Tübingen: M. Niemeyer, 1953), p. 28. Cf. the English translation, *An Introduction to Metaphysics*, tr. Ralph Manheim (Garden City, N.Y.: Anchor-Doubleday, 1961), p. 30.

[3]The sections have been numbered in the present edition to facilitate reference.

two stages, "will to power" and "art," cover the ground staked out in the title *Wille zur Macht als Kunst,* why the third stage at all? Why especially the preoccupation with Plato's own texts? What is the significance of the fact that in the Foreword Heidegger designates "Plato's Doctrine of Truth" and "On the Essence of Truth" as the first milestones along the route traversed in his lectures and essays on Nietzsche?

Perhaps we have already taken a first step toward answering these questions when we notice that the analysis of the course's three stages leaves two sections out of account, section 11, "The Grounding Question and the Guiding Question of Philosophy," and section 19, "The Raging Discordance between Truth and Art." These two sections are not mere *entr'actes* preceding and succeeding the central discussion of art; they are in fact, altering the image, the hinges upon which the panels of the triptych turn. Heidegger's lecture course on will to power as art is joined and articulated by a question that is presupposed in all the guiding and grounding of philosophy since Plato, that of the essence of truth. By advancing through a discussion of Nietzsche's metaphysics of will to power to his celebration of art in the grand style, a celebration conducted within the dreadfully raging discordance of art and truth, Heidegger tries to pinpoint Nietzsche's uncertain location on the historical path of metaphysics. That is the only way he can estimate his own position, the only way he can discern the task of his own thinking. But if the "last 'name' in the history of Being as metaphysics is not Kant and not Hegel, but Nietzsche,"[4] the first "name" is Plato. And if Nietzsche's situation at the end of philosophy is ambiguous, so is that of Plato at the beginning. Plato dare not be confounded with Platonism; Nietzsche dare not be confounded with anyone else. Heidegger designs the structure and initiates the movement of his lecture course in such a way as to let the irreducible richness of both thinkers come to light.

---

[4] Eckhard Heftrich, "Nietzsche im Denken Heideggers," *Durchblicke* (Frankfurt/Main: V. Klostermann, 1970), p. 349. Cf. H.-G. Gadamer, *Wahrheit und Methode* (Tübingen: Mohr und Siebeck, 1960), p. 243.

The structure and movement of the course may become more palpable if we recall the task undertaken in each section, reducing it to bare essentials and ignoring for the moment the amplitude of each section. Only when we arrive at the jointures or hinges (sections 11 and 19) will the summary become more detailed.

Heidegger begins (section 1) by asserting that "will to power" defines the basic character of beings in Nietzsche's philosophy. That philosophy therefore proceeds in the orbit of the guiding question of Occidental philosophy, "What is a being (*das Seiende*)?" Yet Nietzsche "gathers and completes" such questioning: to encounter Nietzsche is to confront Western philosophy as a whole—and therefore to prepare "a feast of thought." Nietzsche's philosophy proper, his fundamental position, is in Heidegger's view ascertainable only on the basis of notes sketched during the 1880s for a major work. That work was never written. The collection of notes entitled *The Will to Power* may not be identified as Nietzsche's *Hauptwerk,* but must be read critically. After examining a number of plans for the *magnum opus* drafted during the years 1882–88 (section 3), Heidegger argues for the unity of the three dominant themes, will to power, eternal recurrence of the same, and revaluation of all values (section 4). For Nietzsche all Being is a Becoming, Becoming a willing, willing a will to power (section 2). Will to power is not simply Becoming, however, but is an expression for the *Being* of Becoming, the "closest approximation" to Being (WM, 617). As such it is eternal recurrence of the same and the testing stone of revaluation. Thus the thought of eternal recurrence advances beyond the guiding question of philosophy, "*Was ist das Seiende?*" toward its grounding question, "*Was ist das Sein?*" Both questions must be raised when we try to define Nietzsche's basic metaphysical position or *Grundstellung* (section 5).

After discussing the structural plan employed by the editors of *The Will to Power,* Heidegger situates his own inquiry in the third book, "Principle of a New Valuation," at its fourth and culminating division, "Will to Power as Art." Why Heidegger begins here is not obvious. Nor does it become clear in the sections immediately following (6–10), which recount the meaning of Being as "will" in metaphysics prior to

Nietzsche and in Nietzsche's own thought. Heidegger wrestles with the notions of "will" and "power," which must be thought in a unified way and which cannot readily be identified with traditional accounts of affect, passion, and feeling. Nor does it help to trace Nietzsche's doctrine of will back to German Idealism or even to contrast it to Idealism. The sole positive result of these five sections is recognition of the nature of will to power as *enhancement* or *heightening,* a moving out beyond oneself, and as the original *opening* onto beings. But what that means Nietzsche alone can tell us.

Section 11, "The Grounding Question and the Guiding Question of Philosophy," the first "hinge" of the course, initiates the interpretation of "Will to Power as Art" by asserting once more that the designated starting point is essential for the interpretation of will to power as a whole. In order to defend that assertion Heidegger tries to sharpen the "basic philosophical intention" of his interpretation. He reiterates that the guiding question of philosophy is "What is a being?" That question inquires into the grounds of beings but seeks such grounds solely among other beings on the path of epistemology. But the grounding question, "What is Being?," which would inquire into the meaning of grounds as such and into its own historical grounds as a question, is not posed in the history of philosophy up to and including Nietzsche. Both questions, the penultimate question of philosophy, and the ultimate question which Heidegger reserves for himself, are couched in the words "What is . . . ?" The "is" of both questions seeks an *ouverture* upon beings as a whole by which we might determine what they *in truth, in essence,* are. Both questions provoke thought on the matter of truth as unconcealment, *alētheia;* they are preliminaries to the question of the "essence of truth" and the "truth of essence." Nietzsche's understanding of beings as a whole, of what *is,* is enunciated in the phrase "will to power." But if the question of the essence of truth is already implied in the guiding question of philosophy, then we must ascertain the point where "will to power" and "truth" converge in Nietzsche's philosophy. They do so, astonishingly, not in knowledge (*Erkenntnis*) but in art (*Kunst*). The way Nietzsche completes and gathers philosophy hitherto has to do with that odd conjunction "truth and art" for which no *tertium comparationis* seems possible.

Heidegger now (section 12) begins to sketch out the central panel of the triptych. He turns to a passage in *The Will to Power* (WM, 797) that identifies the "artist phenomenon" as the most perspicuous form of will to power. Grasped in terms of the artist and expanded to the point where it becomes the basic occurrence of all beings, art is proclaimed the most potent stimulant to life, hence the distinctive countermovement to nihilism. As the mightiest *stimulans* to life, art is *worth more* than truth. Heidegger now tries to insert this notion of art into the context of the history of aesthetics (section 13) with special reference to the problem of form-content. Nietzsche's attempt to develop a "physiology of art," which seems to militate against his celebration of art as the countermovement to nihilism, focuses on the phenomenon of artistic *Rausch* (section 14). After an analysis of Kant's doctrine of the beautiful (section 15), Heidegger defines rapture as the force that engenders form and as the fundamental condition for the enhancement of life (section 16). Form constitutes the actuality of art in the "grand style" (section 17), where the apparent contradiction between physiological investigation and artistic celebration dissolves: Nietzsche's physiology is neither biologism nor positivism, however much it may appear to be. Even aesthetics it carries to an extreme which is no longer "aesthetics" in the traditional sense. At this point (section 18) Heidegger returns to the outset of his inquiry into Nietzsche's view of art and tries to provide a foundation for the five theses on art. Things go well until the third thesis: art in the expanded sense constitutes the "basic occurrence" (*Grundgeschehen*) of beings as such. A host of questions advances. What *are* beings as such in truth? Why is truth traditionally viewed as supersensuous? Why does Nietzsche insist that art is worth more than truth? What does it mean to say that art is "more in being" (*seiender*) than are other beings? What *is* the "sensuous world" of art? These questions evoke another which "runs ahead" of both the guiding and grounding questions of philosophy and which therefore may be considered the "foremost" question: truth as unconcealment, *alētheia,* the question broached in section 11.

Heidegger analyzes Nietzsche's anticipation of that question in section 19, "The Raging Discordance between Truth and Art," the second "hinge" of the course. Nietzsche stands "in holy dread" before the discordance. Why? To answer that we must inquire into the history of the *Grundwort* or fundamental word "truth." The decisive development in that history, argues Heidegger, is that "truth" comes to possess a dual character quite similar to that of Being. Truth can mean a truth, "truths" of various kinds, such as historical judgments, mathematical equations, or logical propositions. Yet each of these can be called a truth only if it participates in a single essence, traditionally designated as "the universal," always valid, hence "immutable and eternal, transcending time." According to Heidegger, Nietzsche's response to the question of truth holds to the route which deviates from the essential one:

> It is of decisive importance to know that Nietzsche does not pose the question of truth proper, the question concerning the essence of the true and the truth of essence, and with it the question of the ineluctable possibility of its essential transformation. Nor does he ever stake out the domain of the question.

But if that is so, how can Nietzsche's philosophy gather and complete all philosophy hitherto? According to the tradition, "the true" is what is *known* to be: truth is knowledge. We recall that this is not the answer for Nietzsche, whose notes on *Erkenntnis* in the first part of Book III Heidegger deliberately bypasses in order to find in those on *Kunst* the essential source of the philosophy of will to power. The implication is that, although Nietzsche does not formulate the question of the essence of truth, he removes "the true" from the realm of knowledge to the domain of art. Heidegger does not at this point draw out the consequences of such a removal, but initiates the final stage of the inquiry.

In order to elaborate the meaning of "the true" as an object of knowledge, Heidegger inquires into the doctrines of Platonism and positivism (section 20). For the former, the standard for knowledge is the supersensuous *idea;* for the latter, it is the sensible *positum.* Each doctrine understands itself as a way of attaining certain knowledge of beings, acquiring truths; the second is merely the inversion of the first. If Nietzsche describes his own philosophy as "inverted Platonism," is it then nothing other than positivism? Nietzsche's *manner* of overturning, inspired by insight into the fundamental *Ereignis* of Western history (i.e., nihilism) and by recognition of art as the essential countermovement, distinguishes his thought from positivism. Nietzsche's philosophy is not merely upside-down Platonism.

Heidegger now (sections 21–23) turns to a number of Platonic texts where the supersensuous character of *truth* and the duplicitous nature of *art* become manifest. Art haunts the sensuous realm, the region of nonbeing, which nonetheless is permeated by beauty: because it shares in beauty, art is a way of letting beings appear. However fleeting its epiphanies may be, art is reminiscent of stable Being, the eternal, constant, permanent *ideai.* The upshot is that if there is a discordance between truth and art in Platonism it must be a felicitous one; by some sort of covert maneuver Platonism must efface the discordance as such. When Nietzsche overturns Platonism, removing "the true" from knowledge to art, he exposes the maneuver and lets the discord rage (section 24). Such exposure arouses dread. For it eradicates the horizon which during the long fable of Occidental thought has segregated the true from the apparent world. Although Nietzsche treads the inessential path of "the true" and does not pose the question of the essence of truth, he pursues that path to the very end (section 25): "the true," "truth" in the traditional metaphysical sense, is fixation of an apparition; it clings to a perspective that is essential to life in a way that is ultimately destructive of life. Art, on the contrary, is transfiguration of appearances, the celebration of all perspectives, enhancing and heightening life. Nietzsche's philosophy rescues the sensuous world. In so doing it compels a question that Nietzsche himself cannot formulate: since all appearance and all apparentness are possible "only if something comes to the fore and shows itself at all," how may the thinker and artist address himself to the *self-showing* as such?

.   I have ignored the amplitude of each section in Heidegger's lecture course for much more than a moment. But certain questions have forced their way to the surface. Why art, in the question of truth? Why Nietzsche, in the question of art?

II. CONTEXTS

In the final hour of the lecture course Heidegger alludes to that generation—his own—which studied at German universities between 1909 and 1914. He complains that during those years Nietzsche's "perspectival optics" of creative art and life implied little more than an aesthetic "touch-up" of traditional academic disciplines and that Nietzsche's significance in and for the history of philosophy remained unrecognized.

Long before he was taken seriously as a thinker, Nietzsche achieved fame as an essayist and acerbic critic of culture. For the prewar generation in all German-speaking countries Nietzsche reigned supreme as the definitive prose stylist and as a first-rate lyric poet. He was a literary "phenomenon" whose work and fate caused his name continually to be linked with that of Hölderlin. It was the time when Georg Trakl could recite a number of verses to the aspiring poets of Salzburg's "Minerva Club" and after his confreres began to disparage the poems, believing they were his, could rise and sneer "That was Nietzsche!" and storm out of the place, abandoning them to their public confessions of incompetence.

Writing in 1930 of the "transformation" taking place in Nietzsche interpretation, Friedrich Würzbach looked back to the earliest responses to Nietzsche as a philosopher.[5] He described them as the plaints of wounded souls whose "holiest sentiments" Nietzsche had ravaged and who were now exercising vengeance. A second wave of books and articles endeavored to show that what Nietzsche had to say was already quite familiar and hence harmless; when that did not work a third wave advanced, stressing Nietzsche's utterly novel and peculiar

---

[5]Friedrich Würzbach, "Die Wandlung der Deutung Nietzsches," *Blätter für deutsche Philosophie*, IV, 2 (Berlin, 1930), 202–11.

character, as if to say that he was but a flaw on the fringes of culture which left the fabric of things intact.

It is not until the publication in 1918 of Ernst Bertram's *Nietzsche: An Essay in Mythology* that Würzbach sees a decisive transformation in Nietzsche interpretation.[6] For at least a decade afterward no book on Nietzsche could ignore Bertram's alternately fascinating and infuriating but always dazzling essay. Bertram's Nietzsche is a legendary "personality" whose individuality transcends the customary confinements of a single human life to ascend "through all the signs of the zodiac" and become a "fixed star" in the memory of man. Such legends rise of themselves in spite of all that scientific demythologizing can do, assuming for each succeeding generation a special meaning, representing a particular "mask of the god." Nietzsche, whose legend has only begun, is a mask of Dionysus crucified. He embodies "the incurability of his century." Nietzsche is torn in two; his *mythos* is "duality."

The style of Bertram's essay seems a German counterpart to the prose of Yeats' middle period. It is the "extravagant style" which the poet, according to Robartes, "had learnt from Pater." Bertram's fascination with myth and legend also is reminiscent of Yeats' *A Vision.* (Both Bertram's *Versuch einer Mythologie* and Yeats' "The Phases of the Moon" appeared in 1918.) Yeats' poem contains the following lines, spoken by Robartes but expressing Ernst Bertram's principal theme:

> . . . Eleven pass, and then
> Athene takes Achilles by the hair,
> Hector is in the dust, Nietzsche is born,
> Because the hero's crescent is the twelfth.
> And yet, twice born, twice buried, grow he must,
> Before the full moon, helpless as a worm.[7]

---

[6] Ernst Bertram, *Nietzsche: Versuch einer Mythologie* (Berlin: Georg Bondi, 1918). For the quotations in the text see pp. 7–10, 12, and 361–62.

[7] William Butler Yeats, "The Phases of the Moon," *The Collected Poems of W. B. Yeats,* Definitive Edition (New York: Macmillan, 1956), p. 161. See also William Butler Yeats, *A Vision* (New York: Collier, 1966), p. 60; note the references to Nietzsche on pp. 126 ff. and 299. Cf. Bertram, p. 10

Unlike Yeats, however, Bertram dispenses with much of Nietzsche's thought. He derides eternal recurrence—which in Heidegger's view is Nietzsche's central thought—as a "fake revelation," the "deceptively aping, lunatic *mysterium* of the later Nietzsche."

Würzbach voices the complaint of all those who struggled to free themselves from Bertram's bewitchment: however convincing his insertion of Nietzsche into the tradition of Luther, Novalis, and Hölderlin, of Eleusis and Patmos may be, it manacles Nietzsche to a moribund tradition and lets him sink with it. Bertram's extravagant style therefore seems an elaborate *Grabrede* or obsequy, soothing, mystifying, mesmerizing, in a word, Wagnerian. Ernst Gundolf and Kurt Hildebrandt reject Bertram's "supratemporal" approach to Nietzsche.[8] They are writing (in 1922) at a time of "dire need" in Germany and see in Nietzsche not the stuff of myths but "the judge of our times" and "guide to our future." For Nietzsche is the legislator of new values. His "office" is juridical. "His basic question was not 'What is?' " writes Gundolf, in opposition to what Heidegger will later assert, "but the far more compelling question, 'What is to be done?' " Yet for Kurt Hildebrandt, as for all members of the Stefan George circle, Nietzsche is ultimately a legend of the Bertramesque sort. He is a hero who wills to supply a "norm" to replace the dilapidated structures of Platonic ideality but whose role as opponent consumes him. He would be *Vollender*, apotheosis, and is but *Vorläufer*, precursor. Rejecting the Platonic *idea*, perhaps "out of envy toward Plato," Nietzsche does not achieve the heights to which Platonic eros alone could have conducted him; he remains foreign to the *Phaedrus* and is banned from the *Symposium*. Liberator he may be; creator he is not. "He was not Hölderlin, who was able to mold a new world in poetry, but the hero who hurled himself upon a despicable age and so became its victim."[9] Neither is he Stefan George. "What Nietzsche frantically craved to be

---

[8]Ernst Gundolf and Kurt Hildebrandt, *Nietzsche als Richter unsrer Zeit* (Breslau: F. Hirt, 1922). For the quotations in the text, unless otherwise noted, see pp. 4, 89, 96, and 103.

[9]Ibid., p. 92.

George *is.*"[10] Still, whatever the outcome of his contest with Plato and Socrates,[11] and of his battle against the nineteenth century, which became a battle against Wagner,[12] Nietzsche remains the "judge of our times" in search of values which will halt the degeneration of man and the decline of the state.

The outcome of preoccupations with Nietzsche as "judge" is of course hardly a fortunate one. Stefan George and his circle dream of a grandiose *politeia,* "a new 'Reich,' " as one writer puts it, created along the guidelines of "the *Dionysian Deutsch*"; they foresee the development of a supreme race combining elements of Greek and Nordic civilization, flourishing on German soil.[13] That same writer recognizes in Alfred Baeumler's *Nietzsche: Philosopher and Politician* a giant stride in the right direction.[14]

To summarize: Nietzsche first gained notoriety as a literary phenomenon; his writings were exemplary for the generation that came to maturity during the Great War; by the end of that conflict Nietzsche was a legend, a Cassandra whose prophecy was fulfilled in Europe's ruin. Interest in Nietzsche as a philosopher remained overshadowed by interest in his prophecy and personal fate. Symptomatic

---

[10]Ibid., p. 102.

[11]Kurt Hildebrandt, *Nietzsches Wettkampf mit Sokrates und Plato* (Dresden: Sibyllenverlag, 1922).

[12]Kurt Hildebrandt, *Wagner und Nietzsche: Ihr Kampf gegen das neunzehnte Jahrhundert* (Breslau, 1924). Heidegger refers to the work in section 13 of *The Will to Power as Art.*

[13]Cf. Theodor Steinbüchel, "Die Philosophie Friedrich Nietzsches, ihre geistesgeschichtliche Situation, ihr Sinn und ihre Wirkung," *Zeitschrift für deutsche Geistesgeschichte,* III (Salzburg, 1937), 280–81.

[14]Alfred Baeumler, *Nietzsche der Philosoph und Politiker* (Leipzig: P. Reclam, 1931). This is of course the work that Heidegger criticizes in section 4, above. Heidegger's opposition to the Nietzsche interpretation of Baeumler, professor of philosophy and a leading ideologue in Berlin from 1933 to 1945, I will discuss in the Analysis of *Nietzsche IV: Nihilism.* Baeumler's arguments concerning the Nietzschean *Nachlass,* which appear to have influenced Heidegger, I will take up in the Analysis of *Nietzsche III: Will to Power as Knowledge and as Metaphysics.* Baeumler's thesis on the contradiction between will to power and eternal recurrence I will consider in the Analysis of *Nietzsche II: The Eternal Recurrence of the Same.*

of that interest was the fascination exerted by his medical history, especially his insanity, and reflected in the studies by P. J. Möbius (1902), Kurt Hildebrandt (1926), Erich Podach (1930), and Karl Jaspers (1936). Only as a critic of culture, as the philosopher of *cultural* revaluation, was Nietzsche's voice heard.

But a second strain of interest in Nietzsche develops alongside that of *Kulturphilosophie,* mirrored in the title "Nietzsche and the philosophy of 'life.' "[15] Here Nietzsche is acclaimed as the passionate advocate of life and opponent of the "paralyzed, soulless formulas" of the contemporary "transcendental" philosophy. Nietzsche struggles to find a new scale of values, not in some schema imposed upon life by a transcendent world, but in life itself. He must define the *quality* of life that is desirable, yet must select criteria that are *immanent* in life. His physiology, rooted in a metaphysics of will to power, even though it fails to remain absolutely immanent in life, influences a large number of philosophers of vitalism and organism, such as Eduard von Hartmann, Henri Bergson, Hans Driesch, and Erich Becher. If Baeumler is the noxious blossom of the first strain, however, then Ludwig Klages' philosophy of "orgiastics" is the exotic bloom of *Lebensphilosophie.*[16] Klages exalts life with even wilder abandon than Zarathustra, recognizing in all forms of *Geist* (including the will) an enemy of man's embodied life or "soul." Nietzsche's "psychological achievement," according to Klages' influential book, is to demarcate the "battleground" between the "ascetic priests" of Yahweh and the "orgiasts" of Dionysus.[17] His psychological *faux pas* is that the doctrine of will remains ensnared in the machinations of those priests. Klages' final judgment is that Nietzsche's best consists of "fragments of a philosophy of orgiastics" and that everything else in his thought "is

---

[15]Cf. Theodor Litt, "Nietzsche und die Philosophie des 'Lebens,' " *Handbuch der Philosophie,* eds. A. Baeumler and M. Schröter (Munich and Berlin: R. Oldenbourg, 1931), Abteilung III D, pp. 167–72.

[16]See especially Klages' three-volume work entitled *Der Geist als Widersacher der Seele* (1929–1932), available in Ludwig Klages, *Sämtliche Werke* (Bonn: Bouvier, 1964 ff.).

[17]Ludwig Klages, *Die psychologischen Errungenschaften Nietzsches* (1926), p. 210. Cited by Theodor Steinbüchel, pp. 275–76.

worthless."[18] If Heidegger goes to great lengths to rescue Apollo, and Nietzsche too, by organizing his central discussion of art about the theme of *form* in the grand style, he does so against the din of the Dionysian *Klage* (= lament) whose bells and timbrels owe more to Bayreuth than to Thebes.

Finally, there is a nascent third strain of Nietzsche appreciation already stirring when Heidegger begins his lecture series on that philosopher, an "existentialist" appreciation. The publication of Karl Jaspers' *Reason and Existence* in 1935 and *Nietzsche: Introduction to an Understanding of His Philosophizing* in 1936 marks its advent.[19] Jaspers' work resists rapid depiction. Yet its main thrust may be felt in the third book, "Nietzsche's Mode of Thought in the Totality of Its Existence." Jaspers measures Nietzsche's significance neither in terms of biography nor on the basis of doxography; neither the life nor the doctrines alone constitute the *Ereignis* which for subsequent thinkers Nietzsche indisputably is. It is Nietzsche's dedication to the task of thought throughout the whole of his existence that elevates him to enormous heights—that dedication, plus his passion to communicate and his skill in devising masks for his passion. Ultimately it is the courage he displays in posing to *Existenz* the question of the meaning of the whole: *warum? wozu?* why? to what end? By asking about the worth of the whole Nietzsche executes a radical break with the past, past morality, past philosophy, past humanity. No one can surpass the radicality of that break. Nietzsche, writes Jaspers, "thought it through to its ultimate consequences; it is scarcely possible to take a step farther along that route." Yet what drives Nietzsche to that protracted and painful rupture with the past is something powerfully affirmative, the "yes" to life, overman, and eternal recurrence; it is in the formulation

---

[18]Ibid., p. 168. Cited by Steinbüchel, p. 276.

[19]Theodor Steinbüchel's mammoth article provides a "Christian existentialist" view of Nietzsche's "situation" in 1936–37. Karl Jaspers' *Nietzsche: Einführung in das Verständnis seines Philosophierens* (Berlin: W. de Gruyter, 1936) serves as Steinbüchel's principal source, but his article refers to much of the literature. Especially valuable in the present context is part six of Steinbüchel's essay, "Current Interpretations of Existence under the Influence of Nietzsche," pp. 270–81. For the quotations in the text see Jaspers' *Nietzsche,* pp. 393–94.

of the positive side of Nietzsche's philosophy that Jaspers foresees a successful career for subsequent philosophy. Thus he lauds Nietzsche's critique of morality as that which "*cleared the path* for the philosophy of existence." Although Nietzsche denies transcendence with every fiber of his existence, Jaspers concludes that the fury of his denial testifies willy-nilly to the embrace of the encompassing.

Of course, Jaspers is not the only philosopher of *Existenz*. Steinbüchel mentions Jaspers only after he has discussed the writer he takes to be the chief representative of the new philosophy—Martin Heidegger.[20] The works by Heidegger which Steinbüchel was able to refer to, whether explicitly or implicitly, are *Being and Time, What is Metaphysics?, On the Essence of Ground,* and *Kant and the Problem of Metaphysics.* What Heidegger was teaching in Freiburg as Steinbüchel composed his article Steinbüchel could not know. Hence what is fascinating about his remarks is that they betray what one might well have expected from a lecture course by Heidegger on Nietzsche. The gap between expectation and reality is considerable.

According to Steinbüchel, Heidegger's philosophy understands man, and Being itself, to be essentially finite; it is Nietzsche who has pointed to human finitude in an unforgettable way. That Heidegger radically extrudes man's "transcendent being toward God" is therefore due to Nietzsche. Nevertheless, Heidegger promulgates "a concealed ethics" according to which man must resolutely assume the burden of his own being. Steinbüchel sees here the "Nietzschean imperative" that man become who he most properly is, scorning the "last man" who remains steeped in "everydayness." Yet Heidegger's secret ethics, his "yes" to the Self, does not preserve Nietzsche's "tremendous faith in life." Nietzsche transfigures Dionysian insight into dithyramb, while Heidegger, in the face of the "thrownness" and "fallenness" of Dasein, can only muster a "reticent resignation."

Whatever value Steinbüchel's remarks on Nietzsche's role in Heidegger's thought may have, what remains striking is the variance between his and Heidegger's own accounts of that role. The former

---

[20]Cf. T. Steinbüchel, pp. 271–73.

mentions neither art nor truth; Nietzsche's importance for the history of metaphysics does not become conspicuous there; and that the *telos* of Heidegger's inquiry into Nietzsche should be Platonism and Plato seems on the basis of Steinbüchel's account altogether out of the question.

Yet it is only fair to say that even forty years later the context of Heidegger's inquiry into Nietzsche is not readily discernible. His investigation has little or nothing to do with Nietzsche as *littérateur,* iconoclast, legend, legislator, judge, inmate, orgiast, or existentialist. My analysis must therefore turn to Heidegger's own writings which are contemporary with or prior to the Nietzsche lectures, in search of a more relevant context.

Heidegger first studied Nietzsche during his student years in Freiburg between 1909 and 1914. He discovered the expanded 1906 edition of notes from the *Nachlass* selected and arranged by Heinrich Köselitz (pseud. Peter Gast) and Frau Elisabeth Förster-Nietzsche and given the title *Der Wille zur Macht.* That book, indispensable because of the quality of Nietzsche's unpublished notes, unreliable because of editorial procedures and unscrupulous manipulations by Nietzsche's sister, eventually occupied a central place in Heidegger's developing comprehension of Western metaphysics as the history of Being. Although he would refer to the whole range of Nietzsche's published writings during his lectures and essays two decades later, *Der Wille zur Macht* is the text he was to assign his students and the source of his principal topics: will to power as art and knowledge (from Book Three, sections I and IV), the eternal recurrence of the same (Book Four, section III), and nihilism (Book One).

That volume's influence on Heidegger is visible already in his "early writings," not as an explicit theme for investigation but as an incentive to philosophical research in general. In his *venia legendi* lecture of 1915, "The Concept of Time in Historiography," Heidegger alludes to philosophy's proper "will to power."[21] He means the urgent need for

---

[21] Martin Heidegger, *Frühe Schriften* (Frankfurt/Main: V. Klostermann, 1972), p. 357.

philosophy to advance beyond theory of knowledge to inquiry into the goal and purpose of philosophy as such, in other words, the need to advance in the direction of metaphysics. In the habilitation thesis which precedes the *venia legendi* lecture Heidegger wrestles with the problem of the historical (as opposed to the systematic) approach to philosophy.[22] Here too Nietzsche's influence is unmistakable. Philosophy possesses a value for culture and exhibits a historical situation, as Dilthey saw; it also puts forward the claim of validity, as Husserl and the Neo-Kantians argued. But Heidegger stresses a third factor, namely, philosophy's "function as a *value for life.*" Philosophy itself exists "in tension with the living personality" of the philosopher, "drawing its content and value out of the depths and the abundance of life in that personality." In this connection Heidegger refers to Nietzsche's formulation "the drive to philosophize," citing that philosopher's "relentlessly austere manner of thought," a manner enlivened, however, by a gift for "flexible and apt depiction."

That Heidegger's own drive to philosophize receives much of its impulse from Nietzsche is not immediately obvious to the reader of *Being and Time* (1927). During the intervening Marburg years Nietzsche was set aside in favor of Aristotle, Husserl, Kant, Aquinas, and Plato. Perhaps Heidegger now wished to distance himself from the Nietzsche adopted by *Lebensphilosophie* and philosophies of culture and value. His rejection of the category "life" for his own analyses of Dasein is clearly visible already in 1919–21, the years of his confrontation with Karl Jaspers' *Psychology of Weltanschauungen.*[23] And although Nietzsche's shadow flits across the pages of the published Marburg lectures, Heidegger's vehement rejection of the value-

[22]Ibid., pp. 137–38.

[23]See Martin Heidegger, "Anmerkungen zu Karl Jaspers' *Psychologie der Weltanschauungen,*" *Karl Jaspers in der Diskussion,* ed. Hans Saner (Munich: R. Piper, 1973), pp. 70–100, esp. pp. 78–79. (The essay now appears as the first chapter of *Wegmarken* in the new *Gesamtausgabe* edition, Frankfurt/Main, 1977.) See also D. F. Krell, "Toward *Sein und Zeit:* Heidegger's Early Review (1919–21) of Jaspers' *Psychologie der Weltanschauungen,*" *Journal of the British Society for Phenomenology,* VI, 3 (October 1975), 147–56; and the "Discussion" article on "The Heidegger-Jaspers Relationship" in the same journal, IX, 2 (May 1978), pp. 126–29.

philosophy of Wilhelm Windelband and Heinrich Rickert undoubtedly delayed his public confrontation with the philosopher who
demanded the revaluation of all values.[24]

In *Being and Time* itself only three references to Nietzsche's
thought appear, only one of them an essential reference, so that it
seems perverse to argue that Nietzsche lies concealed "on every printed
page of *Sein und Zeit.*"[25] Yet we ought to postpone discussion of
Nietzsche's role in awakening the question of *Being and Time* until
Heidegger's own Nietzsche lectures provide the proper occasion for
it.[26] By way of anticipation I may cite one introductory remark by
Heidegger in "The Word of Nietzsche: 'God is Dead' ": "The following commentary, with regard to its intention and according to its scope,
keeps to that one experience on the basis of which *Being and Time* was
thought."[27] If that one experience is the oblivion of Being, which
implies forgottenness of the nothing in which Dasein is suspended, we
may ask whether in *Being and Time* Heidegger tries to complete
Nietzsche's task by bringing the question of the death of God
home—inquiring into the death of Dasein and the demise of
metaphysical *logos,* both inquiries being essential prerequisites for the
remembrance of Being.

If Nietzsche's role in the question of *Being and Time* is not obvious,
neither is the role played there by art. References in Heidegger's major
work to works of art are rare, although we recall the extended reference

---

[24]See for example volume 21 of the *Gesamtausgabe* (Frankfurt/Main, 1976), which
reprints Heidegger's course on "logic" delivered in 1925–26. By Nietzsche's "shadow"
I mean such analyses as that of the development of psychology (p. 36) or that of the
protective vanity of philosophers (p. 97). Heidegger's contempt for *Wertphilosophie*
emerges throughout the course, but see esp. pp. 82–83 and 91–92.

[25]I argued this way, correctly (as I believe) but perhaps unconvincingly, in my dissertation "Nietzsche and the Task of Thinking: Martin Heidegger's Reading of Nietzsche"
(Duquesne University, 1971). Cf. D. F. Krell, "Nietzsche in Heidegger's *Kehre,*" *The
Southern Journal of Philosophy* XIII, 2 (Summer 1975), 197–204. The three references
to Nietzsche in *Being and Time* appear (in Niemeyer's twelfth edition, 1972) on p. 264,
lines 15–16, p. 272 n. 1, and, the essential reference, to Nietzsche's "On the Usefulness
and Disadvantage of History for Life," p. 396, lines 16 ff.

[26]See for example NII, 194–95 and 260.

[27]Martin Heidegger, *Holzwege* (Frankfurt/Main: V. Klostermann, 1950), p. 195.

to Hyginus' fable of *Cura* in section 42. But for the most part literature and art appear as occasions where "they" come and go talking of Michelangelo. If enjoying works of art as "they" do is symptomatic of everydayness, we might well ask how art is to be properly encountered. Yet the fact remains that art is little discussed. The distance covered between the years 1927 and 1937 in Heidegger's career of thought is enormous: Steinbüchel's expectations are evidence enough of that.

From his earliest student days Heidegger had displayed an interest in literature and art: the novels of Dostoevsky and Adalbert Stifter, the poetry of Hölderlin, Rilke, and Trakl (whose poems Heidegger read when they were first published prior to the war), and the Expressionist movement in painting and poetry. Such interest at that time did not and could not irradiate the sober, somber halls of *Wissenschaft*. But in the 1930s literature and art came to occupy the very center of Heidegger's project, for they became central to the question of truth as disclosure and unconcealment. A glance at Heidegger's lecture schedule during the decade of the 1930s suggests something of this development.

Schelling, for whose system art is of supreme importance, is taught many times, as are Hegel's *Phenomenology* and Kant's third critique. (Kant's importance for Heidegger in this respect, ignored in the literature because of the overweening significance of Heidegger's publications on the first critique, we may gauge from his stalwart defense of Kant in section 15 of *The Will to Power as Art*.) Plato, the artist of dialogue, dominates all those courses where the essence of truth is the focus. It is unfortunate that we know nothing of Heidegger's 1935–36 colloquium with Kurt Bauch on "overcoming aesthetics in the question of art." We might hazard a guess that the "six basic developments in the history of aesthetics" (section 13, above) mirror the outcome of that colloquium. It is also unfortunate that we do not know what transpires in Heidegger's seminar on "selected fragments from Schiller's philosophical writings on art," which runs parallel to these Nietzsche lectures. Perhaps the references to Schiller (pp. 108 and 113) provide clues. But of all these lectures and seminars surely the most instructive would be the 1934–35 lectures on Hölderlin's Hymns,

"The Rhine" and "Germania." From the single lecture "Hölderlin and the Essence of Poetry" (1936) we derive some "indirect light," as Heidegger says in his Foreword to the *Nietzsche* volumes, on the parallel rise of Nietzsche and of art in his thought on *alētheia.* Perhaps further light will be shed if we consider three other works stemming from the same period. "The Anaximander Fragment" (composed in 1946 but drawing on a course taught during the summer semester of 1932), "Plato's Doctrine of Truth" (published in 1943 but based on courses held from 1930 on, especially that of the winter semester of 1931–32), and "The Origin of the Work of Art" (published in 1950 but composed in 1935–36 and revised while the first Nietzsche course was in session). But in examining these four essays I cease the work of background and try to limn the figures of the matter itself.

III. QUESTIONS

Why art, in the question of truth?
Why Nietzsche, in the question of art?
On the occasion of the publication of the fourth, expanded edition of *Erläuterungen zu Hölderlins Dichtung* (1971) Heidegger remarked that those commentaries sprang from *einer Notwendigkeit des Denkens,* "a necessity of thought."[28] But the phrase is ambiguous. I take it to mean that Heidegger's thought turns to Hölderlin out of need, *Not-wendig,* in much the same way as Nietzsche's thought of eternal recurrence is "a cry out of need," *Aufschrei aus einer Not* (NI, 310). If Hölderlin's times are destitute, the epoch of Nietzsche and Heidegger is desperate. While Hölderlin can aver, "Indeed, the gods live," Nietzsche must conclude, "God is dead." The latter refrain dominates Heidegger's lectures and essays on Nietzsche; the phrase appears in his *Rektoratsrede* as a signal of urgency; it is the key to

---

[28]Martin Heidegger, *Erläuterungen zu Hölderlins Dichtung* (Frankfurt/Main: V. Klostermann, 1971), p. 7. Cf. Beda Allemann, *Hölderlin und Heidegger* (Zurich: Atlantis, 1956), parts II–IV.

Nietzsche's precarious position at the end of metaphysics and to Heidegger's before the task of his thinking.[29]

Two remarks in Heidegger's Hölderlin essay are particularly revealing with respect to Heidegger's turn to that poet. First, Heidegger insists that the being and essence of things, hence the naming of the gods, can never be derived from things that lie at hand. They must be "freely created."[30] As the motto for his lecture course on will to power as art Heidegger chooses a phrase from *The Antichrist*: "Well-nigh two thousand years and not a single new god!" Is it then a matter of concocting novel divinities? Or of lighting a lantern in broad daylight to search out old familiar ones? A second remark from the Hölderlin essay silences these overhasty questions and redirects the inquiry. Man possesses language in order to say who he is and to give testimony. About what is he to testify? "His belonging to the earth."[31] All creation, *poiēsis,* testifies to man's dwelling on the earth, remaining in Zarathustran fashion "true to the earth." Yet it is an earth cut loose from her sun and deprived of her horizon and a dwelling that hovers in holy dread before the raging discordance of art and truth.

Heidegger's "turn out of need" to the poetry of Hölderlin should not, however, be reduced to an incident of biography. It is not merely a necessity in Heidegger's intellectual life but a turning in the history of the question of Being. Heidegger speaks of that turning in many essays composed during the 1930s and 1940s. Of special consequence here are "The Anaximander Fragment" and "Plato's Doctrine of Truth." To the situation of the former essay Heidegger gives the name "eschatology of Being." By that he means the outermost point in the history of the Occident or evening-land from which he descries the dawn. (Whether it is the dawn of Anaximander's epoch or that of a new age is impossible to tell: Heidegger can only attempt to "ponder the

---

[29]Otto Pöggeler writes, "Ever since 1929–30, when Nietzsche became a matter of 'decision' for Heidegger, his new starting point for thinking the truth of Being was dominated by the all-determining presupposition that God is 'dead.' " Otto Pöggeler, *Philosophie und Politik bei Heidegger* (Freiburg and Munich: Karl Alber, 1972), p. 25.

[30]Martin Heidegger, *Erläuterungen,* p. 41.

[31]Ibid., p. 36.

former dawn through what is imminent."[32]) The name that recurs in the opening pages of the Anaximander essay, designating the *eschaton* of the history of Being, is "Nietzsche."[33] Even if we reduce matters to biography there is no obvious reason why the name "Nietzsche" and no other must appear here. Indeed the reason is highly complex. Heidegger attempts to uncover it during his protracted lecture series on Nietzsche.

A further hint of Nietzsche's significance as a figure of dusk and dawn, *Abendland* and *Morgenröte*, and as our point of entry into the issue of Western history as a whole, emerges from the essay on "Plato's doctrine of Truth." Here too Heidegger speaks of a turning and a need.[34] But it is not merely a turning or a need apropos of Heidegger himself. It is rather "a turning in the determination of the essence of truth" and a need for "not only beings but Being" to become "worthy of question." Much later in his career Heidegger comes to doubt the validity of the thesis expounded in his Plato essay, to wit, that a transformation in the essence of truth from *unconcealment* to *correctness* occurs as such in Plato; yet his early inquiry into Plato's doctrine of truth as portrayed in the Allegory of the Cave remains a highly thought-provoking effort.[35] It is an effort to confront the

---

[32]Martin Heidegger, *Holzwege*, p. 302. Cf. the English translation, *Early Greek Thinking*, tr. D. F. Krell and F. A. Capuzzi (New York: Harper & Row, 1975), p. 18.

[33]See *Early Greek Thinking*, pp. 13–14, 17, and 22–23. See also my remarks in the Introduction to the volume, pp. 9–10.

[34]See the first and last pages of the essay in Martin Heidegger, *Wegmarken* (Frankfurt/Main: V. Klostermann, 1967). pp. 109 and 144.

[35]In "The End of Philosophy and the Task of Thinking" Heidegger explicitly rejects the thesis of his earlier essay on Plato. (See Martin Heidegger, *Zur Sache des Denkens* [Tübingen: M. Niemeyer, 1969], p. 78.) The assertion that in Plato we find an "essential transformation of truth" from unconcealment to correctness is "untenable." Heidegger apparently accedes to the arguments of Paul Friedländer and others that in Greek literature and philosophy *alēthes* always modifies verbs of speech. Although *alētheia* may indeed derive from *lēthō* (*lanthanō*) and the alpha-privative, the sense of "unconcealment" seems to have evanesced even before Homer sang. Hence there is no essential transformation of truth from unconcealment to correctness; at least, none that can be located in Plato. There is instead an essential continuity in the history of "truth," a tendency to regard the true as correctness of assertion or correspondence of statement and fact, without asking about the domain in which words and things so wondrously converge.

consequences of Plato's conjunction of *alētheia,* interpreted as *orthotēs* or correctness of viewing, and *paideia,* education in the broadest possible sense. Essential to the allegory are the transformations or rites of passage undergone by the prisoners of the cave on their way to and from the Ideas, their liberation, conversion, ascent and descent, and the attendant bedazzlements, adjustments, and insights. Heidegger emphasizes that liberation is not simply an unshackling: the liberated prisoner does not run amok but confronts fire and sun, growing accustomed to "fixing his view upon the fixed boundaries of things affixed in their forms."[36] Those rites of passage, and the correctness of viewing that underlies them, determine the history of Being as truth from Aristotle to Neo-Kantian philosophies of value. Heidegger mentions three junctures of that history in which the correspondence of assertion and state of affairs progressively obscures the sense of truth as unconcealment. Thomas Aquinas locates truth "in the human or divine intellect"; Descartes adds his peculiar emphasis, asserting that "truth can be nowhere but in the mind"; and Nietzsche, "in the epoch of the incipient consummation of the modern age," intensifies to the explosion point the assertion concerning truth's place.[37] Heidegger now cites *The Will to Power* number 493, discussed often in the Nietzsche lectures (see section 25, above): "*Truth is the kind of error* without which a certain kind of living being could not live. The value for *life* ultimately decides." Nietzsche's interpretation of truth comprises "the last reflection of the uttermost consequences of that transformation of truth from the unconcealment of beings to correctness of viewing," a transformation which devolves from the interpretation of Being as *idea.* Nietzsche's "intensification" accordingly manifests both continuity and radical departure. To identify truth as error is to persist in the paideiogogical project of correctness; yet it also displays the vacuity of that project. Similarly, to attempt a revaluation of all values is to persist in pursuit of *to agathon,* it is to be "the most unbridled Platonist in the history of Occidental metaphysics"; yet to adopt the

[36]Martin Heidegger, *Wegmarken,* p. 128.
[37]Ibid., pp. 138–39.

standard of "life" itself for the revaluation is to grasp *to agathon* in a way that is "less prejudicial" than the way taken by other philosophies of value.[38] The vacuity of Plato's educative project, and Nietzsche's "less prejudicial" understanding of the Good, are expressions of a crisis in the meaning of Being. Nietzsche's fundamental experience of the death of God implies the collapse of the ontotheological interpretation of Being, for which God was the cause of beings, the failure of metaphysics' envisionment of the divine *ideai,* and the evanescence of that domain of beings once thought to be most in being. It implies the disappearance of all that once was "viewed in a nonsenuous glance . . . beyond the grasp of the body's instruments."[39]

Heidegger had long recognized that doubts surrounding the very meaning of "body" and "soul," "matter" and "spirit," "sensuous" and "supersensuous," "psychical" and "ideal" concealed in themselves the collapse of the meaning of Being.[40] In Nietzsche he found the keenest eyewitness to that collapse. Nietzsche's efforts to "rescue" the sensuous world, to reinterpret its reality outside the Platonic context, and to celebrate art as the fitting means of rescue exhibited most dramatically the critical pass—or impasse—to which the history of Being since Plato had come. "Art, and nothing but art!" Nietzsche had said. Perhaps that was the direction in which the question of the meaning of Being would have to go.

The last of Heidegger's three lectures on "The Origin of the Work of Art," delivered at Frankfurt on December 4, 1936, bears the title "Truth and Art."[41] After reading the text of his contemporaneous

---

[38]Ibid., p. 133.

[39]Ibid., p. 141.

[40]See for example his remarks during the summer semester of 1927, in Martin Heidegger, *Die Grundprobleme der Phänomenologie* (Frankfurt/Main: V. Klostermann, 1975), pp. 30–31. See also his discussion of truth, Being, and Time during the winter semester of 1925–26 (cited in note 24, above), esp. §§ 4, 8, and 9. Traces of such doubt appear even in the *Habilitationsschrift* of 1915–16 and the doctoral dissertation of 1914: cf. M. Heidegger, *Frühe Schriften,* pp. 348, 35, and 117–120. The key text of course is *Being and Time:* see esp. chap. 3.

[41]Published as Martin Heidegger, *Der Ursprung des Kunstwerkes* (Stuttgart: P. Reclam, 1960). See pp. 63 ff.

course on will to power as art we immediately want to add the words ". . . in raging discordance." But in "The Origin of the Work of Art" it is not a question of discordance *between* truth and art; Heidegger uncovers discord or strife *at the heart of both* truth and art. For they share in the creative struggle for Being, presence, in the arena of disclosure and concealment.[42]

Heidegger begins the final hour of his lectures on the origin of the artwork by citing "art itself" as the origin of both work and artist. Art is not a mere general concept under which objets d'art and artists are subsumed. It is the origin of the essential provenance of a work, which is neither a mere thing nor a piece of equipment but a place where truth occurs. Such occurrence Heidegger conceives as the instigation of strife between a historical world and the sustaining earth. Such strife is gathered in the work, which possesses a peculiar autochthony and calm, and which leads a life of its own. Only at the very end of his lecture cycle does Heidegger mention the obvious fact of the work's createdness, its creation by an artist. That suggests the major difference between the Nietzschean and Heideggerian approaches to art, a difference which the Nietzsche lectures explore thoroughly. Heidegger offers no physiology of the artist. He presents no account which could be rooted in subjectivistic metaphysics. Nietzsche's defenders—at least the unliberated ones—might complain that by remaining an observer of the artwork Heidegger regresses to "feminine aesthetics." Heidegger could only rejoin that his lectures try to leave aesthetics of both stereotyped sexes behind—and that in so doing they merely elaborate Nietzsche's understanding of art in the grand style, where the artist himself becomes a work of art and where the distinction between subject and object, active and passive, blurs. But what is entailed in the abandonment of aesthetics? Why must inquiry into art undergo radical change?

In his Frankfurt lectures Heidegger tries to distinguish between the kinds of production appropriate to handicraft and to art. His procedure

---

[42]See D. F. Krell, "Art and Truth in Raging Discord: Heidegger and Nietzsche on the Will to Power," *boundary 2*, IV, 2 (Winter 1976), 379–92.

and insight are those exhibited in the Nietzsche lectures: the *technitēs* or craftsman brings beings forth into presence and so reveals them, his labors being a kind of *alētheuein,* bringing an entity to stand in the openness of its Being. Such openness quickly narrows when the thing produced is absorbed in sheer serviceability or usefulness as a piece of equipment. In the artwork, however, the fate of openness is different. Here openness itself achieves what Heidegger calls *Ständigkeit.* Recalling that for Platonism the Being of beings is interpreted as "permanence," which is one way to translate *Ständigkeit,* we must ask whether Heidegger's interpretation of art is not only female but also metaphysical: if art brings a being to stand and lends it constancy, then is not Heidegger merely affirming the "transcendent value" of art, as aesthetics has always done? And if Nietzsche exposes Platonic "permanence" as the "permanentizing" of perspectival life, as an instinct that preserves life but at some critical point petrifies it, so that an appeal to *Ständigkeit* is ultimately fixation on an apparition, there would be reason to ask whether in his lectures on the origin of the artwork Heidegger has at all learned from Nietzsche.

He has. For the "stand" to which the truth of beings comes in the work of art is by no means to be understood as permanence or constancy.

> Only in the following way does truth happen: it installs itself within the strife and the free space which truth itself opens up. Because truth is the reciprocal relation [*das Gegenwendige*] of lighting and concealing, what we are here calling installation [*Einrichtung*] is proper to it. But truth does not exist ahead of time in itself somewhere among the stars, only subsequently to be brought down among beings, which are somewhere else.... Lighting of openness and installation in the open region belong together. They are one and the same essential unfolding of truth's occurrence [*Geschehen*]. Such occurrence is in manifold ways historical [*geschichtlich*].[43]

Why art, in the question of truth? Truth happens in the work of art. Both truth and art are historical; they stand in time. The work of

---

[43]Martin Heidegger, *Der Ursprung,* p. 68.

art brings forth a being "that never was before and never will come to be afterwards."[44] Its "stand" is not only no guarantee against a fall, it marks the inception of the fall. Hence the need for preservation—which itself lapses into art appreciation and the art trade. If there is something that "stands" in a more perdurant sense it is the Heraclitean and Empedoclean strife, the Anaximandrian usage, which itself becomes present only through the being that rises and falls, emerges, lingers awhile, and disappears, in that way alone announcing what *is*. Thus the "workliness" of the work of art is not supratemporal *Wirklichkeit* but the "*becoming and happening of truth.*"[45] Never renounced, always affirmed is the relation of workliness to the nothing, that is, to a source beyond all beings but achieved only in a being. To dwell in nearness to the source is to be mindful of the double shadow that each thing, in becoming, casts before and behind itself.

Why Nietzsche, in the question of art? When we speak of the rise of art in Heidegger's thought, citing Nietzsche, Hölderlin, Schelling, Schiller, and others as the instigators of such a rise, we must be careful not to subordinate one thinker or poet to another, transforming contexts into causes and questions into answers. We simply cannot say who or what comes first, whether Nietzsche's decisive importance for Heidegger—and the decisive importance of art for Nietzsche—induce Heidegger to turn to Hölderlin and to the art of Greece or of Van Gogh, or whether the lyre of Hölderlin or Trakl or Sophocles sets the tone for Heidegger's turn to Nietzsche. All of these themes reinforce and refine one another long before Heidegger speaks of them publicly. All betray the central tendency of Heidegger's thought on art: the painting, poem, statue, or symphony is not a decorative piece with an assignable cultural value but the major way in which truth, the unhiddenness of beings, transpires. Such truth is not normative but disclosive; not eternal but radically historical; not transcendent but immanent in the things wrought; not sheer light but chiaroscuro. Disclosure, historicity, immanence, and the play of light and shadow

---

[44]Ibid., p. 69.
[45]Ibid., p. 81.

occur upon a new horizon that forms and dissolves and forms again where the epoch of metaphysics wanes and no other epoch is visible. Nietzsche—the *matter of thought* for which that name stands—is a giant on the horizon. His stature, always as incalculable as the horizon itself, remains monumental for the particular reason that his philosophy, more than that of anyone since Plato, is itself a work of art.

Heidegger therefore began his lecture series on Nietzsche by tracing the profile of will to power as art. His next step was to examine the work that displays the effulgence of Nietzsche's own art, *Also sprach Zarathustra.* During the summer semester of 1937 he lectured on that book's fundamental teaching, the eternal recurrence of the same, thereby attaining the summit of his own lecture series.

Glossary

Translation should not and cannot be one-to-one substitution. If it is done that way it may be *wortwörtlich* but can never be *wortgetreu;* although literal, it will not be faithful.

The following list of words gives the options most often taken in the translation of this volume. But the only way readers can be certain about the original of any given rendering is to check the German text.

abscission	*die Zerrissenheit*
absence	*die Abwesenheit*
abyss	*der Abgrund*
actual	*wirklich*
advent, arrival	*die Ankunft*
affect	*der Affekt*
apparent world, world of appearances	*die scheinbare Welt*
apparition	*der Anschein*
at hand	*vorhanden*
attunement	*die Gestimmtheit*
basic experience	*die Grunderfahrung*
basic occurrence	*das Grundgeschehen*
basically	*im Grunde*
the beautiful	*das Schöne*
beauty	*die Schönheit*
Being	*das Sein*
being(s)	*das Seiende*
being(s) as a whole	*das Seiende im Ganzen*

care	*die Sorge, hē epimeleia*
cohere	*zusammengehören*
conception	*die Auffassung*
concordance	*der Einklang*
configuration	*die Gestalt*
confrontation	*die Aus-einander-setzung*
continuance	*die Beständigung*
copying	*das Nachmachen, mimēsis*
countermovement	*die Gegenbewegung*
to create	*schaffen*
creative	*schöpferisch*
to define	*bestimmen*
definitive	*massgebend*
delight	*das Wohlgefallen*
destiny	*das Geschick*
to determine	*bestimmen*
development	*die Entwicklung, die Tatsache*
discordance	*der Zwiespalt*
disinterestedness	*die Interesselosigkeit*
dread	*das Entsetzen*
duration	*der Bestand*
to be embodied	*leiben*
embodying life	*das leibende Leben*
emergence	*das Aufgehen, physis*
enhancement	*die Steigerung*
enigmatic	*rätselhaft*
envisionment	*das Sichtige*
essence	*das Wesen*
essential determination	*die Wesensbestimmung*
to esteem	*schätzen*
to estimate	*abschätzen*
eternal recurrence	
of the same	*die ewige Wiederkehr des Gleichen*
eternal return	*die ewige Wiederkunft*
event	*das Ereignis*

eventuality	*das Vorkommnis*
to excel	*sich überhöhen*
explicit	*ausdrücklich*
expression	*der Ausdruck*
expressly	*eigens*
feeling	*das Gefühl*
felicitous	*beglückend*
fixation	*die Festmachung*
fleeting appearances	*der Anschein*
force	*die Kraft*
form	*die Form*
frame	*das Gestell*
frenzy	*der Rausch*
fullness	*die Fülle*
fundament	*der Grund*
fundamental position	*die Grundstellung*
genuine	*echt, eigentlich*
the grand style	*der grosse Stil*
to grasp	*fassen, begreifen*
ground(s)	*der Grund*
grounding question	*die Grundfrage*
guiding question	*die Leitfrage*
to heed	*achten, beachten*
hierarchy	*die Rangordnung*
historicity	*die Geschichtlichkeit*
illusion	*der Anschein*
imitation	*das Nachahmen, mimēsis*
immutability	*die Unveränderlichkeit*
inversion	*die Umdrehung*
jointure	*der Fug*
know-how, knowledge	*das Wissen, technē*

law	*das Gesetz*
lawfulness	*die Gesetzlichkeit*
to let-lie-before	*vor-liegen-lassen*
to light up	*aufleuchten*
lighting	*die Lichtung*
to linger	*verweilen*
lived experience	*das Erlebnis*
lucid	*durchsichtig*
main *or* major work,	
magnum opus	*das Hauptwerk*
manifold validity	*die Vielgültigkeit*
to manufacture	*anfertigen*
matter (of thought)	*die Sache (des Denkens)*
meditation	*die Besinnung*
metamorphosis	*die Verwandlung*
mood	*die Stimmung*
nondistortion	*die Unverstelltheit,* alētheia
oblivion	*die Vergessenheit*
openness, openedness	*die Offenheit, die Offenbarkeit*
opening up	*die Offenbarung, Eröffnung*
original	*ursprünglich*
outer, outward appearance	*das Aussehen,* eidos
overturning	*die Umdrehung*
particular, individual	*einzeln*
passion	*die Leidenschaft*
perdurance	*die Dauer*
permanence	*die Beständigkeit*
perspicuous	*durchsichtig*
plenitude	*die Fülle*
poetize, write creatively	*dichten*
presence	*die Anwesenheit*
presencing,	
becoming present	*das Anwesen*

what is present	*das Anwesende*
presentative	*vorstellend*
prevail	*herrschen, walten*
to pro-duce	*her-stellen*
proper	*eigentlich*
to be proper to	*gehören*
psychical	*seelisch*
radiance	*der Schein*
the most radiant	*das Hervorscheinendste, to ekphanestaton*
rapture	*der Rausch*
reality	*die Realität*
realm	*der Bereich*
to reign	*walten*
representation	*die Vorstellung*
resolute openness	*die Entschlossenheit*
to revere	*verehren*
reversal	*das Umkehren*
rule	*die Regel, das Gesetz*
to rule	*walten*
the same	*das Selbe*
to scintillate	*aufscheinen, aufleuchten*
to seem	*scheinen*
self-assertion	*die Selbstbehauptung*
semblance	*der Schein*
the sensuous	*das Sinnliche*
severance	*die Entzweiung*
state	*der Zustand*
statement	*der Satz*
strength	*die Kraft*
the supersensuous	*das Übersinnliche*
to surpass	*sich überholen*
sway	*das Walten*
to transfigure	*verklären*
transformation	*der Wandel*

transparent	*durchsichtig*
the true	*das Wahre*
truth	*die Wahrheit*
ultimately	*im Grunde*
unconcealment	*die Unverborgenheit*
unconstrained favoring	*die freie Gunst*
the unsaid	*das Ungesagte*
valuation	*die Wertsetzung*
valuative thinking	*das Wertdenken*
the view upon Being	*der Seinsblick*
to will, want	*wollen*
will to power	*der Wille zur Macht*